Survival

GLOBAL POLITICS AND STRATEGY

Volume 61 Number 5 | October–November 2019

T0332614

'Right-sizing the American ̵̶̶̶ ̵̶̶̶̶ ̵̶̶̶̶ ̵̶̶̶̶ the greater Persian Gulf requires a prudent but steady drawdown from the military commitments in Iraq and Afghanistan. The nation-building experiments there have failed.'

F. Gregory Gause, III, Should We Stay or Should We Go? The United States and the Middle East, p. 18.

'It is unhappily the case that the chances of war have increased because an incentive for war not present 20 years ago has emerged in the second decade of the twenty-first century: the need on the part of dictatorial governments to generate public support through foreign policies of aggressive nationalism. Still, the three revisionist powers have carried out these policies with extreme caution.'

Michael Mandelbaum, Is Major War Still Obsolete?, p. 69.

'Economic connections, from cyberspace to financial links, are becoming the primary areas of great-power competition and are at risk of being weaponised. Increasingly, the US and China follow neither the letter nor the spirit of the rules in their relationships with the EU and its member states.'

Mark Leonard, Jean Pisani-Ferry, Elina Ribakova, Jeremy Shapiro and Guntram Wolff, Securing Europe's Economic Sovereignty, p. 76.

Survival

GLOBAL POLITICS AND STRATEGY

Volume 61 Number 5 | October–November 2019

Contents

On the cover
A US Army C-47 *Chinook* flies over the village of Oreij, Iraq, in advance of a February 2017 assault on the Islamic State stronghold of Mosul.

On the web
Visit www.iiss.org/ publications/survival for brief notices on new books on South Asia, the Middle East and Economy.

***Survival* editors' blog**
For ideas and commentary from *Survival* editors and contributors, visit www.iiss.org/blogs/ survival-blog.

Survival
GLOBAL POLITICS AND STRATEGY

The International Institute for Strategic Studies

2121 K Street, NW | Suite 801 | Washington DC 20037 | USA

Tel +1 202 659 1490   Fax +1 202 659 1499   E-mail survival@iiss.org   Web www.iiss.org

Arundel House | 6 Temple Place | London | WC2R 2PG | UK

Tel +44 (0)20 7379 7676   Fax +44 (0)20 7836 3108   E-mail iiss@iiss.org

14th Floor, GBCorp Tower | Bahrain Financial Harbour | Manama | Kingdom of Bahrain

Tel +973 1718 1155   Fax +973 1710 0155   E-mail iiss-middleeast@iiss.org

9 Raffles Place | #51-01 Republic Plaza | Singapore 048619

Tel +65 6499 0055   Fax +65 6499 0059   E-mail iiss-asia@iiss.org

Survival Online www.tandfonline.com/survival and www.iiss.org/publications/survival

Aims and Scope *Survival* is one of the world's leading forums for analysis and debate of international and strategic affairs. Shaped by its editors to be both timely and forward thinking, the journal encourages writers to challenge conventional wisdom and bring fresh, often controversial, perspectives to bear on the strategic issues of the moment. With a diverse range of authors, *Survival* aims to be scholarly in depth while vivid, well written and policy-relevant in approach. Through commentary, analytical articles, case studies, forums, review essays, reviews and letters to the editor, the journal promotes lively, critical debate on issues of international politics and strategy.

Editor **Dana Allin**

Managing Editor **Jonathan Stevenson**

Associate Editor **Carolyn West**

Assistant Editor **Jessica Watson**

Editorial Intern **Jan Zdrálek**

Production and Cartography **John Buck, Kelly Verity**

Contributing Editors

Ian Bremmer	Bill Emmott	Jeffrey Lewis	Teresita C. Schaffer	Ruth Wedgwood
Rosa Brooks	Mark Fitzpatrick	Hanns W. Maull	Steven Simon	Lanxin Xiang
David P. Calleo	John A. Gans, Jr	Jeffrey Mazo	Angela Stent	
Russell Crandall	John L. Harper	'Funmi Olonisakin	Ray Takeyh	
Toby Dodge	Erik Jones	Thomas Rid	David C. Unger	

Published for the IISS by

Routledge Journals, an imprint of Taylor & Francis, an Informa business.

About the IISS The IISS, a registered charity with offices in Washington, London, Manama and Singapore, is the world's leading authority on political–military conflict. It is the primary independent source of accurate, objective information on international strategic issues. Publications include *The Military Balance*, an annual reference work on each nation's defence capabilities; *Strategic Survey*, an annual review of world affairs; *Survival*, a bimonthly journal on international affairs; *Strategic Comments*, an online analysis of topical issues in international affairs; and the *Adelphi* series of books on issues of international security.

SUBMISSIONS

To submit an article, authors are advised to follow these guidelines:

- *Survival* articles are around 4,000–10,000 words long including endnotes. A word count should be included with a draft.
- All text, including endnotes, should be double-spaced with wide margins.
- Any tables or artwork should be supplied in separate files, ideally not embedded in the document or linked to text around it.
- All *Survival* articles are expected to include endnote references. These should be complete and include first and last names of authors, titles of articles (even from newspapers), place of publication, publisher, exact publication dates, volume and issue number (if from a journal) and page numbers. Web sources should include complete URLs and DOIs if available.
- A summary of up to 150 words should be included with the article. The summary should state the main argument clearly and concisely, not simply say what the article is about.
- A short author's biography of one or two lines should also be included. This information will appear at the foot of the first page of the article.

Please note that *Survival* has a strict policy of listing multiple authors in alphabetical order.

Submissions should be made by email, in Microsoft Word format, to survival@iiss.org. Alternatively, hard copies may be sent to *Survival*, IISS–US, 2121 K Street NW, Suite 801, Washington, DC 20037, USA.

The editorial review process can take up to three months. *Survival*'s acceptance rate for unsolicited manuscripts is less than 20%. *Survival* does not normally provide referees' comments in the event of rejection. Authors are permitted to submit simultaneously elsewhere so long as this is consistent with the policy of the other publication and the Editors of *Survival* are informed of the dual submission.

Readers are encouraged to comment on articles from the previous issue. Letters should be concise, no longer than 750 words and relate directly to the argument or points made in the original article.

ADVERTISING AND PERMISSIONS

For advertising rates and schedules

USA/Canada: The Advertising Manager, Taylor & Francis Inc., 530 Walnut Street, Suite 850, Philadelphia, PA 19106, USA Tel +1 (800) 354 1420 Fax +1 (215) 207 0050.

UK/Europe/Rest of World: The Advertising Manager, Routledge Journals, Taylor & Francis, 4 Park Square, Milton Park, Abingdon, Oxfordshire OX14 4RN, UK Tel +44 (0) 207 017 6000 Fax +44 (0) 207 017 6336.

SUBSCRIPTIONS

Survival is published bi-monthly in February, April, June, August, October and December by Routledge Journals, an imprint of Taylor & Francis, an Informa Business.

Annual Subscription 2019

Institution	£607	$1,062	€890
Individual	£153	$258	€208
Online only	£524	$917	€769

Taylor & Francis has a flexible approach to subscriptions, enabling us to match individual libraries' requirements. This journal is available via a traditional institutional subscription (either print with online access, or online only at a discount) or as part of our libraries, subject collections or archives. For more information on our sales packages please visit http://www.tandfonline.com/page/librarians.

All current institutional subscriptions include online access for any number of concurrent users across a local area network to the currently available backfile and articles posted online ahead of publication.

Subscriptions purchased at the personal rate are strictly for personal, non-commercial use only. The reselling of personal subscriptions is prohibited. Personal subscriptions must be purchased with a personal cheque or credit card. Proof of personal status may be requested.

Dollar rates apply to all subscribers outside Europe. Euro rates apply to all subscribers in Europe, except the UK and the Republic of Ireland where the pound sterling rate applies. If you are unsure which rate applies to you please contact Customer Services in the UK. All subscriptions are payable in advance and all rates include postage. Journals are sent by air to the USA, Canada, Mexico, India, Japan and Australasia. Subscriptions are entered on an annual basis, i.e. January to December. Payment may be made by sterling cheque, dollar cheque, euro cheque, international money order, National Giro or credit cards (Amex, Visa and Mastercard).

Survival (USPS 013095) is published bimonthly (in Feb, Apr, Jun, Aug, Oct and Dec) by Routledge Journals, Taylor & Francis, 4 Park Square, Milton Park, Abingdon, OX14 4RN, United Kingdom.

The US annual subscription price is $842. Airfreight and mailing in the USA by agent named WN Shipping USA, 156-15, 146th Avenue, 2nd Floor, Jamaica, NY 11434, USA. Periodicals postage paid at Jamaica NY 11431.

US Postmaster: Send address changes to Survival, C/O Air Business Ltd / 156-15 146th Avenue, Jamaica, New York, NY11434.

Subscription records are maintained at Taylor & Francis Group, 4 Park Square, Milton Park, Abingdon, OX14 4RN, United Kingdom.

ORDERING INFORMATION

Please contact your local Customer Service Department to take out a subscription to the Journal: **USA, Canada:** Taylor & Francis, Inc., 530 Walnut Street, Suite 850, Philadelphia, PA 19106, USA. Tel: +1 800 354 1420; Fax: +1 215 207 0050. **UK/Europe/Rest of World:** T&F Customer Services, Informa UK Ltd, Sheepen Place, Colchester, Essex, CO3 3LP, United Kingdom. Tel: +44 (0) 20 7017 5544; Fax: +44 (0) 20 7017 5198; Email: subscriptions@tandf.co.uk.

Back issues: Taylor & Francis retains a two-year back issue stock of journals. Older volumes are held by our official stockists: Periodicals Service Company, 351 Fairview Ave., Suite 300, Hudson, New York 12534, USA to whom all orders and enquiries should be addressed. *Tel* +1 518 537 4700 *Fax* +1 518 537 5899 *e-mail* psc@periodicals.com *web* http://www.periodicals.com/tandf.html.

The issue date is October–November 2019.

The print edition of this journal is printed on ANSI-conforming acid-free paper.

THE
ARMED CONFLICT SURVEY
THE WORLDWIDE REVIEW OF POLITICAL, MILITARY AND HUMANITARIAN TRENDS IN CURRENT CONFLICTS
2019

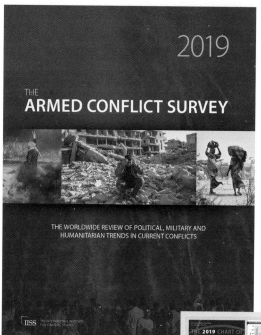

The Armed Conflict Survey 2019 provides in-depth analysis of the political, military and humanitarian dimensions of 33 armed conflicts in six world regions over 2018. This review allows the reader to reflect on the events of the past year and to hone their understanding of the drivers and dynamics of today's wars. It identifies what features set each conflict apart and what dynamics recur across different theatres, tracing how key trends may shape short- and long-term developments.

The growing challenge of criminal networks, the merging of transnational and local dynamics and the targeting of civilians characterised armed conflict in 2018. Climate change and displacement complicated these relationships, while provision of humanitarian aid was used as a weapon of war and urban settings changed the incentives of armed groups.

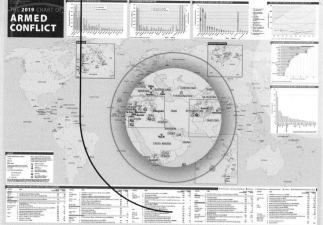

The Armed Conflict Survey 2019 includes maps, infographics and multi-year data, as well as The Chart of Armed Conflict

Should We Stay or Should We Go? The United States and the Middle East

F. Gregory Gause, III

The Clash made that kind of binary choice the centrepiece of their nearly eponymous 1982 hit song, and Americans have been having a more concentrated debate along those very lines about the Middle East. Elites have lagged behind the general public on this issue. Fatigue over the seemingly endless wars in Iraq and Afghanistan was reflected by the American electorate in the last three presidential elections, in which the more dovish candidate on Middle East interventions won. A 2017 poll found that, while a strong majority of Americans believed that the US should stay engaged in the Middle East, 50% of those polled believed that Washington should 'let Middle Easterners resolve their own conflicts' and 25% said that the US should just get out of the region altogether.[1] Yet the American military commitment to the greater Persian Gulf region continues, although reduced from the levels prevailing at the height of the Iraq War in the mid-2000s. But important voices in the American foreign-policy community are now catching up to the public, calling for a reassessment of the extent of American involvement in the region. Meanwhile, American allies in the Middle East itself seem to think that the US is already exiting the region.

The debate about the future American role in the Persian Gulf is a somewhat confused mixture of normative recommendations and questionable empirical assertions. Accordingly, forging a coherent policy requires parsing

F. Gregory Gause, III, is Professor and John H. Lindsey '44 Chair at the Bush School of Government and Public Service, Texas A&M University, and a faculty affiliate of the School's Albritton Center for Grand Strategy.

Survival | vol. 61 no. 5 | October–November 2019 | pp. 7–24   DOI 10.1080/00396338.2019.1662114

the major arguments for a downgrading of the American commitment to the region, examining how the current level of commitment is viewed both in the region and by the US foreign-policy community, and considering both in light of the actual American military presence. Only then can that presence be right-sized by matching a sustainable level of commitment to a realistic set of policy goals.

Staying or going?

In the academic and think-tank communities, there has always been substantial opposition to the militarisation of the American presence in the Persian Gulf. The striking increase in US oil production over the last decade has, in the minds of many observers and more than a few American politicians, reduced the strategic importance of the Gulf to the United States. Those politicians include the current president of the United States.[2] But some analysts follow an older strand of argument against the general notion that the security of oil supplies and transit requires a substantial American military presence.[3] The logic is directly cost–benefit. According to these analysts, such a presence costs the United States more in military spending than the value of the oil that comes out of the Gulf. Charles Glaser and Rosemary Kelanic argued recently that the United States could reduce its defence budget by 15% if it gave up its military presence in the region. The more than four billion barrels of oil stored in strategic reserves by the United States and other countries could mitigate the economic effects of any short- to medium-term shut-off of Gulf oil exports on consumers. It just does not make economic sense, by this logic, to permanently station American military forces and assets in the oil patch.[4]

The very specific energy arguments for an American withdrawal dovetail with more global strategic perspectives arguing that the United States' concentration on the Middle East is taking American resources away from more important strategic concerns such as East Asia. This was the rationale behind the Obama administration's only partially realised 'pivot', or 'rebalancing', to Asia. The Trump administration adopted much the same logic in its 2018 National Defense Strategy, which defined the 'central challenge' to American security as the 'reemergence of long-term, strategic competition' with 'revisionist powers' China and Russia.[5] Analysts in the community of 'restrainers', who call for husbanding American military and diplomatic resources for potential great-power conflicts, have taken particularly sharp aim at the intense military involvement of the United States in the Middle East in the last two decades.[6] Their calls for a strategy of 'offshore balancing' are predicated on a significant reduction in, if not a total withdrawal of, American forces in the Middle East.

This position might not be surprising. But liberal internationalists – past supporters of the Arab Spring and sympathisers in principle if not methodology with George W. Bush's agenda of promoting democracy in the Muslim world – are now picking up this theme. Tamara Cofman Wittes has been a leading voice for a strong American commitment to democratic reform in the Middle East. In her 2008 book on the subject, she called for American elites to overcome the 'deep-seated ambivalence' she saw in the Bush administration's regional 'Freedom Agenda' about pushing friendly Arab states to democratise.[7] As deputy assistant secretary of state for Near Eastern affairs in Barack Obama's first term and then director of the Center for Middle East Policy at the Brookings Institution, she advocated putting democracy promotion at the forefront of American foreign-policy goals in the region. But in the January/February 2019 issue of *Foreign Affairs*, she and co-author Mara Karlin, another veteran of the Obama administration, ran up the white flag. They argued that, while the Middle East matters to the United States, 'it matters markedly less than it used to … [I]t is time for Washington to put an end to wishful thinking about its ability to establish order on its own terms or to transform self-interested and short-sighted regional partners into reliable allies.' They stuck to Wittes's earlier argument that 'lasting stability and security for the Middle East will come only if the relationship between rulers and the ruled is changed', but concluded that such change 'cannot be driven by the United States without far more carrots and sticks than Washington is prepared to deploy'.[8]

There are still voices in the Washington debate who support extensive American military and diplomatic involvement in the Middle East. Neoconservatives, even those who now see the Iraq War as a mistake, favour a regional posture of readiness for a long-term military campaign against anti-American forces.[9] Some neocons in important government positions continue to see that war as having been good and necessary, and regard the decision to withdraw American forces from Iraq in 2011 as wrong-headed.[10] Regional experts attached to institutions favouring the neoconservative version of democracy promotion or a strong American relationship with Israel tend to back continued American commitment.[11] But the tide of the debate has turned from the immediate post-9/11 period, when it was hard to find anyone in 'the blob' who did not think that the Middle East was central to American interests.

These are arguments about what should be done. Yet it is remarkable how many observers, both in the United States and in the Middle East, think that the United States is *already* in the midst of withdrawing from the region. Israeli Prime Minister Benjamin Netanyahu thought that the Obama administration was curtailing US security commitments in the Middle East, to Israel's detriment. He carried his campaign against Obama's policies to the floor of the US House of Representatives, delivering unprecedented direct criticism of an American president and American policy in an address to a joint session of Congress. Israeli officials wondered about American steadfastness in light of its policy toward the Mubarak regime in Egypt during the Arab Spring upheaval of 2011 and in the Syrian 'red line' crisis of 2013. Regarding the first issue, former Mossad chief Danny Yatom commented that 'the way Obama and Hillary Clinton abandoned Mubarak is at once very problematic, and I think hints to other allies – for instance Israel – that these things can happen under certain circumstances to us as well, and to others'.[12] This despite what even Netanyahu and other members of his government acknowledged as the 'unstinting military and security cooperation' between the countries under Obama.[13]

Many observers think the US is already withdrawing

US partners in the Persian Gulf also thought that the Obama administration was leaving them in the lurch given its policies toward Egypt, Syria and Iran. Mohammed bin Zayed Al Nahyan, the crown prince of Abu Dhabi and effective decision-maker in the United Arab Emirates (UAE), told Americans that Obama was 'untrustworthy'. King Abdullah II of Jordan complained privately that 'I think I believe in American power more than Obama does.' Adel al-Jubeir, the Saudi ambassador in Washington during the Syria crisis and now minister of state for foreign affairs, told his superiors in Riyadh that 'Iran is the new great power of the Middle East, and the US is the old.'[14] In reaction to Obama's criticism of Saudi Arabia as a 'free rider' and his call for Riyadh to recognise that it must share the region with Tehran in his 2016 interview in the *Atlantic*, Prince Turki al-Faisal, former head of Saudi foreign intelligence and a former Saudi ambassador to Washington, accused Obama of having 'pivoted to Iran so much that you equate the Kingdom's 80 years of constant friendship with America to an Iranian leadership that continues to describe America as the biggest enemy'.[15] One Saudi commentator contrasted the Obama doctrine, which 'not only represents the president's extreme hesitation toward American military intervention, but also evinces his specific abandonment of the Arab world and his now declared support for a more powerful Iran', with Saudi Arabia's 'Salman Doctrine', which fills this 'deadly vacuum' by taking a more aggressive stance on regional issues.[16] After the 2016 US election, 'Gulf Arab leaders counted the seconds to see the end of the Obama administration, a presidency viewed by many in the region as a stab in the back'.[17] Yet under Obama the United States made substantial arms sales to the Gulf monarchies, attended numerous summit meetings with their leaders and lent support for the Saudi–Emirati intervention in Yemen.

Given their views of Obama, it is hardly surprising that Israel and the Gulf monarchies embraced the Trump administration. President Donald Trump has certainly reciprocated their affections. He moved the American embassy in Israel to Jerusalem and recognised the Israeli annexation of the Golan Heights, asking nothing from Netanyahu in return. He made Saudi Arabia the destination of his first foreign trip as president and has assiduously shielded Crown Prince Muhammad bin Salman from the consequences of the state-sanctioned Saudi killing of dissident journalist Jamal Khashoggi at the Saudi consulate in Istanbul in October 2018. He withdrew from the Joint Comprehensive Plan of Action (JCPOA) – the Iran nuclear deal – and adopted a hard line toward Iran. On the issue of American military power in the Middle East, however, the Trump administration has not been much different than the Obama administration. Israel was surprised and dismayed when Trump announced in December 2018 that he was going to withdraw the small American military force in Syria.[18] The fact that Trump subsequently decided to keep a few hundred US troops in the country could hardly mask his impulse, made clear in the presidential campaign, to reduce the American military role in the region.[19] Saudi Arabia and the smaller Gulf monarchies cannot be heartened by Trump's frequent exhortations to them to pay more to the United States for their security.[20] In June, his stand-down from a military strike on Iran that would have retaliated for its shootdown of a US drone evoked comparisons with Obama's backing away from his pledge to punish Syria for crossing the red line of chemical-weapons use in 2013.[21] While Israel and Saudi Arabia are more than disposed to give Trump the benefit of the doubt, his aversion to American military action in the region is well established.

That an American pullback from the region is under way is also a commonly held view in the academic and analytical communities in the US. Geoffrey Kemp, who served as a Middle East director on Ronald Reagan's National Security Council staff and has witnessed decades of American policy in the region, told a Capitol Hill audience in April 2019 that 'I can't remember a time when US influence in the Middle East was so weak'.[22] The president of the Middle East Institute, America's oldest think tank dedicated to the region, wrote an article in early 2019 entitled 'America's Mideast Retreat'.[23] In January 2019, the consensus of the Brookings Institution's Middle East experts was that 'the perception of US withdrawal from the Middle East overstates the reality, but American influence in the region is certainly on the decline'.[24] Two distinguished American specialists in the politics of the Middle East, in reviewing recent academic work on US policy in the region, concluded that 'the conventional wisdom takes the retreat of US power as a given'.[25]

More and more people, both in the United States and in the Middle East, think that the US is withdrawing from the region or should be doing so. But the empirical reality is not in line with the perception of withdrawal. Should the US nevertheless move in that direction?

More staying than going

At the end of the Obama administration, which by the accounts above marked a substantial decline in the American commitment to the Middle East, there were more than 58,000 American military personnel stationed in the region on land and sea, including more than 5,000 in the campaign against the Islamic State (ISIS) in Syria and Iraq and 8,400 in Afghanistan.[26] Compare that figure to the number of American forces deployed in the region in 1995, just four years after the victory in the First Gulf War and certainly not a time when anyone was talking about an American withdrawal from the Middle East: just below 7,800.[27] The number has not decreased under the Trump administration. According to the International Institute for Strategic Studies, at the end of 2018 there were roughly as many American forces in the region as there were at the end of 2016, at just under 60,000.[28]

There are large and active US military bases in Kuwait, Bahrain, Qatar and the UAE. US forces have access to military facilities in Jordan, Egypt, Iraq and Oman, among other places. There are NATO bases in Turkey.[29] The US continues to engage in Syria and Iraq against what is left of al-Qaeda and ISIS there. The war in Afghanistan, America's longest, is ongoing. None of this has the smell of a country that is looking to leave the greater Middle East.

The argument about American withdrawal from the region turns less on capabilities, of which the US retains a substantial amount, and more on baselines and intentions. It might not be that remarkable that the United States' Middle East allies think it is withdrawing from the region, if their baseline for comparison is 2005. America then had more than 200,000 troops in theatre and was occupying a major regional country. But that is an ahistorical and unrealistic baseline year.[30] The 9/11 attacks led, more for ill than for good, to an unprecedented American military involvement in the greater Middle East. The intense commitment to war in the region was bound to end, and there is every indication that the American involvement in the wars in Iraq (now including Syria) and Afghanistan is, however slowly, coming to an end. One of the many negative consequences of the Iraq War was the sense it left with America's Gulf Arab allies that, when Washington was serious, it would deploy tens of thousands of troops to take care of a problem. If they still believe that, they do need a wake-up call. The real question is how the American military presence in the region compares to the pre-9/11 period. As demonstrated above, even if the Afghan and Iraq–Syria deployments are excluded, that presence is still much greater than it was before 9/11. By any reasonable baseline comparison, the US is not leaving the Middle East.

Those who see a degree of American withdrawal from the region are not wrong, especially when intentions are factored in. As noted, the last three American presidential elections were won by the candidate who was more dovish on the Middle East. Obama was able to wrest the Democratic nomination from Hillary Clinton in 2008 in part because he opposed the Iraq War and she supported it. Both Obama and Trump chose not to use military force in instances when many in the US foreign-policy community thought that they should, or would – Obama in Syria, and Trump in Iran. Neither president was looking for new military engagements in the Middle East, and both were very publicly seeking to avoid such engagements.

Yet, under both the Obama and the Trump administrations, those engagements came. Obama might now regret his decision to intervene in Libya, but intervene he did.[31] He increased the number of troops in Afghanistan at first, before drawing their number down later. He sent troops back into Iraq and into Syria to fight ISIS. He accelerated the American use of drones in locations such as Yemen, increasing American firepower in the regional conflict with Salafi jihadists while minimising the prospects of American casualties.[32] Trump bombed Damascus twice in retaliation for the Assad regime's use of chemical weapons in the civil war. Like Obama, he increased the number of American troops in Afghanistan upon taking office, while also opening talks with the Taliban about an eventual withdrawal. Trump's policy of 'maximum pressure' on Iran brought the two countries to the brink of military conflict in June 2019, with the president sending more troops to the Persian Gulf as tensions ratcheted up.[33] While there is a slender chance that this policy will bring the Iranians to the bargaining table, as Trump clearly hopes, it is more likely to lead to more military crises.

Both presidents discovered that what Marc Lynch calls the 'structural realities' of the American position in the Middle East make a military withdrawal very difficult to realise.[34] As long as the United States is implementing an active counter-terrorism campaign and courting partners that desire continued American involvement, withdrawal will be difficult. If Washington establishes the containment (or, in the Trump administration's case, rollback) of Iranian power as a key foreign-policy goal, leaving the region makes no sense. Important domestic lobbies support an American regional role. The US foreign-policy and military communities see that American role as standard. They are grooved into it by decades of behaviour – base construction, military rotations, arms sales and diplomatic initiatives. Changing those habits would require more political determination than either Obama or Trump has been willing to muster.

Right-sizing the American presence

The preceding observations should squelch any argument that the United States is withdrawing from the greater Persian Gulf region. It is doing no such thing. As in other areas of the world, the post-Cold War period of US dominance of the region is over. But that is a far cry from an end to US involvement there. The question remains: should the United States be withdrawing from the region? The Clash, in 'Should I Stay or Should I Go', sang that 'if I go there will be trouble, and if I stay there will be double'. That balance of trouble might not apply exactly to the Middle East, but the lads had it right that both staying and going involve risks. Foreign military bases in the Middle East have been lightning rods for domestic opposition since before the Second World War. The British discovered that in Egypt, Iraq and Aden. Osama bin Laden pointed to the American military presence in Saudi Arabia as a major motivation for his campaign against the United States, culminating in the 9/11 attacks.[35] ISIS emerged from the chaos in Iraq that accompanied the US military occupation there.[36]

The costs of a military presence can go beyond the financial. Therefore, America's military posture in the Middle East should follow from its interests and be sustainable in terms of American resources and local sensibilities. What is not sustainable is a policy of war against and occupation of regional states, with the aim of changing their domestic politics. The post-9/11 wars have, by one credible estimate, cost the United States $4.933 trillion, with about $1trn in estimated future obligations for veterans' medical and disability costs.[37] US military, civilian and contractor casualties in Iraq and Afghanistan–Pakistan have totalled almost 15,000. Direct civilian deaths in those theatres are estimated to be around 250,000.[38] Given these results, it is hard to make the case that these wars have been a good investment. The United States needs to scale down its ambitions and fix a force presence to match more modest and achievable goals, based on a realistic assessment of its interests.

The key American interest in the Persian Gulf remains the free flow of oil and natural gas. It is certainly true that the United States imports less oil from the region now than in the recent past, given the revolution in fracking and therefore in American energy production. But America's need for Persian Gulf oil has always been modest. It is the Gulf's role in the global oil market that counts. Disruptions there can substantially reduce world oil production, with price effects that immediately ripple through world markets. Oil producers in Canada, Mexico and even Texas are not going to give American consumers a price break if they can get a better deal in China or Japan. Saudi Arabia and its partners Kuwait and the UAE are still the oil producers that have the spare production capacity that can most easily bring extra oil to the market in times of crisis and cut production to support prices. Thus, the Gulf remains centrally important in the world oil market, despite increased American oil production.

> *The Gulf remains important in the world oil market*

Critics of the US military presence in the Gulf are right to question just how necessary the US Navy and Air Force are to the commercial flow of energy. All of the Gulf states want to get their products to market. It is the United States, through sanctions, that has been the chief cause of politically motivated oil-supply restrictions in recent decades. Interruptions of supply, if they are short-term, can be dealt with relatively easily through strategic petroleum reserves and the normal operation of markets. Prices might spike, but over time they will come down. Oil prices since the 1970s have been extremely volatile.[39] The US presence in the Gulf has done nothing to change that. Military basing also cannot guarantee political stability in oil-producing states. The United States has demonstrated no desire to intervene militarily in Middle Eastern states to bolster its partners against domestic uprisings. That did not happen with the shah, despite the oil-price spike that accompanied the Iranian Revolution. It did not happen with Hosni Mubarak in 2011. It is unlikely to happen in the face of comparable domestic upheavals in Saudi Arabia, no matter what the short-term effects on the oil market might be.

But there are still some oil-related American interests that an appropriately sized military presence in the Persian Gulf might assist in securing. Regional actors have used military power to disrupt oil flows – in particular, by way of the tanker war of the 1980s during the Iran–Iraq War and Saddam Hussein's invasion of Kuwait in 1990. A US military presence in the Gulf could discourage similar events and, if they occur anyway, facilitate an effective military response. These are rare events, to be sure. So is a house catching fire, but that does not mean homeowners should forgo insurance. More generally, the United States has a strategic interest in preventing any other state from dominating the Gulf. A dominant power could be tempted to use the vast oil resources of the region for political purposes. This was the primary motivation behind the George H.W. Bush administration's decision to intervene against Saddam's invasion of Kuwait. If the Iraqi leader had been able to control both Iraqi and Kuwaiti oil, and consequently been in a position to intimidate Saudi Arabia into following his lead on oil issues, the temptation to let non-economic considerations drive his oil decisions would have been impossible to resist. An American military presence in the Persian Gulf makes any other power's control over a preponderance of the region's oil resources much less likely.

There is another high-risk, low-probability scenario in which a US military presence in the Gulf could serve American interests. The US gets very little oil from the region. China, however, gets 44% of its crude oil from the Gulf.[40] Right now, Beijing and Washington basically share an interest in the unfettered flow of energy from the Gulf. If geopolitics become more conflictual, that might not be the case. In the event of a conflict in East Asia involving the United States, the ability to control Chinese access to Gulf energy would be a strategic plus. More generally, American influence in the oil patch cannot but help to afford it leverage if relations with China deteriorate.

There is also a more normal kind of influence that American administrations like to exercise on Gulf oil producers, regarding oil prices. Every president since Richard Nixon has attempted to affect oil production and price decisions by Gulf states closely tied to the US, whether it be Saudi Arabia, Iran under the shah or the smaller Gulf monarchies.[41] Trump is merely the first to do it on Twitter. Usually American presidents push the Gulf allies to keep prices low; on rare occasions they cajole them into raising prices.[42] It is hard to imagine that Gulf states would be receptive to these American influence efforts if the United States were not playing a role in their security. The US military presence in the Gulf is the warrant for that role. The same goes for American efforts to prod the Gulf allies on other issues, from counter-terrorism to nuclear proliferation to the Arab–Israeli peace process. These are small (with the exception of Saudi Arabia) and militarily weak (not excepting Saudi Arabia) states. They will seek out great-power protectors elsewhere if the United States does not play that role, with a concomitant reduction in American influence and rise in that of some other great power.

It is hard to calculate on a purely cost–benefit basis whether the insurance-policy elements and the everyday-influence aspects of the American military presence in the Gulf justify the expense of the deployments. It is safe to assume that an appreciable share of the in-country basing costs in Kuwait, the UAE and Qatar are covered by the host countries, though how much is shrouded in secrecy.[43] Qatar built Al Udeid Air Base, the largest American base in the Middle East, for the United States in 1996, and will spend $1.8bn to upgrade it under a 2018 agreement with the United States.[44] Poorer governments in Bahrain (home to the US Fifth Fleet), Oman and Jordan undoubtedly contribute a much smaller share of the basing costs, Iraq and Afghanistan even less. Exiting these facilities would unquestionably save the United States money, but the assumption that such savings would lead to a large overall reduction in the Pentagon's budget is far from certain.

Right-sizing the American force presence in the greater Persian Gulf requires a prudent but steady drawdown from the military commitments in Iraq and Afghanistan. The nation-building experiments there have failed. Washington should be looking to give those governments help in securing themselves against their domestic enemies, but on a flexible timetable aimed clearly at ultimate withdrawal. If transnational Salafi jihadist groups such as al-Qaeda or ISIS are threatening to re-establish themselves in these countries, US forces can deploy to help those governments on a temporary basis from more secure bases elsewhere in the region.

The United States has been wise to avoid establishing permanent bases in Egypt and to end its long-term combat deployments in Saudi Arabia, which lasted from the end of the First Gulf War to the fall of Saddam's regime in Iraq. The domestic politics of those countries are too complex to sustain foreign-military presences, which have in the past become focal points for the mobilisation of political opposition. Permanent bases in those countries would also link the United States to an even greater extent with regimes that, though broadly friendly, have interests that do not completely match American ones.

The US basing and access arrangements in the smaller Gulf monarchies avoid most of these complications. These are small states with a history of political stability. Having been protectorates of the British Empire, they have a long and overwhelmingly accepting tradition of foreign-military presences. Their elites, and appreciable portions of their populations, recognise the need for foreign protection in a dangerous neighbourhood. Kuwait is the only one among the states that has free elections to a legislature with real, if limited, powers. In no election since the First Gulf War in 1991 has the American military presence been raised as a serious issue, despite the success of Islamist candidates of various stripes (Muslim Brotherhood, Salafi and Shia) in some of those elections. Bahrain is the most politically troubled of the small monarchies, with an occasionally mobilised Shia majority ruled by a Sunni ruling family. It saw massive protests during the uprisings of 2011, and serious tensions remain.[45] But there have been no protests against the Fifth Fleet presence or attacks on its base. Many of these states are very wealthy and can subsidise the American basing structure, as they do today. Arguably, American protection has allowed Qatar and the UAE to pursue adventurous foreign policies that have not always been in accord with American interests. But the American military presences there also afford Washington at least some leverage to dial back the outsized ambitions of these small countries.

*   *   *

On balance, the American ground-force base in Kuwait, the Fifth Fleet naval base in Bahrain, Al Udeid Air Base in Qatar, Al Dhafra Air Base in the UAE and the access arrangements in Oman provide the United States with a politically and financially sustainable military presence in a part of the world that, as long as oil remains a strategic commodity, will still be central to the world economy. The US presence in the region yields important benefits in terms of regional and global influence. The basing structure is sufficient for a more modest set of American goals in the region. By itself, it cannot support a policy of military intervention and occupation in the interest of democracy promotion or regime change in larger regional states. But it can support a robust counter-terrorism strategy, afford Washington influence with regional governments, and act as a deterrent to efforts by other actors to disrupt or dominate the world's most important oil patch. This should be enough for an America that should be looking to rock many fewer casbahs in the Middle East.

Notes

1   Middle East Institute, 'American Attitudes on Middle East Policies', MEI/Ipsos Poll, October 2017, https://www.mei.edu/sites/default/files/publications/IpsosMEIPoll_Oct2017.pdf. Different polls give different slants on the general question. A 2018 poll conducted by the Chicago Council on Foreign Relations found that majorities of those polled supported the use of American troops to stop Iran from supporting terrorist groups and to fight 'Islamic extremist groups in Iraq and Syria', while fewer than 50% of those polled would support the use of American troops to support Israel if it were to bomb Iran's nuclear facilities and Iran were to retaliate against Israel or to overthrow Syrian President Bashar al-Assad. Dina Smeltz et al., 'America Engaged: American Public Opinion and US Foreign Policy', 2018 Chicago Council on Foreign Relations Survey, Appendix Figure 3, p. 26, https://www.thechicagocouncil.org/sites/default/files/report_ccs18_america-engaged_181002.pdf.

2   President Trump called the attacks attributed to Iran on oil tankers in June 2019 'very minor' and said that the region was less strategically important to the United States than it used to be. 'Other places get vast amounts of oil there. We get very little … So we are not in the position that

we used to be in in the Middle East.' Tessa Berenson, 'Exclusive: President Trump Calls Alleged Iranian Attack on Oil Tankers "Very Minor"', *Time*, 18 June 2019, https://time.com/5608787/iran-oil-tanker-attack-very-minor/. For somewhat more analytical takes, see Thomas P.M. Barnett, 'America's Post-Oil Grand Strategy', 18 February 2016, http://thomaspmbarnett.squarespace.com/globlogization/2016/2/18/americas-post-oil-grand-strategy.html; and Willis L. Krumholz, 'Petroleum Powerhouse: Why America No Longer "Needs" the Middle East', *National Interest*, 29 April 2019, https://nationalinterest.org/feature/petroleum-powerhouse-why-america-no-longer-needs-middle-east-55012.

3 See Eugene Gholz and Daryl G. Press, 'Protecting "The Prize": Oil and the US National Interest', *Security Studies*, vol. 19, no. 3, 2010, pp. 453–85; and Joshua Rovner and Caitlin Talmadge, 'Hegemony, Force Posture and the Provision of Public Goods: The Once and Future Role of Outside Powers in Securing Persian Gulf Oil', *Security Studies*, vol. 23, no. 3, 2014, pp. 548–81. For another political perspective with much the same conclusion, see Toby C. Jones, 'Don't Stop at Iraq: Why the US Should Withdraw from the Entire Persian Gulf', *Atlantic*, 22 December 2011, https://www.theatlantic.com/international/archive/2011/12/dont-stop-at-iraq-why-the-us-should-withdraw-from-the-entire-persian-gulf/250389/.

4 Charles L. Glaser and Rosemary A. Kelanic, 'Getting Out of the Gulf: Oil and US Military Strategy', *Foreign Affairs*, vol. 96, no. 1, January/February 2017, pp. 122–31.

5 US Department of Defense, 'Summary of the 2018 National Defense Strategy of the United States of America', https://dod.defense.gov/Portals/1/Documents/pubs/2018-National-Defense-Strategy-Summary.pdf.

6 For two recent examples, see Emma Ashford, 'Unbalanced: Rethinking America's Commitment to the Middle East', *Strategic Studies Quarterly*, Spring 2018, pp. 127–48; and Jasen J. Castillo, 'Passing the Torch: Criteria for Implementing a Grand Strategy of Offshore Balancing', in Center for a New American Strategy, 'New Voices in Grand Strategy', Michael J. Zak Lecture Series, April 2019, https://www.cnas.org/publications/reports/new-voices-in-grand-strategy.

7 Tamara Cofman Wittes, *Freedom's Unsteady March: America's Role in Building Arab Democracy* (Washington DC: The Brookings Institution, 2008), particularly chapter 6; quote on p. 102.

8 Mara Karlin and Tamara Cofman Wittes, 'America's Middle East Purgatory', *Foreign Affairs*, vol. 98, no. 1, January/February 2019, pp. 88–100, quotes from pp. 89–90 and 99–100.

9 See Max Boot, 'Why Winning and Losing Are Irrelevant in Syria and Afghanistan', *Washington Post*, 30 January 2019, https://www.washingtonpost.com/opinions/global-opinions/the-us-cant-win-the-wars-in-afghanistan-and-syria--but-we-can-lose-them/2019/01/30/e440c54e-23ea-11e9-90cd-dedb0c92dc17_story.html?utm_term=.2851bdde992d.

10 See David M. Drucker, 'John Bolton: No Regrets About Toppling Saddam',

Washington Examiner, 14 May 2015, https://www.washingtonexaminer.com/john-bolton-no-regrets-about-toppling-saddam.

11 See Mark Dubowitz and Ray Takeyh, 'The United States Finally Has an Aggressive Plan to Defang Iran', *Foreign Policy*, 21 May 2018, https://foreignpolicy.com/2018/05/21/the-united-states-finally-has-an-aggressive-plan-to-defang-iran-trump-pompeo/; and Robert Satloff, 'Don't Pull Back', *Foreign Affairs*, vol. 98, no. 3, May/June 2019, pp. 188–90.

12 Quoted in Ilai Z. Saltzman, 'Not So "Special Relationship"? US–Israel Relations During Barack Obama's Presidency', *Israel Studies*, vol. 22, no. 1, Spring 2017, p. 55.

13 Dana H. Allin and Steven N. Simon, 'Trump and the Holy Land', *Foreign Affairs*, vol. 96, no. 2, March/April 2017, pp. 37–45.

14 Quotes from Jeffrey Goldberg, 'The Obama Doctrine', *Atlantic*, April 2016, https://www.theatlantic.com/magazine/archive/2016/04/the-obama-doctrine/471525/.

15 Prince Turki al-Faisal, 'Mr. Obama, We Are Not "Free Riders"', *Arab News*, 14 March 2016, http://www.arabnews.com/columns/news/894826.

16 Nawaf Obaid, 'The Salman Doctrine: The Saudi Reply to Obama's Weakness', *National Interest*, 30 March 2016, https://nationalinterest.org/feature/the-salman-doctrine-the-saudi-reply-obamas-weakness-15623.

17 Mohammed Alkhereiji, 'No Tears Shed in Gulf Cooperation Council over Obama's Exit', UPI, 31 January 2017, https://www.upi.com/Top_News/Voices/2017/01/31/No-tears-shed-in-Gulf-Cooperation-Council-over-Obamas-exit/5421485880741/.

18 See David M. Halbfinger, 'Syria Pullout by US Tilts Mideast Toward Iran and Russia, Isolating Israel', *New York Times*, 20 December 2018, https://www.nytimes.com/2018/12/20/world/middleeast/syria-us-withdrawal-iran.html.

19 Former US ambassador to Israel Daniel Shapiro, now a distinguished fellow at the Institute for National Security Studies in Tel Aviv, wrote that 'Trump is doubling down on reducing US involvement in the Middle East in an even more brutal fashion [than Obama]: bashing regional allies as freeloaders, demanding payment for US protection, and loudly declaiming against any plausible logic for a US military presence in the region'. Daniel Shapiro, 'Trump Leaves Israel in the Lurch', *Atlantic*, 28 December 2018, https://www.theatlantic.com/ideas/archive/2018/12/israelis-arent-happy-trumps-syria-withdrawal/579103/.

20 For one recent example, see Ben Hubbard, 'Trump Accuses Saudis of Giving US a Bad Deal. Is That True?', *New York Times*, 28 April 2019, https://www.nytimes.com/2019/04/28/world/middleeast/trump-saudi-arabia-military.html.

21 See Eliana Johnson and Wesley Morgan, 'Trump Fudges His Red Line as Iran Takes Out a US Drone', Politico, 20 June 2019, https://www.politico.com/story/2019/06/20/trump-iran-drone-1374227.

22 Joan Polaschik, Geoffrey Kemp and Daniel Benaim, 'The Future of US Engagement in the Middle

East', *Middle East Policy*, vol. 26, no. 2, Summer 2019, pp. 5–30, https://onlinelibrary.wiley.com/doi/full/10.1111/mepo.12418.

23 Paul Salem, 'America's Mideast Retreat', *World Today*, February–March 2019, https://www.chathamhouse.org/publications/twt/americas-mideast-retreat.

24 Jeffrey Feltman et al.,'The New Geopolitics of the Middle East: America's Role in a Changing Region', Brookings Institution, January 2019, https://www.brookings.edu/wp-content/uploads/2019/01/FP_20190107_new_geopolitics_of_mena_final.pdf.

25 Marc Lynch and Amaney Jamal, 'Introduction: Shifting Global Politics and the Middle East', in 'POMEPS Studies 34 – Shifting Global Politics and the Middle East', March 2019, https://pomeps.org/wp-content/uploads/2019/03/POMEPS_Studies_34_Web.pdf.

26 Ash Carter, 'The Logic of American Strategy in the Middle East', *Survival*, vol. 59, no. 2, April–May 2017, pp. 13–24.

27 US Department of Defense, 'Active Duty Military Personnel Strengths by Regional Area and by Country', 30 September 1995, accessed from Defense Manpower Data Center, DoD Personnel, Workforce Reports and Publications, Historical Publications, Worldwide Manpower Distribution by Geographical Area (M05), https://www.dmdc.osd.mil/appj/dwp/dwp_reports.jsp.

28 International Institute for Strategic Studies, *The Military Balance 2019* (Abingdon: Routledge for the IISS, 2019), Chapter 3 ('North America'), https://www.iiss.org/publications/the-military-balance/the-military-balance-2019/north-america. Calculated by totalling troops reported in the 'Deployment' section for the US order of battle in Afghanistan, Bahrain, Iraq, Jordan, Kuwait, Qatar, Saudi Arabia, Syria and the United Arab Emirates.

29 Matthew Wallin, 'US Military Bases and Facilities in the Middle East', American Security Project, June 2018, https://www.americansecurityproject.org/wp-content/uploads/2018/06/Ref-0213-US-Military-Bases-and-Facilities-Middle-East.pdf.

30 For a similar argument, see Steven Simon and Jonathan Stevenson, 'The End of Pax Americana: Why Washington's Middle East Pullback Makes Sense', *Foreign Affairs*, vol. 94, no. 6, November/December 2015, pp. 2–10.

31 'President Obama: Libya Aftermath "Worst Mistake" of Presidency', BBC News, 11 April 2016, https://www.bbc.com/news/world-us-canada-36013703.

32 Andreas Krieg, 'Externalizing the Burden of War: The Obama Doctrine and US Foreign Policy in the Middle East', *International Affairs*, vol. 92, no. 1, January 2016, pp. 97–113.

33 Anthony Capaccio and Margaret Talev, 'US Sends 1,500 Troops to Mideast After Blaming Attacks on Iran', Bloomberg, 24 May 2019, https://www.bloomberg.com/news/articles/2019-05-24/trump-to-send-1-500-more-troops-to-mideast-as-iran-tensions-rise.

34 Marc Lynch, 'Belligerent Minimalism: The Trump Administration and the

Middle East', *Washington Quarterly*, vol. 39, no. 4, Winter 2017, p. 128.

35 See in particular his 1996 'Declaration of Jihad Against the Americans Occupying the Land of the Two Holy Mosques' and his 1998 'Declaration of the World Islamic Front' in Bruce Lawrence (ed.), *Messages to the World: The Statements of Osama bin Laden*, trans. James Howarth (New York: Verso, 2005), pp. 23–30, 58–62.

36 See William McCants, *The ISIS Apocalypse: The History, Strategy and Doomsday Vision of the Islamic State* (New York: St. Martin's Press, 2015), chapters 1 and 2.

37 Watson Institute for International and Public Affairs, 'Summary of War Spending, FY2001–FY2019', Costs of War Project, Brown University, November 2018, https://watson. brown.edu/costsofwar/figures/2018/ budgetary-costs-post-911-wars-through-fy2019-59-trillion.

38 Watson Institute, 'Direct Deaths in Major War Zones: Afghanistan & Pakistan (October 2001– October 2018) and Iraq (March 2003–October 2018)', Costs of War Project, Brown University, November 2018, https://watson. brown.edu/costsofwar/figures/2018/ direct-war-death-toll-2001-480000.

39 For remarkably graphic evidence of that volatility, see BP, 'Statistical Review of World Energy 2019', 68th edition, p. 24, https://www. bp.com/content/dam/bp/business-sites/en/global/corporate/pdfs/ energy-economics/statistical-review/ bp-stats-review-2019-oil.pdf.

40 *Ibid.*, p. 28.

41 For an account of American oil diplomacy in the Gulf in the 1970s, see Andrew Scott Cooper, *Oil Kings: How the US, Iran and Saudi Arabia Changed the Balance of Power in the Middle East* (New York: Simon & Schuster, 2011).

42 That was the case in 1986, when the Saudis had crashed world prices in an effort to discipline other OPEC members for cheating on production quotas. George H.W. Bush, then the US vice president, went to Riyadh in April of that year to argue for more 'stability' in the market – at higher prices. See Daniel Yergin, *The Prize: The Epic Quest for Oil, Money and Power* (New York: Simon & Schuster, 1991), pp. 755–8.

43 David S. Cloud, 'How Much Do Allies Pay for US Troops? A Lot More than Donald Trump Says', *Los Angeles Times*, 1 October 2016, https://www. latimes.com/nation/la-na-trump-allies-20160930-snap-story.html.

44 Paul McCleary, 'Can Trump Find a Better Deal than the US Air Base in Qatar?', *Foreign Policy*, 20 July 2017, https://foreignpolicy.com/2017/07/20/ can-trump-find-a-better-deal-than-the-u-s-air-base-in-qatar/; and Karen DeYoung and Dan Lamothe, 'Qatar to Upgrade Air Base Used by US to Fight Terrorism', *Washington Post*, 24 July 2018, https://www.washingtonpost. com/world/national-security/qatar-to-upgrade-air-base-used-by-us-to-fight-terrorism/2018/07/23/19e04c84-8eb7-11e8-b769-e3fff17f0689_story. html?utm_term=.2da2845f5802.

45 See Ronald Neumann, 'Bahrain's Rulers' Last Chance to Save Their Country', *National Interest*, 20 June 2019, https://nationalinterest.org/ feature/bahrains-rulers-last-chance-save-their-country-63532. Neumann was the US ambassador to Bahrain from 2001 to 2004.

Towards a More Prudent American Grand Strategy

John Glaser, Christopher A. Preble and A. Trevor Thrall

In its conduct of foreign policy, the Trump administration has been impulsive, ad hoc and incompetent. Where the president has been able to wrench the debate to better reflect his world view, the result has been a mixture of backlash, false starts and foolish policies. In other cases, the broken and outdated grand strategy of primacy has continued apace, though with considerably less strategic coherence and greater resistance from both allies and adversaries. The reputation of the United States has plunged since Trump's election, making it much more difficult to successfully pursue US interests, however they are defined. In this dynamic and crowded international arena, resistance to US power and influence is growing, and America's capacity for overcoming this resistance is diminishing.[1]

Given the ineptitude of this White House, and the inability of this president to unite even his own cabinet around a clear strategy, it is hard to escape the conclusion that US foreign policy is undergoing an irreversible shift. Yet many in the foreign-policy establishment, at whom Trump has directed so much of his bluster, continue to believe a return to the status quo ante is imperative. The world under American primacy has grown safer, richer and freer, they point out, and that benefits the United States. They argue that the costs of maintaining the current system – a loosely liberal

John Glaser is director of foreign-policy studies, **Christopher A. Preble** is vice-president for defence and foreign-policy studies, and **A. Trevor Thrall** is a senior fellow at the Cato Institute. They are the co-authors of *Fuel to the Fire: How Trump Made America's Broken Foreign Policy Even Worse (and How We Can Recover)* (Cato Institute, 2019), from which this article is adapted.

Survival | vol. 61 no. 5 | October–November 2019 | pp. 25–42   DOI 10.1080/00396338.2019.1662131

order dependent on US military predominance – are either not onerous or are clearly outweighed by the benefits. We should look past Donald Trump, ignore calls for the United States to change direction and focus instead, they insist, on making primacy work better – including by explaining its benefits more clearly to the American people.

A better-concerted marketing campaign, however, is unlikely to make the pre-Trump foreign policy popular. Americans, particularly younger ones who have reached adulthood during the post-9/11 'global war on terror', doubt that American military dominance has delivered safety and security. They are eager to continue and even expand America's engagement with the rest of the world, but sceptical that such engagement must be primarily military in nature – as it was during most of the past quarter-century. A sober, clear-eyed assessment, one that looks past Trump's late-night Twitter rants and the false bravado of his campaign-style rallies, would take account of the changes taking place around the world, and focus on America's unique ability to adapt. These advantages have been weakened during the Trump era, but they certainly have not vanished.

Reimagining US foreign policy

Over the past 70 years, under US leadership, the world has indeed changed – and mostly for the better. People around the world are living longer, healthier and more fulfilling lives. The benefits are not limited solely to those living in advanced economies; living standards have improved even for the world's poorest. Though pockets of chaos and violence persist, organised, state-on-state conflict has nearly disappeared. That does not mean, however, that American hard power is responsible for all this progress.[2]

Relative peace between the great powers since 1945 also coincides with the emergence of nuclear weapons. And inter-state war has further declined, in large measure due to modern conventional weapons that have created an environment of defence dominance. Together, these trends explain why the threat and use of force plays a much smaller role in international politics than a generation ago: offence is risky, conquest is hard, and the costs of conflict often seem to outweigh any possible benefits to the national interest.

Norms have also evolved to tame the war-prone nature of the international system. The United Nations Charter affirmed the importance of sovereign equality and explicitly proscribed the use of force except in self-defence or unless authorised by the UN Security Council. That doesn't mean that inter-state war has ended, but occasional transgressions – from the Soviet Union's invasion of Afghanistan to the United States' overthrow of Saddam Hussein's Iraq – inevitably generate criticism and recrimination from the international community.

Global trade has thrived within the international system that emerged after the Second World War, and globalisation accelerated after the fall of the Berlin Wall. Today, for the most part, states aim to preserve and expand global trade, both because it is economically beneficial and because it is broadly conducive to peace. The belief that global trade depends on US military might is widespread, but unsubstantiated.[3] At the very least, America's current commitments and force posture far exceed what is necessary to secure a global commons safe enough for states to engage in mutually beneficial trade.[4]

In short, although the American foreign-policy establishment sees US power as the linchpin of the global order and the United States as an indispensable nation, the truth is that many of the trends contributing to stability and economic growth are emergent phenomena, occasionally helped and occasionally hurt by US foreign policy, but driven by factors largely exogenous to US designs. Fortunately, many countries benefit from the relative peace and prosperity that prevails today and are therefore motivated to help preserve it. At this pivotal moment in history, America's leaders should seek to lock in those attitudes and build a more resilient global order that is not overly dependent on a single dominant state.

Defenders of primacy regularly decry the crisis of America's diminishing military power and exhort their fellow Americans to support cuts to domestic spending and to tolerate the higher taxes that would be required in order to pay for a military budget approaching $1 trillion. There is considerable evidence that the American people's willingness to sustain such a massive military build-up simply doesn't exist and cannot be easily mobilised. Though most Americans don't know how much they are already paying for the US military, either in absolute terms or relative to major rivals such as China and Russia, a mere one in three thinks we should be spending more.[5]

The debate over the organising principles that should guide American foreign policy once Trump leaves office is already under way. The expert community is engaged, for the first time in a long time, in a healthy conversation about the future of US grand strategy.[6] On the right, establishment politicians such as former Ohio governor John Kasich and several conservative academics have sharply criticised Trump's foreign policy, issuing calls for the United States to renounce Trump's unilateralism and to reaffirm America's commitment to active global leadership.[7] On the left, resistance to Trump's 'America First' agenda is often accompanied by calls for a renewed commitment to use US power to promote a liberal human-rights agenda and to challenge corrupt, authoritarian capitalism around the world.[8] But among progressives there has also been a growing sentiment that the United States relies too much on military force.[9] In a speech at Westminster College in 2017, Senator Bernie Sanders called on Americans to confront the fact that 'American intervention and the use of American military power has produced unintended consequences which have caused incalculable harm'.[10] In a related vein, Peter Beinart has made a strong case for bringing the 'war on terror' to an end and substantially reducing America's overseas military presence.[11]

No new cold war

Bridging much of the left and right, however, is perhaps the most popular motivation for a new guiding principle in US foreign policy: the fear of a rising China. Observers across the political spectrum argue that the United States should once again use containment as the model, this time assigning China the role of superpower nemesis.[12]

Though the temptation to replay America's greatest hits is understandable, the Cold War is a poor guide to grand strategy in the twenty-first century. China is not the Soviet Union, and the conditions of today's international system are not those of the post-Second World War era. Unlike the Soviet Union, China has not declared its intention to destroy the United States or capitalism, or to overturn democratic governments around the world. Debate over China's exact intentions will persist, but there are good reasons to believe that China's best strategy is to continue working within the same global system that helped it grow and prosper over the past several decades. Any efforts by China to add to its territory through conquest would not only incur the direct costs of war, but also raise the threat of confrontation with the United States and others, as well as risk negative economic consequences.

Beyond that, despite its impressive and still-growing economic and military might, China does not present a direct security threat to the United States. Though China's neighbours must be wary of its growth, the risk of war between China and the United States would be vanishingly low even if China's intentions were ambitious, mostly due to geography and nuclear weapons. Even in the extreme scenario in which China re-absorbs Taiwan by military force, little would change for the United States. Moreover, aggressive efforts to deny Chinese influence in its own neighbourhood would make cooperating with China on other important matters – including trade – more difficult.[13]

Though the United States has long relied on buttressing its Asian allies – South Korea and Japan – as well as special partners like Taiwan against potential threats from China, all of them today have economies capable of supporting competent militaries, and they are also trading partners of great importance to China. While little trade took place between the American- and Soviet-bloc nations during the Cold War, China's largest trading partner is the United States, followed by various Asian neighbours. As a result, a Cold War-style mobilisation, complete with separate trading blocs, would be unwise economically, and may be impossible.

So, where should the debate over US foreign policy go? Restraint has gradually gained traction in the academic community. More recently, fatigue from almost two decades of costly post-9/11 wars has generated public support for a less interventionist foreign policy. 'The American public', explains Ian Bremmer, 'is less convinced than ever that it is the US's responsibility to guarantee global security and prosperity in the 21st century.'[14] At times, Trump has seemed to tap into this discontent. Over the course of his 2016 presidential campaign, he adopted positions that enthused his base – including promises to end wars, forgo nation-building missions and extract more value from US alliances – but that were deeply unpopular with the men and women responsible for US foreign policy over the past several decades. His victory signalled that the politics of foreign policy were undergoing a seismic shift. Positions that would have once rendered a candidate for high office unelectable might even have helped Trump win.

The danger today is that reactions to Trump will cause another shift, but in the wrong direction. To the extent that both Democrats and Republicans oppose Trump, some have also become more hawkish in their opposition to his perceived (but apocryphal) retrenchment. Trump's Beltway detractors have erroneously associated him with isolationism and retreat, rendering sensible adjustments to US foreign policy increasingly unwelcome. They would create a false dichotomy, explains the University of Birmingham's Patrick Porter, 'between primacy or "global leadership" on one hand and inward-looking isolation on the other'.[15] The 'advocates of primacy', Porter notes, 'brand today's realists who call for retrenchment as Trumpian', in the hope that even a tenuous association with Trump's many other unpopular policy positions and unpleasant character traits would forever discredit calls to rein in the excesses of US foreign policy. Americans should reject this false binary choice in favour of a third option.

Embracing restraint

The United States should embrace a foreign policy of restraint grounded in three core principles. The first concerns the scope of American ambitions. The United States should reject the myths of primacy and the hyperactive foreign policy it has promoted. The United States is not the indispensable nation. Nor is it insecure. Nor is it capable of micromanaging the world's affairs efficiently and effectively from Washington. In this light, the United States should pursue a more modest foreign-policy agenda that facilitates global trade and focuses more narrowly on the physical security of the homeland, while worrying less about trying to police the world.

The United States enjoys so many geographic, economic and military advantages that it does not need to do much to ensure its own security. Civil wars and unrest in the Middle East, for example, may compromise

American interests such as the stability of oil prices or the spread of democracy, but they do not threaten American national security much, if at all. US troops should not be sent to try to pick winners in these internecine fights, nor should they be expected to remain in these places for years or decades on the pretext of stabilising the region or, even worse, building nations in America's image.

Similarly, US security does not depend upon maintaining permanent alliances.[16] To be sure, countries friendly to the United States continue to feel threatened by predatory or potentially hostile neighbours. It is important to remember, however, that the primary Cold War motivation to create alliances was to deter the military threat posed by a Soviet Union that most believed intended to dominate Europe and threaten the existence of the United States. Without such a justification today, the United States gains little from its alliances and instead puts itself at risk of having to cope with crises and fight wars on behalf of other nations.

Rethinking and reforming the US alliance system is therefore of primary importance. A considerable share of US military spending does, in fact, go to protecting allies from harm. In that sense, Americans are essentially paying for the privilege of defending others. Trump is not the first to acknowledge this: in 1963, then-president John F. Kennedy insisted that the United States 'cannot continue to pay for the military protection of Europe while the NATO states are not paying their fair share … We have been very generous to Europe and it is now time for us to look out for ourselves' and 'consider very hard the narrower interests of the United States'.[17] Nearly every administration since has acknowledged the problem of allied burden-sharing in both Europe and Asia.[18]

Primacists fear that without US security commitments, allies will take insufficient steps to defend themselves from harm, choosing instead to capitulate to regional rivals such as China or Russia. But restructuring, and even rescinding, America's security commitments to allies to reflect modern realities would not ineluctably mean their domination by neighbouring powers. With proper encouragement, formerly weak and fragile US partners could become capable and empowered ones. A regional descent into arms races and insecurity spirals is by no means the most likely scenario.

When common security challenges emerge, the United States can always work with others to address them. We need not be permanently locked into alliances to do so.

Although terrorist groups such as al-Qaeda and the Islamic State (ISIS) remain a concern, the terrorist threat cannot serve as a guiding principle for foreign policy. Not only is the eradication of terrorism impossible in a practical sense, but over time terrorist threats have proven less substantial than many believed immediately after the attacks of 9/11.[19] Moreover, the 'war on terror' has illustrated that continuous military intervention is not the answer and has in fact exacerbated the problem.[20]

The terrorist threat cannot guide foreign policy

Instead, the United States should address the threat of terrorism by continuing to improve its homeland-security measures, maintaining vigilance on the intelligence front, and using diplomacy and other tools to discourage conflict where possible.

Contrary to what some critics of restraint argue, doing less in foreign policy does not mean retreat or isolationism. It simply means that the United States should recognise – and take advantage of the fact – that it does not need to fight most wars, meddle in the internal affairs of other nations, or worry about who owns which oilfield in the Middle East or which island in the South China Sea. Restraint means realising that although it is easy to care about such issues, most things that happen in the world don't have a significant impact on the security of the United States or the well-being of American citizens. Restraint means appreciating that, when the United States does intervene in the affairs of other nations, its ability to manage outcomes is very limited, often bitterly contested and usually expensive.

The second principle undergirding restraint concerns the means America uses to achieve its foreign-policy goals. The primary tools of US engagement should be diplomacy, commerce and cooperation, rather than military force. War and intervention have played a disproportionately large role in US foreign policy since the Second World War. Looking back on the Cold War, Kenneth Waltz noted that 'in the roughly thirty years following 1946, the United States used military means in one way or another to intervene in the affairs of other countries about twice as often as did the Soviet Union'.[21] In the post-Cold War era, US military action has been even more ubiquitous. The Congressional Research Service lists more than 200 instances of the use of US armed forces abroad since 1989.[22]

While the United States will always need a strong military for deterrence and self-defence, the use of force should be seen as a last resort. The current American addiction to military intervention reflects both the desire to manage the world's affairs and the belief that war or the threat of it is the best way to do it. In fact, the effectiveness of military force is far more limited. As America's efforts to use force to spread democracy, fight terrorism and build nations abroad have shown, the liberal application of force can make small conflicts bigger, create new enemies and pull the United States into unwinnable situations.

Restraining the impulse to use force may require Washington to accept that the United States can't always get the results it wants. Nor will the dividends always come quickly. Diplomacy is a slow business in the best of times and cannot always prevent or resolve conflicts. But, as the Syrian case shows, military intervention often is not a sensible option for the United States. The Syrian civil war did not represent a direct threat to the United States, certainly not one that justified risking American lives, and the underlying problems in Syria were not susceptible to resolution through US military action. The only responsible course was to encourage negotiations among the various factions in the hope of eventually producing a durable peace.

More importantly, diplomacy, commerce and cooperation are the most direct paths to achieving most of what Americans want from foreign policy: good relations with friendly nations, increasing levels of mutually beneficial trade, and the ability to work multilaterally to set global standards and solve global problems. While advocates of primacy argue that a global US military presence is necessary to protect world markets, for example, in fact the trade policies of the United States and international cooperation among nations are far more important. Trade will survive if the United States pulls its military out of South Korea, but not if the US pulls out of the World Trade Organization and abandons all of its trade agreements.

Diplomacy is also the best first step when dealing with contentious issues and 'rogue nations'. The Obama administration's negotiation of the Joint Comprehensive Plan of Action – the Iran nuclear deal – was a good example of how diplomacy can resolve problems that might otherwise look like candidates for the use of force. Rather than bombing or invading Iran, Washington combined global economic sanctions with multilateral diplomacy, producing an agreement that halted, and rolled back, Iran's nuclear programme. The contrast between this approach and that of the Bush administration to Iraq in 2003 is stark and instructive. In the former case, unlike the latter, there were no lives lost; the United States did not spend hundreds of billions of dollars on a military campaign; and there was no decade-long occupation by American troops, no civil war following regime change and no spike in terrorism.

Primacy has eroded America's moral authority

A successful foreign policy of restraint will require a much greater commitment to diplomacy than the Trump administration has manifested. The United States should upgrade its diplomatic infrastructure and capabilities, which will mean taking some of the excess funds in the Pentagon's budget and devoting them to training, and employing experienced diplomats to do the hard work of nimble statecraft. The State Department must be rebuilt and revitalised after the demoralising 'reorganisation' it suffered on Rex Tillerson's watch and the indifference to diplomacy – bordering on disdain – that Trump and his team have displayed thus far. The US should seek multilateral support for most major international undertakings, especially those involving the potential use of economic sanctions or military force.

The third principle for restraint is to realign US foreign policy with the liberal values and norms of behaviour traditionally espoused by US political leaders. Primacy has eroded America's moral authority and undermined the normative, rules-based character of the international system. It is difficult to make the case that US military power upholds the liberal order while it is being used to help Saudi Arabia, among the world's most regressive authoritarian regimes, commit war crimes in Yemen. America's hardline policy against Iran may be justified in part by its illiberal regime and support for terrorist proxies, but Washington itself chooses to support numerous dictatorships that routinely back violent militants. The United States has repeatedly used force in the name of humanitarian intervention to stop thuggish regimes from slaughtering their own people, despite lending its support to equally reprehensible governments.

The basic liberal principles that underpin today's international institutions and legal regimes are laudable and worthwhile. But in its zeal to police that order, America has weakened the most important conventions of this post-Second World War system: territorial integrity, non-intervention and nonaggression. In a notable 1986 ruling, the International Court of Justice held that the United States violated these very principles of international law by supporting the Contra rebels against the government of Nicaragua and by mining Nicaraguan harbours by way of covert CIA operations. The United States dismissed the legitimacy of the court and refused to pay reparations – just the type of response permitted under exceptionalist logic and one deeply at odds with the internationalist tradition heralded by defenders of the liberal, rules-based international order. Even when the United States has worked within the system, it has often disregarded its constraints. In 2011, the UN Security Council approved a US-led NATO military operation to impose a no-fly zone to protect Libyan civilians from the Gadhafi regime's suppression of armed rebels. But the US-led coalition almost immediately exceeded the largely humanitarian UN mandate and pursued regime change.

Assuming the role of global cop and enforcer of the liberal world order seems to necessitate violating the very rules and norms which the US commands others to follow. In 1974, Turkey invaded and annexed a large portion of Cyprus, going on to ethnically cleanse the area, but Washington never brought itself to condemn the transgressions of a NATO ally. Israel, too, has annexed and occupied territory in violation of international law while receiving significant support from the United States. John Kerry, the US secretary of state at the time, castigated Russia's annexation of Crimea this way: 'You just don't in the 21st century behave in 19th century fashion by invading another country on completely trumped up pretext.'[23] With the illegal invasion of Iraq still ripe in the collective conscience, Kerry's assertion was hardly persuasive. When then-president Barack Obama later condemned Russia's territorial grab on the grounds that international law prohibits redrawing territorial borders 'at the barrel of a gun', reiterating a metaphor Kerry had used, much of the rest of the world baulked: the United States did something similar in the 1999 Kosovo war.[24] Such tone-deaf hypocrisy perverts the so-called liberal order and undermines the legitimacy of US power.[25]

The goal of a world order constrained by international rules and norms and infused with liberal principles is not advanced by a foreign policy that routinely disregards those very constraints. As the most powerful country in the world, the United States has enormous influence over the character of the international system. More than any other nation, its actions determine the basis of international norms. A grand strategy of restraint carries the benefit of being more consistent with both the US constitution and the UN Charter. A less interventionist foreign policy is not only appropriate given the essentially benign security environment we currently inhabit, it would also resurrect the United States' international image and revive the American tradition of serving as an example for other countries to emulate, rather than a ruffian to obey.

Benefits of restraint

A foreign policy of restraint grounded in these three principles – setting modest, achievable objectives; privileging diplomacy, trade and cooperative global engagement over threats; and exemplifying the behaviour Americans expect others to follow – will benefit the United States in several ways. Most obviously, a more restrained foreign policy will reduce the negative side effects of America's hubris. Foreign-policy elites protested when Trump labelled their handiwork a 'disaster', but substantial criticism was warranted. The trouble is that he has mostly compounded his predecessors' errors. The human costs of the past two decades of military intervention have been staggering on all sides. The financial burden has also been enormous: the cost of the 'war on terror' alone could be as high as $6trn.[26] Diminished public confidence in US foreign policy at home and growing anti-Americanism around the world have been another cost of a hyperactive America.

Forgoing the unilateral use of military force and intervening less often would increase America's diplomatic flexibility and its moral capital, boosting the effectiveness of its efforts to foster prosperity and peace. Nations such as Switzerland and Canada play a prominent role in international diplomacy because other states know they have no intention of using military force to coerce others. The United States, by contrast, has frequently encountered resistance. The US does not have to adopt a neutral stance in international affairs. It can and should oppose human-rights violations, wars and terrorism, and its diplomacy should reflect that. Nor does it have to abandon all forms of coercion. Multilateral economic sanctions – or threats thereof – have at times proven to be effective tools of diplomacy. But, on balance, the track record of military and economic coercion in international politics is not a good one, especially when the negotiations centre on issues of great importance to the target country. In such cases, threats of military force are more likely to result in escalation and further violence than to produce the end the US seeks.

Of course, many observers believe just the opposite, that taking military force 'off the table' will hamstring any efforts at diplomacy. Why would Iran or North Korea, for example, be willing to negotiate with the United States about their nuclear programmes if there were not some sort of threat at the end of the line? This logic makes sense in the abstract, but the number of cases in which it is applicable is fewer than many contend. Why did Iran and North Korea seek nuclear weapons in the first place? In large part, the answer is their fear of the United States. If the US had a deeper commitment to diplomacy and cooperation, potential adversaries would have less need for a nuclear deterrent.

A less expansive foreign-policy agenda would also allow the United States to seek significant reductions in military spending. The money saved could be put to the urgent task of rebuilding the United States and restoring some semblance of fiscal responsibility. An enormous chunk of America's defence spending goes to support a military big enough to intervene abroad on a regular basis; to the ongoing support of campaigns in Afghanistan,

Iraq, Syria and elsewhere; and to the upkeep of hundreds of military bases around the world. Right-sizing and optimising the force structure for self-defence, ending the military side of the 'war on terrorism' and pulling back from bases America does not need for its own security could produce savings of hundreds of billions of dollars each year without any reduction in US security.[27]

Furthermore, reforms are required to make the foreign-policy process more transparent to Congress and the public. Democratic theory holds that the free press and the marketplace of ideas help democracies make better policy by subjecting the arguments of political leaders, and the performance of government institutions and policies, to scrutiny and debate. Presidents and the Pentagon, on the other hand, often prefer secrecy because it means they don't have to explain what they're doing or why they are doing it, or be held accountable for things that go wrong. That approach to foreign policy should be anathema in a democracy.

One thing Trump's presidency proves is that even a commander-in-chief averse to the imperial responsibilities of primacy will not readily shirk them. Power does not check itself, either in the international domain or the domestic. The shift from primacy to restraint will therefore require not merely a change in the conception of the US role in the world, but a restoration of the principles embedded in the constitution. Congress needs to rein in the unilateral powers of the executive branch by reasserting its authority under Article I to determine the nation's involvement in foreign conflicts. Too often presidents have waged war and conducted military operations short of war without clear authorisation to do so. This practice not only cuts against the separation of powers set out in the constitution, it also prevents the people's representatives from ensuring that the nation's foreign policy reflects public preferences.

Finally, a restrained foreign policy would align better with the classical liberal values established at the nation's founding and help curb excessive government power at home. It might also increase public confidence in America's moral leadership. The founders wisely noted the connection between America's foreign policy and the health of American democracy at home. Playing the role of global hegemon and habitually using military force abroad undermines liberal norms. At the same time, the pursuit of primacy has fuelled the unhealthy growth of presidential power, which in turn has promoted American tendencies towards intervention and meddling abroad while threatening the rule of law and civil liberties at home.

Donald Trump's ascendance to the highest office in the nation nearly three years ago was perhaps the most compelling illustration of the hazards of vesting the presidency with so much unbridled power. We share many of the concerns voiced by the foreign-policy establishment about what Trump has done, and might yet do, to US foreign policy, and how detrimental it could be to the stability of the international system. But any world order that depends for its survival on the whims of a single person in a single branch of government in a single country is simply untenable. Trump seems to have come along at the tail end of America's 'unipolar moment', and the relative decline in US power is yet another reason to revise American grand strategy to accommodate changing conditions in an increasingly multipolar world.

Notes

1 See Kristen Bialik, 'How the World Views the US and Its President in 9 Charts', Pew Research Center, 9 October 2018, https://www.pewresearch.org/fact-tank/2018/10/09/how-the-world-views-the-u-s-and-its-president-in-9-charts/.

2 See Christopher J. Fettweis, 'Unipolarity, Hegemony, and the New Peace', *Security Studies*, vol. 26, no. 3, May 2017, pp. 423–51.

3 See Duncan Snidal, 'The Limits of Hegemonic Stability Theory', *International Organization,* vol. 39, no. 4, Autumn 1985, pp. 579–614.

4 See Joshua R. Itzkowitz Shifrinson and Sameer Lalwani, 'It's a Commons Misunderstanding: The Limited Threat to American Command of the Commons', in Christopher A. Preble and John Mueller (eds), *A Dangerous World? Threat Perceptions and US National Security* (Washington DC: Cato Institute, 2014).

5 Frank Newport, 'Americans Not Convinced US Needs to Spend More on Defense', Gallup, 21 February 2018, https://news.gallup.com/poll/228137/americans-not-convinced-needs-spend-defence.aspx. See also Jessica T. Mathews, 'America's Indefensible Defense Budget', *New York Review of Books*, vol. 66, no. 12, 18 July 2018, pp. 23–4.

6 See, for example, Richard Fontaine et al., 'New Voices in Grand Strategy', Michael J. Zak Lecture Series, Center for a New American

Security, April 2019, https://www.cnas.org/publications/reports/new-voices-in-grand-strategy.

7   See Hal Brands, *American Grand Strategy in the Age of Trump* (Washington DC: Brookings Institution Press, 2018); Eliot A. Cohen, *The Big Stick: The Limits of Soft Power and the Necessity of Military Force* (New York: Basic Books, 2018); Colin Dueck, 'The Future of Conservative Foreign Policy', *Texas National Security Review*, vol. 2, no. 1, November 2018, https://tnsr.org/roundtable/policy-roundtable-the-future-of-conservative-foreign-policy/#intro; and John Kasich, 'Reclaiming Global Leadership', *Foreign Affairs*, vol. 97, no. 4, July/August 2018, pp. 102–12.

8   See, for example, Elizabeth Warren, 'A Foreign Policy for All', *Foreign Affairs*, vol. 98, no. 1, January/February 2019, pp. 50–61.

9   See 'Policy Roundtable: The Future of Progressive Foreign Policy', *Texas National Security Review*, 4 December 2018, https://tnsr.org/roundtable/policy-roundtable-the-future-of-progressive-foreign-policy/; and Daniel Nexon, 'Toward a Neo-Progressive Foreign Policy', *Foreign Affairs*, 4 September 2018, https://www.foreignaffairs.com/articles/united-states/2018-09-04/toward-neo-progressive-foreign-policy.

10   Alex Ward, 'Read: Bernie Sanders's Big Foreign Policy Speech', Vox, 21 September 2017, https://www.vox.com/world/2017/9/21/16345600/bernie-sanders-full-text-transcript-foreign-policy-speech-westminster.

11   Peter Beinart, 'America Needs an Entirely New Foreign Policy for the Trump Age', *Atlantic*, 16 September 2018, https://www.theatlantic.com/ideas/archive/2018/09/shield-of-the-republic-a-democratic-foreign-policy-for-the-trump-age/570010/.

12   See Emma Ashford and Trevor Thrall, 'The Battle Inside the Political Parties for the Future of US Foreign Policy', War on the Rocks, 12 December 2018, https://warontherocks.com/2018/12/the-battle-inside-the-political-parties-for-the-future-of-u-s-foreign-policy/.

13   See Charles L. Glaser, 'A US–China Grand Bargain? The Hard Choice Between Military Competition and Accommodation', *International Security*, vol. 39, no. 4, Spring 2015, pp. 49–90; and Joshua Shifrinson, 'Should the United States Fear China's Rise?', *Washington Quarterly*, vol. 41, no. 4, Winter 2019, pp. 65–83.

14   Ian Bremmer, 'Americans Want a Less Aggressive Foreign Policy. It's Time Lawmakers Listened to Them', *Time*, 19 February 2019, https://time.com/5532307/worlds-apart-foreign-policy-public-opinion-poll-eurasia/.

15   Patrick Porter, 'A World Imagined: Nostalgia and Liberal Order', Cato Institute Policy Analysis no. 843, 5 June 2018, https://www.cato.org/publications/policy-analysis/world-imagined-nostalgia-liberal-order.

16   See Benjamin H. Friedman, 'Bad Idea: Permanent Alliances', Defense 360, 13 December 2018, https://defense360.csis.org/bad-idea-permanent-alliances/.

17   'Remarks of President Kennedy to the National Security Council Meeting', 22 January 1963, US Department of State, Office of the Historian, Foreign Relations of the United

States, vol. XIII, Western Europe and Canada, https://history.state.gov/historicaldocuments/frus1961-63v13/d168.

18 See James Goldgeier, 'When President Trump Heads to Europe, Discussion Turns to Burden-sharing', *Washington Post*, 14 November 2018, https://www.washingtonpost.com/news/monkey-cage/wp/2018/07/09/president-trump-goes-to-europe-this-week-its-leaders-are-bracing-for-the-impact/?utm_term=.56b2db3338eb.

19 See John Mueller and Mark Stewart, *Chasing Ghosts: The Policing of Terrorism* (New York: Oxford University Press, 2015).

20 See A. Trevor Thrall and Erik Goepner, 'Step Back: Lessons for US Foreign Policy from the Failed War on Terror', Cato Institute Policy Analysis no. 814, 26 June 2017, https://www.cato.org/publications/policy-analysis/step-back-lessons-us-foreign-policy-failed-war-terror.

21 Kenneth N. Waltz, 'The Emerging Structure of International Politics', *International Security*, vol. 18, no. 2, Fall 1993, pp. 44–79.

22 See Barbara Salazar Torreon and Sofia Plagakis, 'Instances of Use of United States Armed Forces Abroad, 1798–2018', Congressional Research Service, 28 December 2018, https://fas.org/sgp/crs/natsec/R42738.pdf.

23 See Reid J. Epstein, 'Kerry: Russia Behaving Like It's the 19th Century', Politico, 2 March 2014, https://www.politico.com/blogs/politico-now/2014/03/kerry-russia-behaving-like-its-the-19th-century-184280; and Michael R. Gordon, 'Kerry Takes Offer of Aid to Ukraine and Pushes Back at Russian Claims', *New York Times*, 4 March 2014, https://www.nytimes.com/2014/03/05/world/europe/secretary-of-state-john-kerry-arriving-in-kiev-offers-1-billion-in-loan-guarantees-to-ukraine.html.

24 Obama is quoted in, for example, Aamer Madhani, 'Obama to Putin: Don't Deal With Ukraine Over "Barrel of a Gun"', *USA Today*, 12 March 2014, https://eu.usatoday.com/story/news/world/2014/03/12/obama-yatsenyuk-white-house-ukraine-crimea/6335573/.

25 See Martha Finnemore, 'Legitimacy, Hypocrisy, and the Social Structure of Unipolarity: Why Being a Unipole Isn't All It's Cracked Up to Be', *World Politics*, vol. 61, no. 1, January 2009, pp. 58–85.

26 See Neta C. Crawford, 'United States Budgetary Costs of the Post-9/11 Wars Through FY2019: $5.9 Trillion Spent and Obligated', Watson Institute for International and Public Affairs, Brown University, 14 November 2018, https://watson.brown.edu/costsofwar/files/cow/imce/papers/2018/Crawford_Costs%20of%20War%20Estimates%20Through%20FY2019%20.pdf.

27 See John Glaser, 'Withdrawing from Overseas Bases: Why a Forward-Deployed Military Posture Is Unnecessary, Outdated, and Dangerous', Cato Institute Policy Analysis no. 816, 18 July 2017, https://www.cato.org/publications/policy-analysis/withdrawing-overseas-bases-why-forward-deployed-military-posture.

Is America Prepared for Great-power Competition?

Brian D. Blankenship and Benjamin Denison

The Trump administration's National Defense Strategy (NDS) and National Security Strategy (NSS) bluntly state that the United States is now back in the business of great-power competition. Chief among the core American security interests identified by these documents is strategic competition with China and Russia. As the NDS puts it, 'the central challenge to U.S. prosperity and security is the *reemergence of long-term, strategic competition* by ... revisionist powers', specifically China and Russia.[1] In response to the growing power of rival states, the NSS recommends a return to Cold War-style strategic competition: 'An America that successfully competes is the best way to prevent conflict. Just as American weakness invites challenge, American strength and confidence deters war and promotes peace.'[2]

Admittedly, the growing competition between the US and China, and the US and Russia, may not directly resemble the strategic competition of the Cold War.[3] During that conflict, the US competed with the Soviet Union not just in the military domain, but also in the economic and political realms as both powers attempted to create orders that were separate and distinct from each other. In this competition, all elements of the state were marshalled to aid in the struggle. Alliances and transnational partners were courted to support the order each superpower preferred. These patterns are unlikely to be repeated today. Nevertheless, given that Washington has begun to stress

Brian D. Blankenship is an Assistant Professor in the Department of Political Science at the University of Miami, and can be contacted via email at brdblank@gmail.com. **Benjamin Denison** is a Postdoctoral Fellow at the Center for Strategic Studies at the Fletcher School of Law and Diplomacy at Tufts University, and can be contacted via email at bcdeniso@gmail.com.

Survival | vol. 61 no. 5 | October–November 2019 | pp. 43–64   DOI 10.1080/00396338.2019.1662134

the centrality of great-power competition, it is important to assess whether the US would be prepared to head towards a similar type of competition, regardless of its precise contours. Understanding how the actions taken during the Cold War period drove American strategic success is essential to evaluating America's capacity for great-power competition today.

We contend that many of the long-term trends shaping America's power base, along with the Trump administration's domestic and foreign policies, are working against the United States' ability to successfully engage in the kind of great-power strategic competition being envisioned in the NDS and NSS. With a fiscal policy that has been dominated by tax cuts more than investment in physical and human infrastructure; stagnant military budgets lacking in robust investment in modernisation and future capabilities; and a foreign policy that has alienated core allies and fostered distrust of American leadership among US strategic partners, efforts to pursue the goals of the NSS and NDS are unlikely to succeed. Given this disconnect between current trends and the geopolitical objectives laid out in the NSS and NDS, further discussion is needed within the Trump administration and the foreign-policy establishment about what American grand strategy should look like and how to match US resources and capabilities to strategic ends that will best secure American interests.

Strategies of great-power competition

While there is a robust debate in the US over the kind of grand strategy the country should adopt,[4] the Trump administration seems to view the coming era of great-power competition as a return to a Cold War-style contest, in this case with China and Russia. Its strategy is intended to prevent these powers from 'contesting [America's] geopolitical advantages and trying to change the international order in their favor'.[5] It seeks to stop them from gaining 'veto authority over other nations' economic, diplomatic, and security decisions' by maintaining US pre-eminence in the international system and preventing other powers from inhibiting American political, economic and military dominance.[6] These goals reflect a strategy of 'primacy', which upholds the view that a great power is most secure when it has no challengers.[7] There are plenty of alternative grand strategies, but as the US has consistently pursued primacy since at least 1991, if not 1945, it is unsurprising that the Trump administration would take a view of great-power competition that is consistent with this strategy.[8]

When great powers engage in strategic competition, they typically undertake both internal balancing and external balancing to help increase their own power within the international system while preventing the rising influence of others. Internal balancing means building military and economic strength, and investing in technologies and other domestic areas that help convert the latent capabilities of the state into material strength. External balancing entails working to build alliances and partnerships with other states to address common threats.[9] Both are aimed at building a state's resources and overall power in order to exert more influence in the international system while denying competitors the ability to assert more influence themselves. Because it is not reliant upon the actions of other actors, internal balancing is more reliable than external balancing, and is therefore favoured by great powers.[10]

Internal balancing can encompass any activity that expands the state's economy, boosts government revenues and builds military capabilities. This could potentially include expanding the tax and fiscal capacity of the state, increasing government revenue and pushing for greater employment. Internal balancing can also be achieved through investments in education and technological innovation; the building up of physical infrastructure and transportation hubs; and the construction of dry docks, aircraft factories and other industrial facilities.

Table 1: **Strategies for great-power competition**

Strategy	Actions	Benefits
Internal balancing	• Increase military spending • Grow domestic economy • Increase state revenues • Invest in technological innovation • Build infrastructure and human capital	• More latent material resources to convert to military power • Modernisation of military technology • Growth of military power
External balancing	• Build and maintain formal military alliances and informal partnerships • Obtain foreign-basing rights • Entice local partners with arms transfers and foreign aid • Work through international institutions	• Increased power-projection capabilities • Cooperative partners willing and able to share the burden of limiting the influence of competitors • Increased legitimacy when acting in concert with other states

Whereas internal balancing can take a great deal of time and involves costly investments, external balancing through the formation of alliances can allow a state to rapidly shift the balance of power in its favour. Moreover, allies can provide a great power with basing access, which is essential for the projection of power over large distances.[11] Iceland, for example, was a valuable member of NATO throughout the Cold War despite not having a standing army because it hosted an important US naval base. Making alliance guarantees is not the only way to sway states to one's side, however; oftentimes, great powers use more transactional means, such as foreign aid and arms transfers, to gain favours. The US base at Camp Lemonnier in Djibouti, for instance, comes at the price of some $63 million per year in rent, in addition to substantial aid and preferential procurement.[12]

In the early Cold War period, the US engaged in both internal and external balancing in its competition with the Soviet Union. Between 1949 and 1969, US military spending averaged 9.1% of GDP.[13] In 1949, the top rate of federal income taxes was 91% (this had decreased to 70% by 1965), and the highest rate of federal estate taxes was almost 80%.[14] Tax revenues promoted economic growth and allowed for robust investment in the state's military capacity. A focus on increasing the domestic sources of US power also allowed for the beginnings of large infrastructure investments, including the interstate highway system, and other federal grant programmes intended to build up the physical and human capital of the country.[15] Increased domestic investment in public research universities and higher education helped improve collegiate education, and in 1950, the National Science Foundation was created as a means of promoting technological and scientific progress.

Externally, the United States established its first peacetime alliance with the formation of NATO in 1949. The following decade, NATO expanded beyond its initial 12 members, and the United States formed a number of other alliances, including bilateral pacts with Japan, South Korea, the Philippines and Taiwan, as well as multilateral pacts such as the Australia–New Zealand–United States Security Treaty (ANZUS), the Southeast Asia Treaty Organization (SEATO) and the Central Treaty Organisation (CENTO). The US also established a number of more informal partnerships – especially in the Middle East, with countries such as Israel, Saudi Arabia and Egypt – based on arms sales and aid. This network of partnerships served not only to deter communist expansion, but also to provide the United States with a network of naval and air bases.[16]

Thus, as the Cold War developed, the United States, like the Soviet Union, began consolidating external allies and shoring up its international commitments. However, the competition between the US and the Soviet Union did not just exist at the inter-German border and in the United Nations Security Council. Rather, both competed to produce superior domestic economic growth, technological innovation, educational outcomes and other direct indicators of predominance and status. Both societies were mobilised in the service of a singular purpose, a level of commitment that has not been duplicated in the US since the Cold War ended.

Internal balancing and domestic capacity

As the Trump administration signals a return to great-power competition, it is unclear whether the United States can replicate the kind of internal balancing that enabled 'peace through strength' in the Cold War. While the White House admits in both the NSS and the NDS that strengthening the American economy and other sources of domestic power will be necessary to prevail in the competition it believes the country faces, it is not at all certain that the administration has the capacity to actually carry out the requisite programme of internal balancing.

The end of the Cold War left the United States in such a strong position internationally that it was hard to imagine how anything could disturb the so-called Pax Americana over which it presided.[17] However, although the American economy has continued to grow, and advancements in weapons technology have created a modern and robust military, increased budget deficits, tax cuts and other factors have undermined America's capacity to mobilise internal resources for great-power competition. The national debt is predicted to hit 100% of GDP in the 2020s and approach 150% by 2048.[18] Given that debt-servicing payments increase over time, this financial burden could harm the United States' ability to fund national priorities, including increased defence spending. Attempts to rein in this financial problem by cutting various forms of discretionary spending, including defence spending through the Budget Control Act, have only harmed military-modernisation programmes and undermined readiness for future great-power contingencies, as well as decreasing investment in research and education.[19]

Beyond mandatory-spending programmes on entitlements such as Medicare and Social Security, the United States' debt problems have had two main causes, both of them political in origin: tax cuts and peripheral wars.[20] Since 2001, the US federal government has cut taxes under presidents George W. Bush, Barack Obama and Donald Trump.[21] As a result, the deficit has grown even as federal revenues have decreased.[22] While supply-side economic theory holds that lower marginal tax rates encourage investment and innovation, the history of the Cold War shows that high levels of public revenue led to increased investment and public spending in areas that contributed to building American power.[23] Today, the highest tax rate in the US is only 37%, compared to 91% in 1955 and 50% in 1985. Likewise, the highest estate-tax rate is only 40% today compared to 77% in 1955 and 55% in 1985.[24] As mandatory spending increases with an ageing population, the federal deficit seems to be stuck in a spiral whereby revenues are being continually trimmed back even as expenditures continue to grow. This limits the availability of shrinking resources for building the country's military infrastructure and other forms of internal balancing for prospective great-power competition.

While tax cuts during a period of unipolarity and American hegemony might make sense in the absence of any US military operations, the supposed peace dividend stemming from a reduced need for military readiness after the Cold War ended did not go to domestic priorities. Nor did it go to keeping the deficit in check.[25] Instead, since the launch of the war in Afghanistan in 2001, the United States has spent more than $6 trillion expanding its military footprint in the Middle East, Africa and elsewhere as part of the 'global war on terror' – spending that happened even as taxes were being cut, and that now accounts for more than 25% of the national debt.[26] President Trump has expressed a desire to end these peripheral wars and campaigned on nation building at home, but has struggled to achieve either goal, illustrating the difficulties the US may face in trying to prioritise great-power competition.[27]

The fiscal situation of the United States has further harmed the country's ability to engage in internal balancing by resulting in lower levels of military spending, which has largely flatlined due to the Budget Control Act. Without a commitment to find revenue elsewhere, it is unclear how military spending could meaningfully increase, or how additional internal resources for defence could be mobilised. Recent projections for the US budget indicate that interest payments on the national debt will exceed defence spending as early as 2023.[28] Reductions in tax revenue, coupled with increased expenditures on foreign adventures and domestic entitlements, have made the economic base of US military power appear increasingly shaky.

This matters because American competitiveness and military strength are ultimately driven by economic sources of power. If these sources become unreliable, tough choices on allocations will need to be made. Retrenchment from commitments abroad is often the most palatable choice. In times of crisis, it may become difficult to surge resources to where they are needed. While the US does not currently face this dilemma, long-term trends suggest that mobilising for great-power competition will become more difficult.[29]

It is unclear how military spending could increase

The decline in America's capacity for internal balancing is not limited to federal defence appropriations. At the state level, governments have increasingly cut funding to higher education, placing public research universities on shakier financial ground and increasing tuition fees for students.[30] This has had the effect of increasing Americans' indebtedness, making it more difficult to fully mobilise the country's human resources. Universities find it necessary to seek out foreign students willing to pay exorbitant tuition fees to make up for budget shortfalls.[31] Unlike during the Cold War, the prioritisation of tax cuts over investment in higher education has made the country's university system – historically an engine of innovation, growth and strategic competitiveness – more likely to falter.[32]

Internal-balancing efforts face major constraints due to increased domestic polarisation as well. Any move to increase tax revenues to reinvest in defence, education, infrastructure, innovation and debt reduction appears unlikely to succeed in the face of staunch bipartisan (and especially Republican) opposition. While the more progressive wing of the Democratic Party has shown greater willingness to increase taxes – especially on the wealthy – its political success is far from guaranteed, and in any case increases in tax revenue are likely to be offset by ambitious spending proposals, leaving the deficit largely intact. Increased polarisation at home has also reduced the chances of achieving a bipartisan consensus on foreign policy or a united domestic front against a common enemy – both of which contributed to the United States' success in the Cold War.[33] Although a desire to mobilise the nation for strategic competition may be present, elected officials appear unable to work together to drive internal-balancing efforts.[34]

Meanwhile, the Trump administration itself does not appear to be promoting the kind of internal-balancing efforts that will be needed for its strategy to succeed. Despite identifying great-power competition as a focus of the nation's foreign and defence policies, the administration has pushed through massive tax cuts that are expected to increase federal deficits by $1.9trn between 2018 and 2028, and to increase the federal deficit by 17% in 2018 alone.[35] It has also called for spending cuts across executive agencies.[36] In addition, the White House has engaged in tariff wars with trade partners that have weakened domestic manufacturing and harmed the domestic economy.[37] Thus, it has undermined the country's strength and prevented the consolidation of a bipartisan consensus to face the great-power competition it says is coming. All in all, the United States does not appear to possess the same capacity, or even desire, to build the kind of domestic unity that it enjoyed during the Cold War.

External balancing and international capacity

If the United States' internal constraints limit its capacity to engage in great-power competition, might its external partnerships make up for this? The Cold War has bequeathed to the United States a global network of alliances that contain many of the world's major economies. For the purposes of great-power competition, Washington could leverage its allies in two ways: politically and militarily. Politically, its alliances provide the United States with an array of partners from which it can solicit support for its preferred policies, such as trade agreements with terms favourable to the US. Allies can also support the US by refusing to cooperate with the country's adversaries, for example by refusing to sell them advanced technologies.[38] Many US allies host American military bases, which helps the United States to project power overseas.[39] Militarily, alliances add to the collective military capabilities the United States can potentially draw upon.

Since launching his presidential campaign, President Trump has questioned the premises of American alliances. He has claimed that NATO is 'obsolete' and indicated that defending NATO partners such as Montenegro might not be in the American national interest.[40] US allies in Asia have hardly fared much better. Trump reportedly weighed the possibility of withdrawing US troops from South Korea and Japan, and considered the merits of striking a nuclear deal with North Korea that would leave it with the capacity to strike its regional neighbours but not the US mainland.[41]

To the extent that Trump does value American alliances, it is in terms of their burden-sharing functions. By itself, Trump's desire for increased allied contributions to the common defence is understandable and hardly unique to him. Such contributions would serve to render the US alliance network more capable. However, Trump's suggestion that the United States might be unwilling to defend allies that do not carry their weight may not be consistent with his administration's desire to engage in great-power competition. Ultimately, there are few – if any – allies with the capacity to act as an independent counterweight to the United States' principal competitors.

In Asia, perhaps the best candidate to serve as a regional counterweight to China is Japan. Yet Japan is hobbled not only by the weight of its history – which has left the country reluctant to take significant steps towards military self-reliance and its neighbours uneasy about Japanese military power – but by long-term demographic trends.[42] After peaking at around 128m in 2008, Japan's population is expected to drop to 100m by 2053, and to 88m by 2060.[43] Other regional candidates face challenges of their own. India is preoccupied with economic development and its rivalry with Pakistan,[44] while Australia would face challenges projecting power into East Asia.

In principle, a coalition of Southeast Asian states – perhaps with the ten members of the Association of Southeast Asian Nations (ASEAN) at its core – could present a formidable check on China's ability to exert influence and project power in the western Pacific. After all, ASEAN represents a combined population of 636m people with the sixth-largest GDP in the world.[45] However, there is little indication that the Southeast Asian nations neighbouring China have any intention of balancing it either individually or collectively. ASEAN members remain highly dependent on China economically: trade with China accounted for nearly 20% of GDP for the average Asian country in 2014, which is nearly ten times the average European country's trade with the Soviet Union as a percentage of GDP during the Cold War, which topped out at 2% in 1983.[46]

The states of Southeast Asia have preferred to hedge

So far, the states of Southeast Asia have preferred to hedge rather than risk China's ire by aligning too closely with the United States.[47] Research indicates that a fear of taking sides and antagonising neighbouring great powers, coupled with collective-action problems, often impede the formation of counterbalancing coalitions among weaker states.[48] This dynamic may change as China's economy and military continue to grow, or if its behaviour becomes significantly more aggressive, but in the near term it is unlikely that the United States will find enough willing partners for a balancing coalition in Southeast Asia. In any case, the Trump administration's policies seem to do more to push allies away than to unite them.

In Europe, the question is less one of resources than of political circumstances. Russia's $1.6trn GDP is dwarfed by that of the European Union ($17.3trn), as well as by the combined GDP of the three largest European NATO members: France, Germany and the United Kingdom ($8.9trn).[49] Many members of NATO have increased their military spending, and eight countries now meet NATO's 2%-of-GDP target for military spending, up from three in 2014.[50] But many allies still lag behind. Of particular note is Germany, which, with a GDP of $3.7trn, has the potential to be the fulcrum of the European balance of power.[51] The Germans, however, have proven reluctant to translate their economic resources into military power: the country spent only 1.2% of GDP on defence in 2017, and it suffers from a shortage of combat-ready equipment.[52] Other key Alliance members, particularly the UK and France, have historically fared better. Yet much of the French military is already tied down in Africa, and both countries have faced declining military budgets in the wake of the Great Recession, with consequences for their military readiness.[53]

None of this is meant to suggest that Europe is at risk of being overrun in the event of a conflict with Russia. However, it is unclear whether NATO's European members have the ability and willingness to defend the Alliance's northern and eastern borders in Poland, Romania and the Baltic countries. Recent polling data shows that the populations in most European countries – including core NATO members France, Germany and the UK – are more concerned with issues such as terrorism, immigration and the Islamic State (ISIS) than they are with Russia, and that majorities in most countries outside the United States and Canada would not support going to war to uphold NATO's Article V.[54] Moreover, the other members of NATO are still heavily dependent on the United States for the strategic-airlift capabilities that would be required to carry large forces over long distances.[55] Indeed, a 2017 RAND report found that France, Germany and the UK would face difficulties sustaining an armoured brigade for combat in the Baltics.[56]

One could argue that these problems could be overcome to the extent that the United States can credibly communicate its willingness to retrench from the continent if its allies do not take on significantly more of the responsibility for defending themselves, in keeping with President Trump's favoured approach. It is perhaps just as likely, however, that a waning faith in US protection would encourage NATO members to pass the buck for deterring Russia among themselves. The most potentially powerful countries in Europe are insulated from Russia thanks to NATO expansion, and it would be unsurprising if they used their margin of security as an excuse to adopt a more passive, wait-and-see approach.[57] Indeed, there would be historical precedent for this, as in the case of France's withdrawal from NATO's military command in 1966. If the French felt they had that much room to manoeuvre in the face of a far more powerful Soviet Union, it would hardly be surprising if the states of Western and Central Europe made a similar judgement about the threat posed by Russia today.

More generally, by emphasising burden-sharing as much as he does and threatening to withdraw US protection as a coercive lever, Trump risks alienating American partners and encouraging them to go their own way.[58] If they do, allies are likely to become less willing to reflexively defer to US preferences and more willing to accommodate and cooperate with US competitors in areas of mutual gain. Indeed, this is likely to be the case if US partners simply become more militarily self-reliant, as Trump has said he wishes for them to do. In the worst-case scenario envisioned by realists such as John Mearsheimer at the end of the Cold War, more military capabilities in the hands of the European states could reawaken pre-1945-style competition among them by stoking regional security dilemmas.[59]

Europe would no longer be beholden to the United States

More capable alliance partners could pose problems for the US even in the most desirable scenarios. Many European leaders – including German Chancellor Angela Merkel and French President Emmanuel Macron – have signalled their desire to move in the direction of a more united and capable Europe, and have suggested that the continent needs an independent army.[60] The prospect seems remote for now, but it is worth considering what the implications would be for great-power competition. The more capable of looking after itself Europe becomes, the more tempted it will be to use its military strength for its own purposes and to create military command structures outside the auspices of NATO.[61] Europe would no longer be beholden to the United States for its defence, and would therefore be more likely to pursue its own interests, even at the expense of US ones.

Moreover, a more independent Europe, as well as one that no longer trusts the United States, would have little incentive to cooperate with the US in areas more peripheral to its interests – such as balancing against China. In recent months, frictions have emerged between the US and its NATO allies over Chinese telecommunications giant Huawei's efforts to build up its 5G internet network, with many European states being resistant to limiting Huawei's access to the European market.[62] While NATO's dependence on US protection gives Washington leverage to shape allied behaviour, this leverage will last only insofar as US protection is sufficiently valuable and credible.

In effect, a more militarily united Europe would represent yet another potential great-power competitor for the United States. In part for this reason, the US government has in previous instances expressed concern that an independent EU defence posture would decouple it from the United States.[63] For example, the European Community's intransigence on trade and other issues prompted then-secretary of state Henry Kissinger to warn in 1970 that an 'independent Europe could prove to be a competitive power center with the U.S.'.[64]

To summarise, then, it is clear that any effort on the part of the United States to encourage allied burden-sharing as a substitute for its own capabilities would run up against two challenges. The first would be collective-action problems.[65] If allies failed to pool their resources, the United States would be faced with a power vacuum that it would need to fill itself if it did not want to risk seeing its competitors do so.[66] This scenario is especially likely in Asia, both because of China's sheer size when compared to its neighbours and because, unlike in Europe, the states of East Asia have few formal security ties, let alone a shared history of belonging to a multilateral alliance. The second challenge would be a problem of alliance control. Even if burden-sharing schemes succeeded and allies formed balancing coalitions with minimal US involvement, Washington could expect that allies capable of defending themselves would have little reason to align their foreign policies with US preferences. Capable partners might cooperate with the United States when their interests aligned, but their collaboration would be far from guaranteed.

If, on the other hand, Washington opted for a more muscular, active approach to great-power competition – one that relied on maintaining a physical deterrent presence abroad both to signal American commitment and to act as a front-line defence – then it would need partners willing to host its forces with sufficient confidence in US protection to risk incurring the displeasure of US competitors such as China and Russia. This would require renewing America's commitment to its allies and devoting resources to their defence, whether in the form of a forward presence or rapid-deployment forces. Such an approach would inevitably run up against the internal constraints described above, and may also undercut US efforts to encourage greater allied burden-sharing.

Of course, China and Russia face challenges of their own. There are many indications that both countries are already facing internal and external constraints that are limiting their ability to mobilise for strategic competition.[67] In Russia, these constraints include an ageing population and a weak economy.[68] China's economic growth rate has also slowed more quickly than expected, and there are growing doubts about the sustainability of its development model.[69] Neither country has alliance partnerships that can compare to the Warsaw Pact or similar alliances during previous episodes of great-power competition, even if they are increasingly working together themselves. Indeed, some have argued that the threat posed by China and Russia is nowhere near as severe as the threat once posed by the Soviet Union, and no challenge to American military preponderance.[70]

Nevertheless, the United States has said that it sees itself in competition with both China and Russia as peer challengers. They may not pose the same threat as did the Soviet Union during the Cold War – though they clearly *do* pose a serious challenge for Washington's ability to project power and defend its allies in their immediate neighbourhoods[71] – but Washington seems poised to behave as though they did. The question is whether the US is capable of doing so.

Is Washington ready?

Although the stated priority of the United States is to focus on great-power competition, there is reason to doubt that the country is willing or able to engage in the kind of internal and external balancing that would be needed to prevail in such a competition. It is true that the defence budget has increased under Trump – though the Defense Department has said that this trend is unlikely to continue.[72] Yet much of the administration's behaviour, coupled with long-standing structural trends, threatens to undermine US efforts to engage in great-power competition. Some US policies suggest a desire for foreign-policy retrenchment, such as Trump's open scepticism of

US alliances and commitments abroad. Others, such as tax cuts and rising entitlement spending combined with an already sizeable national debt, undermine Washington's capacity to devote resources either to American commitments abroad or to internal investments such as education and infrastructure spending. This creates a mismatch of ends and means.

There are a number of ways the US could respond to this disconnect. Firstly, the administration could decide that the United States is unprepared to engage in strategic competition and instead adopt a grand strategy of restraint or offshore balancing. This would reduce American commitments abroad, help to restore fiscal balance at home and better match overseas activities with the economic capacity of the country.[73] Internally, this would entail focusing on reducing the debt and the deficit while making domestic investments intended to foster long-term economic growth. Externally, the United States would reduce its overseas footprint and devolve more of the responsibility for balancing Russia and China to local partners, while retaining what political scientist Barry Posen calls the 'command of the commons' – the United States' pre-eminence in the air, sea and space domains so that it can project power abroad in case a vital American interest comes under threat.[74] Under this strategy, insisting on burden-sharing would make sense, even if this entails threatening to abandon allies or withdrawing from US commitments. The downside to this option is that it would mean admitting that the US is in decline, and allowing China and other great powers to have more of a say in the international order and more leeway in their own regions.

If the US is in fact committed to strategic competition as stated in the NSS and NDS, then the country will have to direct its domestic and foreign policies towards that end. Rather than focusing on restricting immigration, removing funding for education, making further tax cuts or antagonising international partners, the United States should reinvest in the nation's infrastructure, economy and international posture to ensure that it remains the preponderant power. Improving the country's financial health through increasing revenues, reforming mandatory spending and finding ways to remove budget caps on the military would be necessary to maintain the United States' power within the international system, as would sustaining the loyalty of US partners and the country's sizeable overseas footprint.

To be clear, our argument is not that the United States is on the verge of 'losing' a competition for global supremacy with its competitors. Just the opposite: the US still enjoys a number of advantages, while its primary competitors, Russia and China, face their own challenges. Our point is simply that the US faces a range of long-term constraints, many of which are entirely within its power to manage but which the country's policies during the last 20 years have only exacerbated. Neither China nor Russia has yet become a US competitor on a par with the Soviet Union, but neither does the United States enjoy the same dominance that it did in the early years of the Cold War and immediately after it ended.

Strategic competition among great powers has always been a complicated and expensive endeavour. At the height of its power, the US was able to marshal most of its national endowments towards the singular purpose of expanding its economic and military strength, and attracting strategic partners to assist in its competition against Soviet influence and power. However, economic, political and international trends over the past few decades, coupled with the Trump administration's alienation of alliance partners and domestic policies that are driving up the federal deficit, indicate that the US is unprepared to return to the forms of balancing needed to prevail in a strategic competition. As the bipartisan members of the Commission on the National Defense Strategy put it in a recent report, 'America is very near the point of strategic insolvency, where its "means" are badly out of alignment with its "ends".'[75] The United States must re-evaluate the requirements of great-power competition and have an honest national conversation about the forms of investment and international cooperation that will be needed to meet those requirements. Otherwise, the administration will continue to operate at cross purposes, degrading America's strategic position even further and making a return to great-power competition needlessly difficult.

Notes

[1]   Jim Mattis, 'Summary of the 2018 National Defense Strategy of the United States of America', US Department of Defense, 2018, p. 2, https://dod.defense.gov/Portals/1/Documents/pubs/2018-National-Defense-Strategy-Summary.pdf. Emphasis in original.

2   White House, 'National
    Security Strategy of the United
    States of America', 2017, p. 3,
    https://www.whitehouse.gov/
    wp-content/uploads/2017/12/NSS-
    Final-12-18-2017-0905-2.pdf.

3   See Joshua Shifrinson, 'The Rise of
    China, Balance of Power Theory and
    US National Security: Reasons for
    Optimism?', *Journal of Strategic Studies*,
    December 2018, pp. 1–42; and Ali
    Wyne, 'Is This the Beginning of a New
    Cold War?', RAND Blog, 12 December
    2018, https://www.rand.org/
    blog/2018/12/is-this-the-beginning-of-
    a-new-cold-war.html.

4   See, for example, Barry R. Posen and
    Andrew L. Ross, 'Competing Visions
    for U.S. Grand Strategy', *International
    Security*, vol. 21, no. 3, 1997, pp. 5–53;
    Eugene Gholz, Daryl G. Press and
    Harvey M. Sapolsky, 'Come Home,
    America: The Strategy of Restraint in
    the Face of Temptation', *International
    Security*, vol. 21, no. 4, 1997, pp. 5–48;
    and Stephen G. Brooks, G. John
    Ikenberry and William C. Wohlforth,
    'Don't Come Home, America: The Case
    Against Retrenchment', *International
    Security*, vol. 37, no. 3, 2013, pp. 7–51.

5   White House, 'National Security Strategy
    of the United States of America', p. 27.

6   Mattis, 'Summary of the 2018 National
    Defense Strategy of the United States
    of America', p. 2.

7   See Posen and Ross, 'Competing
    Visions for U.S. Grand Strategy'.

8   See Patrick Porter, 'Why America's
    Grand Strategy Has Not Changed:
    Power, Habit, and the U.S. Foreign
    Policy Establishment', *International
    Security*, vol. 42, no. 4, Spring 2018,
    pp. 9–46; and Christopher Layne,

    *The Peace of Illusions: American Grand
    Strategy from 1940 to the Present* (Ithaca,
    NY: Cornell University Press, 2006).

9   See Kenneth Waltz, *Theory of
    International Politics* (New York:
    McGraw-Hill, 1979); and John J.
    Mearsheimer, *The Tragedy of Great Power
    Politics* (New York: W. W. Norton, 2001).

10 See Waltz, *Theory of International
    Politics*, p. 168; Paul K. MacDonald
    and Joseph M. Parent, 'Graceful
    Decline? The Surprising Success
    of Great Power Retrenchment',
    International Security, vol. 35, no. 4,
    2011, p. 20; and Joseph M. Parent
    and Sebastian Rosato, 'Balancing in
    Neorealism', *International Security*, vol.
    40, no. 2, 2015, pp. 51–86.

11 See James D. Morrow, 'Alliances and
    Asymmetry: An Alternative to the
    Capability Aggregation Model of
    Alliances', *American Journal of Political
    Science*, vol. 35, no. 4, 1991, pp. 904–33.

12 Renanah Miles and Brian Blankenship,
    'Djibouti's First, but Will It Last?',
    Lawfare, 3 January 2016.

13 White House, 'Office of Management
    and Budget Historical Tables',
    https://www.whitehouse.gov/omb/
    historical-tables/.

14 See Internal Revenue Service, 'SOI
    Tax Stats Historical Table 23 – U.S.
    Individual Income Tax: Personal
    Exemptions and Lowest and Highest
    Bracket Tax Rates, and Tax Base for
    Regular Tax', https://www.irs.gov/
    statistics/soi-tax-stats-historical-
    table-23; and Darien B. Jacobson,
    Brian G. Raub and Barry W. Johnson,
    'The Estate Tax: Ninety Years and
    Counting', https://www.irs.gov/pub/
    irs-soi/ninetyestate.pdf.

15 As Richard Holbrooke said in 1992,

the Cold War 'made "national security" the justification for everything
– the interstate highway system, the
National Defense Education Act,
the Vietnam War, the foreign aid
program'. Quoted in R.W. Apple,
Jr, 'White House Race Is Recast: No
Kremlin to Run Against', *New York
Times*, 6 February 1992.

16   Stacie L. Pettyjohn, *U.S. Global Defense
Posture, 1783–2011* (Santa Monica, CA:
RAND Corporation, 2012).

17   See Carla Norrlof, *America's Global
Advantage: US Hegemony and
International Cooperation* (New York:
Cambridge University Press, 2010);
Michael Mastanduno, 'Preserving the
Unipolar Moment: Realist Theories
and U.S. Grand Strategy After the Cold
War', *International Security*, vol. 21, no.
4, 1997, pp. 49–88; Stephen G. Brooks
and William C. Wohlforth, *World
Out of Balance: International Relations
and the Challenge of American Primacy*
(Princeton, NJ: Princeton University
Press, 2008); Michael Beckley, 'China's
Century? Why America's Edge Will
Endure', *International Security*, vol.
36, no. 3, 2012, pp. 41–78; and Joseph
S. Nye, 'Limits of American Power',
Political Science Quarterly, vol. 117, no.
4, 2002, pp. 545–59.

18   Sophie Tatum, 'CBO Projects Debt
Could Rise to a Historic 152% of GDP
by 2048', CNN, 28 June 2018.

19   Grant A. Driessen and Megan S.
Lynch, 'The Budget Control Act:
Frequently Asked Questions',
Congressional Research Service, 23
February 2018.

20   On the role of mandatory-spending
programmes in increasing national
debt, see James McBridge and

Andrew Chatzky, 'The National
Debt Dilemma', Council on Foreign
Relations, 20 December 2018; and
Nate Silver, 'What Is Driving Growth
in Government Spending?', *New York
Times*, 16 January 2013.

21   See Zachary A. Goldfarb, 'The Legacy
of the Bush Tax Cuts, in Four Charts',
Washington Post, 2 January 2013;
Michael Cooper, 'From Obama, the
Tax Cut Nobody Heard Of', *New
York Times*, 18 October 2010; and Jim
Tankersley, 'Trump's Tax Cut One
Year Later: What Happened?', *New
York Times*, 27 December 2018.

22   Steve Wamhoff and Matthew Gardner,
'Federal Tax Cuts in the Bush, Obama,
and Trump Years', Institute on Taxation
and Economic Policy, 11 July 2018.

23   Adam Michel, 'Analysis of the 2017
Tax Cuts and Jobs Act', Heritage
Foundation, 19 December 2017.

24   Internal Revenue Service, 'SOI Tax
Stats Historical Table 23'; and Jacobson,
Raub and Johnson, 'The Estate Tax'.

25   See Alex Mintz and Chi Huang,
'Defense Expenditures, Economic
Growth, and the "Peace Dividend"',
American Political Science Review,
vol. 84, no. 4, December 1990, p.
1,283; Steve Chan, 'Grasping the
Peace Dividend: Some Propositions
on the Conversion of Swords into
Plowshares', *Mershon International
Studies Review*, vol. 39, no. 1, 1995,
pp. 53–95; Hugh Rockoff, 'The Peace
Dividend in Historical Perspective',
American Economic Review, vol. 88, no.
2, 1998, pp. 46–50; and Ann Markusen,
'How We Lost the Peace Dividend',
American Prospect, July 1997.

26   Neta C. Crawford, 'United States
Budgetary Costs of the Post-9/11 Wars

Through FY2019: $5.9 Trillion Spent and Obligated', Watson Institute, Brown University, 14 November 2018, https://watson.brown.edu/costsofwar/files/cow/imce/papers/2018/Crawford_Costs%20of%20War%20Estimates%20Through%20FY2019%20.pdf.

27   See Benjamin Denison, 'Confusion in the Pivot: The Muddled Shift from Peripheral War to Great Power Competition', War on the Rocks, 12 February 2019, https://warontherocks.com/2019/02/confusion-in-the-pivot-the-muddled-shift-from-peripheral-war-to-great-power-competition/.

28   Nelson D. Schwartz, 'As Debt Rises, the Government Will Soon Spend More on Interest than on the Military', New York Times, 25 September 2018.

29   See National Defense Strategy Commission, 'Providing for the Common Defense: The Assessments and Recommendations of the National Defense Strategy Commission', 13 November 2018, p. 63.

30   See Peter Mcpherson, Howard Gobstein and David Shulenburger, 'Funding and the Future of U.S. Public Research Universities', Innovations: Technology, Governance, Globalization, vol. 5, no. 2, 2010, pp. 23–30; and Jon Marcus, 'The Fragile State of the Midwest's Public Universities', Atlantic, 15 October 2017.

31   See Rick Seltzer, 'New Study Attempts to Show How Much State Funding Cuts Push Up Tuition', Inside Higher Ed, 24 July 2017; and Phil Oliff et al., 'Recent Deep State Higher Education Cuts May Harm Students and the Economy for Years to Come', Center on Budget and Policy Priorities, 19 March 2013.

32   David F. Labaree, 'Learning to Love the

Bomb: The Cold War Brings the Best of Times to American Higher Education', in Paul Smeyers and Marc Depaepe (eds), Educational Research: Discourses of Change and Changes of Discourse (New York: Springer, 2016), pp. 101–17.

33   See Carroll Doherty, 'Key Takeaways on Americans' Growing Partisan Divide over Political Values', Pew Research Center, 5 October 2017; and Clare Foran, 'America's Political Divide Keeps Getting Wider', Atlantic, 5 October 2017.

34   Dina Smeltz, Joshua Busby and Jordan Tama, 'Political Polarization the Critical Threat to US, Foreign Policy Experts Say', Hill, 9 November 2018.

35   See John McClelland and Jeffrey Werling, 'How the 2017 Tax Act Affects CBO's Projections', Congressional Budget Office, 20 April 2018; and Jim Tankersley, 'No, Trump's Tax Cut Isn't Paying for Itself (at Least Not Yet)', New York Times, 17 October 2018.

36   See, for example, Nancy A. Youssef, 'Trump, After Boosting U.S. Military Budget, Says It Is Too High', Wall Street Journal, 3 December 2018; and Dan De Luce and Robbie Gramer, 'State Department, USAID Face Drastic Budget Cut', Foreign Policy, 12 February 2018.

37   See Neil Baron, 'Trump's Tariffs Are Hurting America', Hill, 26 October 2018; and Mark J. Perry, 'Backfire Economics – Trump's Tariffs Are Hurting US Farmers and Workers and Putting the Entire Economy at Risk', AEI, 9 July 2018.

38   See Norrlof, America's Global Advantage; and Michael Mastanduno, 'CoCom and American Export Control Policy: The Experience of the Reagan Administration', in David A. Baldwin

and Helen V. Milner (eds), *East–West Trade and the Atlantic Alliance* (London: Palgrave Macmillan, 1990), pp. 191–221.

[39] See Brooks, Ikenberry and Wohlforth, 'Don't Come Home, America'; and Pettyjohn, *U.S. Global Defense Posture, 1783–2011*.

[40] 'Trump's "Obsolete" Comment Worries Nato', BBC, 16 January 2017, https://www.bbc.com/news/world-us-canada-38635181; Ben Jacobs, 'Donald Trump Reiterates He Will Only Help Nato Countries that Pay "Fair Share"', *Guardian*, 27 July 2016, https://www.theguardian.com/us-news/2016/jul/27/donald-trump-nato-isolationist; and Sophie Tatum, 'Trump Seems to Question U.S. Commitment to Defending All NATO Allies', CNN, 18 July 2018, https://www.cnn.com/2018/07/17/politics/trump-nato-fox/index.html.

[41] Choe Sang-Hun and Motoko Rich, 'Trump's Talk of U.S. Troop Cuts Unnerves South Korea and Japan', *New York Times*, 4 May 2018, https://www.nytimes.com/2018/05/04/world/asia/south-korea-troop-withdrawal-united-states.html; and Thomas Wright, 'The Biggest Danger of North Korea Talks', *Atlantic*, 3 March 2018, https://www.theatlantic.com/international/archive/2018/03/north-korea-south-korea/555245/.

[42] See Jennifer Lind, *Sorry States: Apologies in International Politics* (Ithaca, NY: Cornell University Press, 2008); and Jeremy Berke, 'Japan's Demographic Time Bomb Is Getting More Dire, and It's a Bad Omen for the Country', *Business Insider*, 5 June 2018, https://www.businessinsider.com/japans-population-is-shrinking-demographic-time-bomb-2018-6.

[43] Tomoko Otake, 'Japan's Population Projected to Plunge to 88 Million by 2065', *Japan Times*, 10 April 2017, https://www.japantimes.co.jp/news/2017/04/10/national/social-issues/japans-population-projected-plunge-88-million-2065/.

[44] Rajan Menon, 'The India Myth', *National Interest*, no. 134, 2014, pp. 46–57.

[45] David Shambaugh, 'U.S.–China Rivalry in Southeast Asia: Power Shift or Competitive Coexistence?', *International Security*, vol. 42, no. 4, 2018, pp. 90–3.

[46] See World Bank, 'GDP (Current US$)', World Development Indicators, https://data.worldbank.org/indicator/NY.GDP.MKTP.CD; and Katherine Barbieri and Omar M.G. Keshk, 'Correlates of War Project Trade Data Set Codebook', http://www.correlatesofwar.org/.

[47] Feng Zhang, 'Is Southeast Asia Really Balacing Against China?', *Washington Quarterly*, vol. 41, no. 3, 2018, pp. 191–204; and Shambaugh, 'U.S.–China Rivalry in Southeast Asia'.

[48] See Waltz, *Theory of International Politics*; Stephen M. Walt, *The Origins of Alliances* (Ithaca, NY: Cornell University Press, 1987); Paul Schroeder, 'Historical Reality vs. Neo-Realist Theory', *International Security*, vol. 19, no. 1, 1994, pp. 108–48; Mearsheimer, *The Tragedy of Great Power Politics*; Robert S. Ross, 'Balance of Power Politics and the Rise of China: Accommodation and Balancing in East Asia', *Security Studies*, vol. 15, no. 3, 2006, pp. 355–95; and William C. Wohlforth et al., 'Testing Balance-of-Power Theory in World History', *European Journal of International Relations*,

vol. 13, no. 2, 2007, pp. 155–85.

49 See World Bank, 'GDP (Current US$)'. Dollar values are from 2017.

50 Michael Birnbaum and Thomas Gibbons-Neff, 'NATO Allies Boost Defense Spending in the Wake of Trump Criticism', *Washington Post*, 28 June 2017, https://www. washingtonpost.com/world/ nato-allies-boost-defense-spending-in-the-wake-of-trump-criticism/2017/06/28/153584de-5a8c-11e7-aa69-3964a7d55207_story. html; and Ryan Heath, '8 NATO Countries to Hit Defense Spending Target', Politico, 5 July 2018, https:// www.politico.eu/article/nato-jens-stoltenberg-donald-trump-8-countries-to-hit-defense-spending-target/.

51 World Bank, 'GDP (Current US$)'.

52 See Georg Löfflman, 'Pulling Germany's Military Back from the Brink', *National Interest*, 16 September 2015, https://nationalinterest.org/ feature/pulling-germanys-military-back-the-brink-13852; Niall McCarthy, 'Defense Expenditures of NATO Members Visualized', *Forbes*, 10 July 2018, https://www.forbes.com/sites/ niallmccarthy/2018/07/10/defense-expenditure-of-nato-members-visualized-infographic/#2efb517114cf; and 'Germany Remains Reluctant to Pull Its Weight in the World', *Economist*, 19 February 2018, https://www.economist.com/ kaffeeklatsch/2018/02/19/ germany-remains-reluctant-to-pull-its-weight-in-the-world.

53 Michael Shurkin, *The Abilities of the British, French, and German Armies to Generate and Sustain Armored Brigades in the Baltics* (Santa Monica, CA:

RAND Corporation, 2017), https:// www.rand.org/pubs/research_reports/ RR1629.html.

54 Andrew Rettman, 'Few Europeans See Russia as "Major" Threat', *EU Observer*, 14 June 2016, https:// euobserver.com/foreign/133815; and Judy Dempsey, 'NATO's European Allies Won't Fight for Article 5', Carnegie Europe, 15 June 2015, http://carnegieeurope.eu/ strategiceurope/?fa=60389.

55 See James D. Hood, *NATO Strategic Airlift: Capability or Continued US Reliance*, MA dissertation, Air War College, 2009; Pierre Tran, 'French Lawmaker Decries Dependence on Russian, Other Foreign Capabilities', *Defense News*, 30 March 2017, https://www. defensenews.com/air/2017/03/30/ french-lawmaker-decries-dependence-on-russian-other-foreign-capabilities/; and Yvonni-Stefania Efstathiou, 'European Strategic Airlift: A Work in Progress', Military Balance Blog, 10 January 2019, https://www.iiss. org/blogs/military-balance/2019/01/ european-strategic-airlift.

56 Shurkin, *The Abilities of the British, French, and German Armies to Generate and Sustain Armored Brigades in the Baltics*.

57 See Wohlforth et al., 'Testing Balance-of-Power Theory in World History'.

58 Glenn H. Snyder, *Alliance Politics* (Ithaca, NY: Cornell University Press, 1997).

59 John J. Mearsheimer, 'Back to the Future: Instability in Europe After the Cold War', *International Security*, vol. 15, no. 1, 1990, pp. 5–56. See also Robert J. Art, 'Why Western Europe Needs the United States and NATO', *Political Science Quarterly*, vol. 111, no.

1, 1996, pp. 1–39.

60 Maia De La Baume and David M. Herszenhorn, 'Merkel Joins Macron in Calling for EU Army to Complement NATO', Politico, 13 November 2018, https://www.politico.eu/article/angela-merkel-emmanuel-macron-eu-army-to-complement-nato/.

61 See Yaroslav Trofimov, 'Is Europe Ready to Defend Itself?', Wall Street Journal, 4 January 2019.

62 David E. Sanger et al., 'America Pushes Allies to Fight Huawei in New Arms Race with China', New York Times, 26 January 2019, https://www.nytimes.com/2019/01/26/us/politics/huawei-china-us-5g-technology.html.

63 See Stanley R. Sloan, 'The United States and European Defence', Chaillot Papers, no. 37, 2000; and Barry R. Posen, 'European Union Security and Defense Policy: Response to Unipolarity?', Security Studies, vol. 15, no. 2, 2006, pp. 149–86.

64 Thomas Robb, A Strained Partnership? US–UK Relations in the Era of Detente, 1969–77 (Manchester: Manchester University Press, 2014), pp. 37–8.

65 See Wohlforth et al., 'Testing Balance-of-Power Theory in World History'.

66 See Mancur Olson, Jr, and Richard Zeckhauser, 'An Economic Theory of Alliances', Review of Economics and Statistics, vol. 48, no. 3, 1966, pp. 266–79.

67 See Michael Beckley, Unrivaled: Why America Will Remain the World's Sole Superpower (Ithaca, NY: Cornell University Press, 2018).

68 See Stephen Fortescue, 'Can Russia Afford to Be a Great Power?', Lowy Institute, 1 June 2017; Denis Pinchuk and Maria Kiselyova, '"No Miracles": Labor Shortage Set to Hit Russia's GDP', Reuters, 3 October 2017; Anna

Andrianova and Jake Rudnitsky, 'World War Still Haunts Putin as Population Decline Taxes Economy', Bloomberg, 4 April 2018; and Kenneth Rogoff, 'Russia's Future Looks Bleak Without Economic and Political Reform', Guardian, 5 July 2017.

69 See Marc Champion and Adrian Leung, 'Does China Have What It Takes to Be a Superpower?', Bloomberg, 30 August 2018; Viola Zhou, 'China's Population Is Going to Shrink. Here's What that Means', Inkstone, 7 January 2019; Anna Fifield, 'Chinese Economy Slows to Lowest Growth Rate in 28 Years', Washington Post, 21 January 2019; and Frances Coppola, 'The Great Chinese Bank Bailout', Forbes, 29 January 2019.

70 See Beckley, Unrivaled; and Stephen G. Brooks and William C. Wohlforth, 'The Once and Future Superpower: Why China Won't Overtake the United States', Foreign Affairs, vol. 95, no. 3, 2016, pp. 91–104.

71 See Thomas Christensen, 'Posing Problems Without Catching Up: China's Rise and Challenges for U.S. Security Policy', International Security, vol. 25, no. 4, 2001, pp. 5–40.

72 National Defense Strategy Commission, 'Providing for the Common Defense', November 2018, p. xii.

73 See Paul K. MacDonald and Joseph M. Parent, Twilight of the Titans: Great Power Decline and Retrenchment (Ithaca, NY: Cornell University Press, 2018).

74 Barry R. Posen, 'Command of the Commons: The Military Foundation of U.S. Hegemony', International Security, vol. 28, no. 1, 2003, pp. 5–46.

75 National Defense Strategy Commission, 'Providing for the Common Defense', November 2018, p. xii.

Is Major War Still Obsolete?

Michael Mandelbaum

Twenty years ago, I published an article with the title 'Is Major War Obsolete?' in *Survival*. The article offered a definite answer to the titular question: yes, major war – that is, 'war fought by the most powerful members of the international system, drawing on all of their resources and using every weapon at their command'[1] – had become obsolete, with 'obsolete' meaning not altogether impossible but going out of fashion and therefore increasingly unlikely.

This year I published a book entitled *The Rise and Fall of Peace on Earth*, the theme of which is that, after 25 years of unprecedentedly deep peace following the fall of the Berlin Wall, the international system has reverted to a less happy but more familiar condition.[2] Security competition – political and military rivalry among the most powerful states – has returned after a hiatus of a quarter-century. This makes the world of 2019 more prone to war than the world of 20 years earlier.

This three-decades-long global trajectory – from the security competition of the Cold War to the deep peace of the post-Cold War era and now back to security competition – raises three questions: how and why did it happen? Could the West have prevented the relapse from an unprecedentedly peaceful international order to one marked by the all-too-familiar conflicting ambitions of its most powerful members? And just how dangerous is the world today?

Michael Mandelbaum is the Christian A. Herter Professor Emeritus of American Foreign Policy at the Johns Hopkins University School of Advanced International Studies and the author of *The Rise and Fall of Peace on Earth* (Oxford University Press, 2019).

Survival | vol. 61 no. 5 | October–November 2019 | pp. 65–71   DOI 10.1080/00396338.2019.1662104

Squandering the deep peace

The deep peace after 1989 did not come about by accident. It did not arise from the fortuitous and entirely unrepeatable circumstances that the end of the Cold War bequeathed, although that outcome did contribute substantially to it. The world enjoyed a deeper peace than ever before in modern history, I argue in *The Rise and Fall of Peace on Earth*, because of the unusually robust presence of three peace-promoting features of the international system: the benign hegemony of the United States; economic interdependence (this was one of the great ages of globalisation); and the widespread practice of democratic politics and government. Neither alone nor together did these three developments guarantee peace. That is because nothing can fully do so: international politics has no iron laws like the laws of physics. Combined as they were in the wake of the Cold War, however, the three did create a higher barrier to major war than had previously existed during the modern era.

The period of deep peace ended because of the confluence of three developments. 'Is Major War Obsolete?' anticipated each of them, but did not foresee the way in which their interaction would make the world less peaceful. As I wrote two decades ago, 'the obsolescence of major war' has turned out to depend on 'the policies and preferences of Russia and China'.[3] It was their adoption of policies designed to overturn the political status quo in Europe and East Asia, respectively, along with similar policies undertaken by Iran in the Middle East, that brought the golden quarter-century of peace to an end. (What happened, and why, in those three regions are the subjects of the three main chapters of *The Rise and Fall of Peace on Earth*.) In addition, and as I also suggested 20 years ago might occur, democracy has proven to have a weaker global appeal and less staying power than it then seemed to, especially in Russia and China.

Moreover, in Russia and China, as elsewhere, the modern state has continued to be 'an economic institution. To spur production and manage redistribution have become its twin missions.'[4] As I argue in *The Rise and Fall of Peace on Earth* but did not anticipate 20 years ago, Russia and China adopted peace-subverting foreign policies because, among other reasons, their respective economic performances have begun to falter in the last ten years, depriving the dictatorships that govern them of their most reliable sources of public support and political legitimacy. Feeling an acute need for an alternative source of such support, they turned to aggressive nationalism, reviving the familiar pattern of rivalry among the world's strongest states. That is, economics turned out to be as significant for politics and foreign policy as I believed, but the consequences of this importance pushed crucial countries away from rather than toward peaceful conduct.

2019 hindsight

Could different Western policies have prevented this reversion? In the Russian case they might well have. Led by the United States, the Western democracies, foolishly and despite assurances to the contrary they had previously conveyed to Soviet and Russian leaders, expanded NATO, their Cold War military alliance, up to Russia's borders while making it clear that Russia itself would never be allowed to join.[5] There followed other initiatives – the abandonment of the 1972 Anti-Ballistic Missile Treaty and the wars in Kosovo, Iraq and Libya among them – that the United States and its allies undertook without regard for Russian preferences and without adequate appreciation that the Russian government and the Russian public interpreted them as being directed against them and their interests. This, in turn, created widespread resentment of the United States and the European democracies in Russia, which made it all too easy for Russian leader Vladimir Putin to enhance his popularity by portraying his aggressive policies toward Ukraine – falsely – as measures undertaken to defend Russia against a hostile, rapacious West.

Had the members of NATO instead included Russia in a pan-European security order in the wake of the Cold War, they would not have alienated the Russians as they did. At a minimum, this inclusion would have provided them with some leverage against Putin that they could have used to try to moderate Russian policies toward its neighbours. In 2019, it is both too late and too early to include Russia in a common, peaceful, Western security order. It is too late because Putin seems irrevocably committed to hostile relations with the West. Indeed, such hostility forms an important part of the foundation of his autocratic and kleptocratic regime, which makes friendly relations and close cooperation with a government he heads impossible. It is too early because a new regime, or at least a new leader, in Moscow is necessary for the approach to Russia that the West should have taken in the 1990s to have any hope of success.

As for China, the rest of the world might, in theory, have forestalled its aggressive twenty-first-century foreign policies by attempting to inhibit the surging economic growth that gave China the military resources and the political confidence to mount its challenge to East Asia's security arrangements. This was never a politically plausible option, however. The Western democracies, above all the United States, firmly believed that economic growth would promote liberal domestic politics in China and peaceful Chinese foreign policies. And so, up to a point, it did: the China of today has moved very far from the political totalitarianism and comprehensive economic central planning of the Maoist era.

Beyond that, Western economies gained major benefits – opportunities for productive investment and a flow of cheap consumer goods – from China's economic progress. Western governments would have encountered political resistance at home if they had attempted to take serious steps to block Chinese growth. The Clinton administration initially tried to make trade with China contingent on the communist government in Beijing respecting the human rights of those it governed. When Beijing refused, and the American business community expressed its displeasure at the prospect of restrictions on their lucrative trade with the People's Republic, Clinton backed down.

In the case of the third revisionist power, Iran, the United States inadvertently contributed to its twenty-first-century political and military strength by conducting military operations that eliminated three of its major Middle Eastern adversaries: the Afghan Taliban, Saddam Hussein of Iraq, and the Islamic State (ISIS) that took root in Iraq and Syria. In addition, by agreeing to looser restraints on its nuclear-weapons programme than the economic pressure imposed on Iran had seemed to make feasible, and by failing to enforce the 'red line' on the Tehran-backed Syrian regime's use of chemical weapons, then-president Barack Obama arguably encouraged Iranian leaders to believe that their campaign to dominate the Middle East would not meet determined resistance from the United States. Tougher American policies could have done more to contain Iran.

On the brink?

Despite the West's missteps, the world has not become unstoppably war-prone since the golden quarter-century of peace ended. Major war is not imminent: the year 2019 is not the twenty-first-century equivalent of 1914 or 1939. The principal causes of the obsolescence about which I wrote 20 years ago remain very much in force. The potential human, environmental and other costs of such a conflict continue to be stratospherically high: the United States, Russia and China all have nuclear weapons. Moreover, the prospective economic costs of even a conflict in which nuclear weapons are not used have, if anything, increased over the last two decades. Contemporary conventional weapons can do vast damage. Each of the three revisionist powers, unlike the communist bloc during the Cold War, is deeply embedded in the global economic order. China has in fact become central to it, meaning that China and other countries with economic connections to it would have a great deal to lose from a war that interrupted commerce in East Asia.

It is unhappily the case that the chances of war have increased because an incentive for war not present 20 years ago has emerged in the second decade of the twenty-first century: the need on the part of dictatorial governments to generate public support through foreign policies of aggressive nationalism. Still, the three revisionist powers have carried out these policies with extreme caution. All three have engaged in what Jakub Griegel and A. Wess Mitchell, in their book *The Unquiet Frontier*, call 'probes': steps calibrated to increase their own power but without provoking a forceful response from the West.[6] They hope in this way gradually to change the regional balance of power in their favour without having to wage a major war. All this means that, as I write in *The Rise and Fall of Peace on Earth*, 'the world in the wake of the post-Cold War era bore a marked resemblance to the world before that unusually peaceful 25-year period. It resembled, that is, the world of the Cold War itself.'[7] Security competition is once more alive and well. To answer the question posed by the title of this essay in a grammatically dubious but politically accurate way: major war is less obsolete today than it was in 1999. It remains forbiddingly expensive and for that reason is not likely. But, as was the case 20 years ago, it is not impossible, and has unfortunately become less unlikely than it was then.

Notes

1   Michael Mandelbaum, 'Is Major War Obsolete?', *Survival*, vol. 40, no. 4, Winter 1998–99, p. 20.
2   Michael Mandelbaum, *The Rise and Fall of Peace on Earth* (New York: Oxford University Press, 2019).
3   Mandelbaum, 'Is Major War Obsolete?', p. 28.
4   *Ibid.*, p. 25.
5   See Michael Mandelbaum, 'Preserving the New Peace: The Case Against NATO Expansion', *Foreign Affairs*, vol. 74, no. 3, May/June 1995, pp. 9–13.
6   Jakub J. Griegel and A. Wess Mitchell, *The Unquiet Frontier: Rising Rivals, Vulnerable Allies, and the Crisis of American Power* (Princeton, NJ: Princeton University Press, 2016), p. 216.
7   Mandelbaum, *The Rise and Fall of Peace on Earth*, p. 133.

Noteworthy

Putin family values

'The liberal idea presupposes that nothing needs to be done. That migrants can kill, plunder and rape with impunity because their rights as migrants have to be protected … So, the liberal idea has become obsolete. It has come into conflict with the interests of the overwhelming majority of the population.'

[…]

'Let everyone be happy, we have no problem with that. But this must not be allowed to overshadow the culture, traditions and traditional family values of millions of people making up the core population.'

[…]

'[Liberals] cannot simply dictate anything to anyone.'

Russian President Vladimir Putin offers his critique of liberalism during an interview with the Financial Times.[1]

'Whoever claims that liberal democracy is obsolete also claims that freedoms are obsolete, that the rule of law is obsolete and that human rights are obsolete. What I find really obsolete are authoritarianism, personality cults, the rule of oligarchs, even if sometimes they may seem effective.'

European Council President Donald Tusk.[2]

So special

'We really don't believe that this administration is going to become substantially more normal; less dysfunctional, less unpredictable, less faction-riven, less diplomatically clumsy and inept.'

Extract from a confidential memo prepared in summer 2017 by Kim Darroch, the UK's ambassador to the US, that was leaked in July 2019.[3]

'I do not know the Ambassador, but he is not liked or well thought of within the U.S. We will no longer deal with him.'

US President Donald Trump tweets on 8 July 2019.[4]

Forest for the trees

'On the question of burning in the Amazon, which in my opinion may have been initiated by NGOs because they lost money, what is the intention? To bring problems to Brazil.'

Brazilian President Jair Bolsonaro blames environmental non-governmental organisations (NGOs) for the large number of forest fires in Brazil since January 2019.[5]

'The policies of the Brazilian government on the Amazon region call into question whether they are still pursuing the goal of consistently reducing deforestation rates. We need certainty on that account before we can continue project cooperation.'

German Environment Minister Svenja Schulze announces a freeze on financial assistance for conservation projects in Brazil.[6]

Survival | vol. 61 no. 5 | October–November 2019 | pp. 72–74   DOI 10.1080/00396338.2019.1662111

Prorogatory

'Do or die, come what may.'
Newly installed British Prime Minister Boris Johnson vows in June 2019 to take the UK out of the EU by the 31 October deadline with or without a deal.[7]

'This morning I spoke to Her Majesty The Queen to request an end to the current parliamentary session in the second sitting week in September, before commencing the second session of this Parliament with a Queen's speech on Monday 14 October.'
Johnson writes to members of the House of Commons on 28 August 2019 to announce the prorogation of Parliament.[8]

'Boris Johnson has detonated a bomb under the constitutional apparatus of the United Kingdom. The prime minister's request to the Queen to suspend parliament for up to five weeks, ostensibly to prepare a new legislative programme, is without modern precedent. It is an intolerable attempt to silence parliament until it can no longer halt a disastrous crash-out by the UK from the EU on October 31.'
From an editorial appearing in the Financial Times.[9]

One country, no system

'We are innocent citizens, passengers on the way home. I am asking for global help for Hong Kong people. We don't trust our government.'
A Hong Kong resident describes an attack by masked men at a train station on 21 July 2019 and accuses the city's police of failing to intervene.[10]

'Take a minute to think, look at our city, our home – do you all really want to see it pushed into an abyss?'
Hong Kong leader Carrie Lam addresses anti-government protesters during a press conference on 13 August.[11]

65
Percentage of the world's babies who were born in Asia in 1965–70

36
Percentage of the world's babies expected to be born in Asia in 2100[12]

Distrust and vilify

'The deadline of the Atomic Energy Organization for passing the production of enriched uranium from the 300 kg border will end tomorrow [27 June 2019]. With the end of this deadline, the speed of enrichment will speed up.'
Behrouz Kamalvandi, a spokesman for the Atomic Energy Organization of Iran, announces the country's intention to breach the nuclear deal (JCPOA) reached in 2015 in response to what it says is the failure of the deal's European signatories to provide economic benefits.[13]

'Contrary to public statements by its detractors on all sides, JCPOA was not built on trust. It was indeed based on explicit recognition of mutual mistrust. That is why it is so long and detailed.'
Iranian Foreign Minister Mohammad Javad Zarif comments on the JCPOA during an interview with the New York Times.[14]

'If you want to participate in the dollar system you abide by US sanctions.'
US Treasury Secretary Steven Mnuchin endorses US sanctions against Iran on 18 July 2019.[15]

Sources

1 'Transcript: "All This Fuss About Spies … It Is Not Worth Serious Interstate Relations"', *Financial Times*, 27 June 2019, https://www.ft.com/content/878d2344-98f0-11e9-9573-ee5cbb98ed36?emailId=5d15ebaa0ab9eb00041b5a2e&segmentId=c393f5a6-b640-bff3-cc14-234d058790ed.

2 'Putin: Russian President Says Liberalism "Obsolete"', BBC, 28 June 2019, https://www.bbc.co.uk/news/world-europe-48795764.

3 Andrew Sparrow, 'What Kim Darroch Is Reported to Have Said About Trump – And What It Means', *Guardian*, 7 July 2019, https://www.theguardian.com/politics/2019/jul/07/what-kim-darroch-is-reported-to-have-said-about-trump.

4 Donald J. Trump (@realDonaldTrump), tweet, 8 July 2019, https://twitter.com/realDonaldTrump/status/1148298497189392384?ref_src=twsrc%5Etfw%7Ctwcamp%5Etweetembed%7Ctwterm%5E1148298497189392384&ref_url=https%3A%2F%2Fwww.theguardian.com%2Fus-news%2F2019%2Fjul%2F08%2Fdonald-trump-we-will-no-longer-deal-with-the-british-ambassador.

5 Jonathan Watts, 'Jair Bolsonaro Claims NGOs Behind Amazon Forest Fire Surge – But Provides No Evidence', *Guardian*, 21 August 2019, https://www.theguardian.com/world/2019/aug/21/jair-bolsonaro-accuses-ngos-setting-fire-amazon-rainforest.

6 German Federal Ministry for the Environment, Nature Conservation and Nuclear Safety, 'BMU Suspends Country Call for Brazil and Reviews Ongoing Climate Action Protests', press release, 13 August 2019, https://www.bmu.de/en/report/bundesumweltministerin-svenja-schulze-zu-iki-projekten-in-brasilien-und-zum-amazonasfonds/.

7 George Parker, 'Boris Johnson Sparks Election Warning with "Do or Die" Pledge on Brexit', *Financial Times*, 25 June 2019, https://www.ft.com/content/403eafe6-972c-11e9-8cfb-30c211dcd229.

8 'Boris Johnson's Letter to MPs in Full', BBC, 28 August 2019, https://www.bbc.co.uk/news/uk-politics-49497667.

9 Editorial Board, 'Boris Johnson's Suspension of Parliament Is an Affront to Democracy', *Financial Times*, 28 August 2019, https://www.ft.com/content/9dbc7852-c9b2-11e9-af46-b09e8bfe60c0.

10 Lily Kuo, '"We Saved Ourselves": Hong Kong Train Attack Victims Describe 30-Minute Ordeal', *Guardian*, 24 July 2019, https://www.theguardian.com/world/2019/jul/24/hong-kong-protests-china-blames-black-hands-of-us-for-unrest.

11 'Hong Kong Leader Warns Protesters Not to Push City into "Abyss"', BBC, 13 August 2019, https://www.bbc.co.uk/news/world-asia-china-49327352.

12 Anthony Cilluffo and Neil G. Ruiz, 'World's Population Is Projected to Nearly Stop Growing by the End of the Century', Pew Research Center, 17 June 2019, https://www.pewresearch.org/fact-tank/2019/06/17/worlds-population-is-projected-to-nearly-stop-growing-by-the-end-of-the-century/?utm_source=Pew+Research+Center&utm_campaign=f4ae2671d3-Global_2019_06_18&utm_medium=email&utm_term=0_3e953b9b70-f4ae2671d3-400005773.

13 Patrick Wintour, 'Iran's Ultimatum on Breaching Nuclear Deal Puts EU3 on the Spot', *Guardian*, 26 June 2019, https://www.theguardian.com/world/2019/jun/26/iran-ultimatum-on-breaching-nuclear-deal-puts-eu-3-on-the-spot.

14 Farnaz Fassihi and David D. Kirkpatrick, 'In His Own Words: Iran's Foreign Minister, Mohammad Javad Zarif', *New York Times*, 4 July 2019, https://www.nytimes.com/2019/07/04/world/middleeast/iran-zarif-interview.html?action=click&module=Top%20Stories&pgtype=Homepage.

15 Victor Mallet, 'Abide by US Sanctions on Iran or Drop the Dollar, Mnuchin Says', *Financial Times*, 18 July 2019, https://www.ft.com/content/09799460-a958-11e9-984c-fac8325aaa04?emailId=5d313ab1e915ce0004bd5f2f&segmentId=22011ee7-896a-8c4c-22a0-7603348b7f22.

Securing Europe's Economic Sovereignty

Mark Leonard, Jean Pisani-Ferry, Elina Ribakova, Jeremy Shapiro and Guntram Wolff

Europeans like to believe that the European Union has the collective economic size and capacity to determine Europe's economic destiny. They think the EU can determine its own rules for economic life, negotiate on an equal footing with partner economies, and even set economic standards and regulations for the rest of the world. But perhaps the EU has been lucky so far. Perhaps its apparent economic independence was always the result of the fortuitous absence of geopolitical interference. Perhaps it could only flourish under the benevolent aegis of a real superpower. Perhaps, in other words, its independence only endured because no serious power was willing to challenge it, and because the United States was willing to protect it. Now the behaviour of other powers is increasingly calling Europe's economic sovereignty into question. China and the US, in particular, do not separate economic interests from geopolitical interests in the same way that the EU does. They are increasingly using economic connections, from cyberspace to financial links, to serve geopolitical goals. Europe's economic sovereignty is now at stake.

Until recently, the EU took for granted that the global system provided a functional framework for international economic relations, which could

Mark Leonard is co-founder and director of the London-based European Council on Foreign Relations (ECFR). **Jean Pisani-Ferry** holds the Tommaso Padoa-Schioppa chair of the European University Institute in Florence and is a Senior Fellow at Bruegel, an economic think tank based in Brussels. **Elina Ribakova** is Deputy Chief Economist of the Institute of International Finance and a former Visiting Fellow at Bruegel. **Jeremy Shapiro** is the research director of the ECFR. **Guntram Wolff** is the Director of Bruegel. This article is adapted from a report prepared and published under the auspices of the ECFR and Bruegel.

Survival | vol. 61 no. 5 | October–November 2019 | pp. 75–98   DOI 10.1080/00396338.2019.1662148

be regarded as separate from the sphere of geopolitics. Of course, the economic rules of the road were determined by power relations that arose in the wake of the Second World War. But in the years that followed, even the US largely followed them. The economic and geopolitical spheres often overlapped, particularly during the Cold War. But the US regarded the economic integration of 'Western' countries as conducive to the strength of the free world, and it stood by this principle even after the Soviet Union ceased to exist. The EU's very construction reflected this disposition: most international economic powers were given to EU-level bodies, and most security and foreign-policy instruments were left to individual member states. Accordingly, the EU was able to conduct an international economic policy that was reasonably insulated from geopolitical concerns.

This separation of the economic was always fragile. It now looks hopelessly outdated. The US and China have fundamentally different relationships with Europe, but neither separates economics from geopolitics. In general, national-security issues are gaining prominence everywhere, as is the relationship between economics and national security. Economic connections, from cyberspace to financial links, are becoming the primary areas of great-power competition and are at risk of being weaponised.[1] Increasingly, the US and China follow neither the letter nor the spirit of the rules in their relationships with the EU and its member states. In the US case, its decision to make full use of the centrality of its currency and its financial system to enforce secondary sanctions against Iran was a major shock to European partners. Washington's abandonment of core principles of the global multilateral trading system and withdrawal from the Paris Agreement on climate change were also disruptive. As for China, the EU now accepts that Beijing is behaving as 'an economic competitor in the pursuit of technological leadership, and a systemic rival promoting alternative models of governance'.[2]

It is essential that Europeans respond to this challenge. The collective capacity of EU countries working together to preserve their economic independence underpins the value of European integration to European citizens. That value is further bolstered by the EU's ability to participate in defining the rules of the game for the global economy – what Germans call *Handlungsfähigkeit* and the French call *Europe puissance*. The challenge for

Europe is substantial but manageable. The EU and its member states should adopt an economic-sovereignty agenda to protect European economic independence through a variety of tools ranging from competition policy to the international role of the euro. To do so, the EU needs to better integrate economic policy and geopolitics.

China's challenge

China has embarked on a path of geopolitical competition that clearly threatens European economic sovereignty. At the same time, the Chinese government professes adherence to the rules of the international economic order. Rather than directly asserting its right to use economic interdependence for geopolitical purposes, the Chinese strategy is to nip around the edges, to find loopholes and blurriness in an incomplete economic order, and to use technicalities in the rules against their original purposes, as in China's continuing insistence on maintaining its developing-country status within the World Trade Organization (WTO).

A key part of this strategy is winning the global competition over emerging technologies such as artificial intelligence, big data and biotech.[3] For China, this is both an economic and national-security imperative. Many emerging technologies have dual uses, and the old paradigm that technologies designed for military use will trickle down into civilian applications often works the other way in China. Chinese plans for industrial and technological development are premised on civilian companies' help to advance military applications. China's resolute industrial policies and subsidies to key sectors (in particular, solar, batteries, autonomous driving and 5G) reflect a clear intention to gain competitive advantage in key sectors that China sees as critical for future geopolitical and economic advantage.

Of course, technological competition as a part of geopolitical struggle is nothing new. During the Cold War, military–technological competition with the Soviet Union provoked great fear in the West. But the current situation is vastly different. China and the West are in each other's business to an extent far beyond anything seen during the Cold War. The huge degree of interconnectedness means there are many more channels through which each side can hurt the other.

China has some structural advantages in that competition. Important parts of the digital infrastructure are controlled by large multinational corporations, which are subject to pressure and control from their home countries. The Chinese National Intelligence Law enables the government to force private companies to collaborate with Chinese intelligence services. Restrictions on foreign investment between the EU and China are asymmetric in favour of Chinese companies entering the EU market. In China, European investors face numerous roadblocks, including the near impossibility of securing arbitration, difficulties in moving capital back from China and challenges to intellectual-property rights. China also leverages market access to force companies to transfer technology, a practice incompatible with the spirit of WTO rules. Finally, China heavily subsidises its own national champions and favours them in terms of access to credit, rendering the playing field uneven. This asymmetry means China can gain influence over technology from the European economy, but Europeans cannot similarly influence Chinese technological developments. Chinese state-owned enterprises, with their enormous financial muscle, are well equipped to exploit Western openness to gain traction in key sectors of the global economy. And because it is not always clear which Chinese funds are used to raise ownership stakes, they are sometimes able to do so with a degree of stealth.[4]

As a rapidly rising power, China is also increasingly present in third markets and often does not follow the EU's approach or existing multilateral principles. China's Belt and Road Initiative (BRI), for example, aims to leverage Chinese trade flows to build infrastructure and create a broad network of partner countries. The BRI is explicitly not conceived as a multilateral framework of trade, investment and financial relations; it is centred on China, lacks transparency and sometimes imposes onerous conditionality. Through the BRI, China has raised its profile in the Middle East in the form of humanitarian aid and infrastructure projects, including a July 2018 pledge of $20 billion for reconstruction in war-torn countries in the region, such as Syria.[5] It has also become an important economic partner and investor in African countries. Its investments are often welcome and can boost much-needed growth to the benefit of Africa and also the EU, which could find new trading opportunities. But it also means Europe faces more competition in advancing its own Africa and Middle East policies. The lack of transparency with respect to Chinese funding could also make it more difficult for Western multilateral development banks to lend in the region and carry out any subsequent debt restructuring.

In particular, China's financial claims over heavily indebted countries could turn into control of strategic infrastructure and political influence. This has led the US and the EU to express concern that China is not following the principles of the Paris Club, which aims to provide multilateral solutions to problems of over-indebtedness. While Beijing has made some efforts to alleviate these concerns, it is important for the EU to clearly establish the facts and not fall into the trap of merely repeating US official statements.

Another worry is China's influence over individual EU countries through foreign investment. China has already induced Hungary, Greece and Slovenia to block or dilute resolutions relating to human rights and to international arbitration over the South China Sea.[6] Similarly, in March 2018, the EU members of the United Nations Human Rights Council felt compelled to abstain on a Chinese resolution that redefined the defence of human rights in terms of state-to-state cooperation according to 'mutual interests'.[7] That vote hardly accorded with EU values or interests, but Chinese pressure on certain vulnerable EU members meant abstention was the only way to avoid an internal EU division. China's 16+1 initiative, aimed at expanding its economic cooperation with 11 EU member states and five Balkan countries, has also undermined EU unity by creating direct bilateral links between some Central and Eastern European countries and China. Italy's signing on 23 March 2019 of a Belt and Road Initiative cooperation agreement will likely increase tensions in the EU on the right approach to China.[8]

The American problem

The United States has been Europe's most important ally since the Second World War, and the problems that it poses for European economic sovereignty are of a very different nature than those posed by China. The US has always had interests and priorities that differ from Europe's. But the primacy of the Atlantic Alliance and the strong belief that US national security and long-term prosperity would be best served by strengthening a global rules-based economic system made infringements of the global rules the exception rather than the rule. Under President Donald Trump, however, US policy has placed much less value on the transatlantic Alliance and has demonstrated on issues as varied as Iran and trade that it is willing to leverage its economic position to secure policy outcomes, even if that implies undermining the global system and EU security.

More broadly, the Trump administration has actively reduced the support it gives to the multilateral order and has sometimes used its advantageous position to extract immediate economic gains from the system. The dollar, the United States' financial system, and its role as a hub for the global digital architecture provide the US with an unrivalled ability to use the global economic order to serve its own security goals. To what extent future US administrations will continue that practice is an open question, but it is clear that the damage the Trump administration has inflicted on the multilateral trading system will be difficult to fully reverse.

Most egregiously, the United States is using its global economic clout to attempt to advance geopolitical objectives – in particular, rolling back Iran. When the Trump administration decided to withdraw from the Iranian nuclear deal and to return to a policy of economically isolating Iran, the European signatories objected and decided that it was in their interests to continue with the deal. But the essence of the deal is that, in exchange for ending its nuclear programme, Iran is allowed to return to global markets. The US government sought not only to exclude Iran from US markets, but also to ensure that other countries did not do business with it, whether or not they shared US goals. To do this, the US used so-called secondary sanctions, threatening to cut off foreign firms that traded with Iran from the US market, the US financial system and the use of the dollar. The US has supplemented this pressure by threatening to prevent the directors of companies that violate US sanctions from entering US territory.[9]

In principle, a 1996 EU regulation protects European companies from US enforcement of secondary sanctions. The EU attempted to leverage this rule to negotiate an EU exception from US secondary sanctions. But the central global position of the US financial system means that such regulations no longer have the deterrent value that they did in 1996. European banks and companies are not confident in the EU's ability to protect them and place too much value on their access to the United States to take the risk. They have pre-emptively complied with US sanctions, even as their governments have urged them not to. Leading EU members have tried to push back. In January 2019, France, Germany and the United Kingdom announced the creation of a special-purpose vehicle called INSTEX that, by netting out gross Iranian exports and imports and thus minimising direct transfers of money, will provide an alternative financial channel for transactions with Iran and thus, in theory, reduce the need for EU–Iranian trade to access the global payments system. But this vehicle is unlikely to lead to a significant resumption of transactions with Iran because any company doing business with the United States can be sanctioned directly. For now, at least, INSTEX is limited to humanitarian goods that are not under US sanctions.

The challenge the EU faces in preserving its economic sovereignty is compounded by its security dependence on the US. Despite efforts to at least pursue an independent defence capacity, EU strategic autonomy remains 'limited to the lower end of the operational spectrum [and] the prospects for significant change are slim over the coming decade based on current government plans'.[10] Without the US, the International Institute for Strategic Studies estimates that Europe would need to invest around $100bn to establish sufficient capacity for a maritime confrontation and $300bn or more to fill the gaps in defending territory against a state-level attack.[11] Rich European countries could afford this large bill if there was political will to do so, but even in that case it would take ten to 20 years to attain the required capabilities. For Central and Eastern European EU members that feel directly threatened by Russia, there is also the issue of how much military assistance the rest of the EU would be ready to provide. Accordingly, many of the more security-conscious Eastern European states reject any sort of overt distancing from US policy.

Europe's task

In responding to these challenges, the EU should not try to emulate the US and China by closely linking economic policy to geopolitics. It will never wield discretionary power in the ways that they do. Its economic system is based on explicit, stable principles, and should remain so. State intervention is and will continue to be bound by the rule of law. These characteristics are strengths, not weaknesses. But in a world of mutual dependence, economic sovereignty hinges on the ability to project economic power in response to economic aggression, and on the robustness and diversification of the domestic economic system in order to minimise damage. In this realm, the EU has to engage in significant retooling with respect to technology, finance and global governance.

Technology

There is no such thing as technological independence in an open, interconnected economy. But an economy of 450 million inhabitants with a GDP of €14 trillion (excluding the UK) can realistically aim to master key generic technologies and infrastructures. This concept of technology sovereignty has inspired major EU initiatives in fields including energy, aviation, aerospace and geopositioning. It applies equally to today's infrastructures – digital networks and cloud computing – and to new fields such as genomics and artificial intelligence.

Proactive instruments to support Europe's technological capacity, such as greater funding for education and research, are expensive but not particularly controversial. Reactive or protective instruments, such as industrial policy, are more contentious. But it is now clear that the EU needs to become better at safeguarding the basis of entrepreneurial success in Europe. In doing so, the EU should remain an economy that is open to foreign investment and competition, which clearly create jobs and increase growth. However, some essential interests deserve protection because Europe's autonomy and sovereignty would suffer if it were dominated by foreign powers.

The control of state aid to domestic industries is one key to ensuring economic sovereignty. Companies that receive generous state support or tax privileges may be able to seize control of critical technologies or even entire industries. Effective control of state aid, in European markets and extraterritorially, is therefore important to guaranteeing European firms a level playing field. In theory, the best way to control state aid would be to build on the WTO Agreement on Subsidies and Countervailing Measures, which provides a platform for international collaboration and could help the EU to react effectively to subsidies that distort international trade.[12] However, the current framework has proved slow, complex and largely incapable of dealing with the complicated subsidies provided to state-owned enterprises.[13] Moreover, the WTO measures apply only to goods, not services. This is insufficient for modern economies driven by services, networks and data. The EU therefore needs to take additional steps to ensure overall fairness in the EU economy. The European Commission vigilantly monitors direct and indirect subsidies provided by EU member states to national companies. The same vigilance should apply to state aid provided by foreign governments. In some circumstances, the EU will need to apply its competition-policy instruments to such aid.

Control of state aid will not be enough to ensure European economic sovereignty in the technologies of the future. In certain areas, increasing returns, network effects and innovation rents contribute to the emergence of winner-take-all markets even without direct state subsidies. Competition policy in such markets affects technological leadership and has implications for sovereignty. What to do about it is a hard question. The German industry association believes that the EU should relax merger control to allow for the market-driven creation of European champions.[14] The German and French economy ministers think the Council of the EU should be given a final political veto on competition-policy decisions.[15] But in trying to strengthen the global competitiveness of European companies, it makes little sense to relax competition principles at home. Strong competition in the domestic market is often conducive to success on global markets. It is unlikely that less competition domestically will make it easier for EU-based companies to enter foreign markets, including the Chinese market. Less competition can also increase inequality.

In practice, this means that EU regulators, in assessing whether a given merger will reduce competition, should take into account the possibility that foreign firms might soon enter a given market. This is not to say that competition rules should allow less competition overall. The very purpose of competition policy is to protect consumers from producer abuse of market power. This principle should be upheld – even more so in a context of increasing concentration and market power at global level – by, among other measures, protecting competition-policy decisions from politicisation. Even in a more geopolitically intense world, competition-policy decisions should retain their judicial character and should be taken by independent authorities.

There might still be instances in which clearly defined security interests could justify relaxation of a merger decision – for example, when disallowing a merger of European producers would permit a foreign company to dominate network infrastructure, with negative implications for security. Accordingly, there should be security control mechanisms for mergers. The dilemma facing the EU, as seen in the debate over a European equivalent to the Committee on Foreign Investment in the United States, is that EU member states define national security, and EU mechanisms allow them to block a merger from a third country. But what body could define security for intra-EU mergers?

One means of redress would be to empower the EU's High Representative for Foreign Affairs and Security Policy to invoke a security clause, which would then lead to a European Commission college decision on whether to overrule a proposal from the Commissioner for Competition. The activation of the clause would have to be based on a clearly defined and limited set of criteria directly relating to security concerns. This measure would not require a treaty change and would avoid the politicisation of competition-policy decisions. However, it would require a strengthening of the High Representative and the European External Action Service.

Protecting European technology also calls for renewed efforts to screen foreign investments in key technologies, as well as to control their export. Several EU member states have individually introduced or are considering national-security exceptions to standard investment rules. In the UK, the government announced in 2018 that foreign-initiated mergers and investments that might raise national-security concerns will be subject to national-security assessments. In the event an assessment concludes that there is a risk to national security, the government will impose remedies or block an investment altogether.[16] Similar provisions have been introduced in Germany.[17]

In February 2019, the European Parliament adopted an EU framework for screening foreign direct investment.[18] The regulation introduces a mechanism for cooperation and information-sharing among member states but stops short of giving the European Commission the power to veto investments. The objective of the framework is greater coordination of national-security-related screening of foreign investment. It will help increase awareness as well as concentrate peer pressure across the EU. But it does not establish an independent EU authority for investment screening, and the list of EU-wide interests over which the European Commission has the right to even issue an opinion is much narrower than in the US.

On export controls, the EU's regime is limited to dual-use exports (that is, items that can be used for both civilian and military purposes) with a clear focus on peace and security and non-proliferation of weapons of mass destruction. A draft regulation proposed in 2016 by the European Commission would broaden the definition to include cyber-surveillance technology, clarify intangible technology transfer and technical assistance, and add a requirement for authorisation of export items not explicitly listed.[19] However, the focus remains on security and human rights rather than on safeguarding technological superiority, as in the US.

The EU is right not to mimic the US in its approach to investment and export controls. But the new European investment-screening framework remains unsatisfactory because it keeps the definition of security concerns at the national level. An integrated single market means that investments in one EU country are effectively investments throughout the EU. It follows that the EU should develop a common approach and common procedures for the screening of foreign investments, and empower the European Commission with the right to recommend on security grounds the prohibition of a foreign investment. The final say should belong to the Council of the EU, deciding by qualified majority. The EU should also develop instruments such as a dedicated investment fund that would offer member states alternatives when foreign investments are deemed undesirable.

Finance

The EU has long regarded global finance as a domain in which the US-led multilateral order reigned supreme. Payment infrastructure has not been a serious issue. The working assumptions have been that the US dollar would remain the reference global currency for trade and investment purposes and that the global financial architecture would remain centred on the Bretton Woods institutions. The Trump administration's use of the United States' central role in the global financial system to impose its policy preferences has cast grave doubt on these assumptions, which were already shaken by the global financial crisis and the euro-area crisis. At the same time, China's declared intention to promote parallel financial and payments systems indicates tectonic changes in the offing. An already heterogeneous global monetary and financial system now faces fragmentation. In turn, the EU faces a series of strategic choices.

The euro is far from challenging the dollar

The first choice is about the international role of the euro. The euro is the second international currency after the US dollar and significantly ahead of other currencies. The euro's share of central-bank reserves in 2017 was 20%, compared to 63% for the US dollar, 5% each for the British pound sterling and the Japanese yen, and 1% for the Chinese renminbi.[20] Clearly, the euro is an important international currency, but is very far from challenging the dominance of the US dollar.

The EU's official doctrine has long been that it neither encourages nor discourages an international role for the euro. However, in 2018, the European Commission adopted a more positive tone and outlined proposals that would contribute to increasing the use of the euro by non-residents.[21] But piecemeal initiatives are unlikely to matter much. If European policymakers want an international currency, they need to consider what really encourages global use of that currency. An international currency requires deep and integrated capital and banking markets at home, but EU markets remain too fragmented to incentivise foreign investors to invest on the necessary scale. An international euro would also require a European-level safe asset (the equivalent of a US Treasury bond), but to date European leaders have baulked at creating one.[22] An international euro would also require the European Central Bank (ECB) to establish swap lines with other central banks to ensure that banks operating in a foreign currency could retain access to liquidity in times of market stress. But the ECB does not believe such swap lines fall within its current mandate for monetary stability.

The second strategic choice concerns the global financial architecture. That architecture was initially conceived as a single system structured around two sister institutions: the International Monetary Fund (IMF) and the World Bank. Regional development banks also provided support, but within the framework established and dominated by the Bretton Woods institutions. Now, however, a web of financial safety nets has supplanted the single net once provided by the IMF. Credit lines potentially available from bilateral swap lines, most significantly from the US Federal Reserve, and regional financing arrangements such as the European Stability Mechanism and the Asian Chiang Mai Initiative, each account for amounts broadly equal to the IMF's total resources. The World Bank has also lost its monopoly. New development-finance institutions have been established, the most notable of which are the Shanghai-based New Development Bank (2014) and the Beijing-based Asian Infrastructure Investment Bank (2015). And of course there is the BRI.

These changes may herald the unravelling of the post-war financial order. Growing tensions between the US and China could, for instance, lead the US to assert dominance over the Bretton Woods system (where it holds a blocking minority) and prompt China to secede from it and build a separate system of bilateral, regional and multilateral financing arrangements. Even short of outright fragmentation, adversarial behaviour within the multilateral institutions is a distinct possibility.

So far, the EU has not formulated a coherent response to this looming crisis. It has two significant financial instruments for doing so: the European Investment Bank (EIB), which is intended to foster infrastructure development, innovation, investment in smaller companies and the transition to a low-carbon economy in the EU; and the recently created European Stability Mechanism, the core mission of which is to provide financial assistance to euro-area countries that risk losing market access. Both institutions are focused on the EU: 90% of EIB lending goes to EU countries, and the European Stability Mechanism's scope is limited to the euro area. But these institutions could help the EU to prepare for the possibility of a politically or geopolitically motivated stalemate over the provision of IMF assistance to a neighbouring country. Currently the EU is not equipped to provide such assistance outside the context of an IMF programme. One way to make it possible would be to amend the treaty establishing the European Stability Mechanism so that it could provide conditional assistance to third countries. Another possible, though financially less potent, alternative would be to make the balance-of-payments instruments for third countries able to be funded by the EU budget.

Europe is also home to several financing institutions, the most significant of which is the London-based European Bank for Reconstruction and Development (EBRD). The EU and its member states account for a majority of the shareholders, but the United States, China and many others are also shareholders, and the bank's scope has gradually extended to North Africa, the Middle East and Mongolia. The EIB and the EBRD have different mandates but also different shareholders.

For the EU to leverage its influence, there are two clear ways forward: to give the EIB, which has so far been mostly focused on investment within the EU, a greater international role; and to broaden the geographical scope of EBRD operations so as to turn it into a sort of European counterpart to the Asian Infrastructure Investment Bank. The first option would have the advantage that the EU would retain total control. The second option would build on the EBRD's international experience and on its wider shareholder base.

The third choice that confronts the EU concerns the international payments system. The United States' exercise of political power over that system has created yet another vulnerability for the EU. At the core of the global payment infrastructure is a financial-messaging service, SWIFT, which is used for almost all cross-border payments. Disconnecting a country's banks from the SWIFT financial-messaging capabilities isolates that country almost completely from the global financial system, curtailing its ability to conduct business even with countries that have not directly sanctioned it. In November 2018, as a result of US pressure, SWIFT, registered and governed under Belgian law, disconnected Iranian banks, saying the step, 'while regrettable, [had] been taken in the interest of the stability and integrity of the wider global financial system'.[23]

China and Russia had already noticed the vulnerability that partici-pation in such an interconnected payment system presented, and started collaborating on a payments system of their own in 2014–15.[24] Each now has a fully functional domestic payments system and intends to connect them. Other countries have expressed an interest in joining the scheme. But the EU cannot separate its financial (and, as a consequence, economic) system from that of the US given their economic and financial interdependence. The cre-ation of a special vehicle for Iran is a political signal rather than an actual channel for significant transactions. The only way for the EU to effectively oppose unilateral US secondary sanctions is direct retaliation. And the size of the European economy is large enough for the threat of proportionate retaliatory measures to weigh significantly on US choices.

Global governance

The EU plays a key role in multilateral organisations including the IMF, the G20 and the WTO. It regards these as fundamental pillars of the rules-based global system. While discontent with globalisation has grown over the last decade, increased interdependence calls for greater cooperation on a global level. The best options for managing these conflicting influences are non-binding coordination procedures and soft pledge-and-review mechanisms rather than new or even reformed institutions. The challenge for the EU is to make effective use of its voice in existing international organisations while also promoting effective global collective action, at times outside of those institutions.

The EU's mixed-representation model could give it significant weight in multilateral forums. The EU28 has 25% of the G20 seats, for example. The EU has been similarly influential at the Financial Stability Board and the Bank for International Settlements. The EU's voting share at the IMF is 29.61% (including the UK's 4.03%), and exceeds by far that of the US, its single-largest shareholder at 16.5%. China has only 6.1% of the voting rights. Thus, the EU has the power to veto any IMF decision. From this perspective, Brussels faces a stark trade-off: fight to preserve the disproportionate power it enjoys within the Bretton Woods system at the risk of precipitating the fragmentation of global governance, or accept a diminished role in that system in favour of greater involvement in, and ownership of, the global institutions sponsored by China and other rising powers. The right path is not obvious. But the perennial and regularly deferred debate on the consolidation of EU or euro-area chairs in the Bretton Woods system should not be postponed much longer.

The problem at the WTO is even more severe. The organisation is at risk of disintegration, with its dispute-resolution framework near collapse. The US has criticised the WTO for being unable to uphold rules and for regulatory overreach, but the Trump administration is also openly defiant of multilateral rules that constrain its freedom of manoeuvre. China has not transformed into the market economy that so many had hoped would result from its membership of the WTO. Its developing-country status, its state capitalism and its lack of protection of property rights all create serious issues for China's WTO partners.

A fundamental goal of international rules on trade is to prevent a large economy from unfairly using its size as an advantage. The United States' use of a national-security clause to impose tariffs is particularly worrying. It leaves it up to the EU to find other partners to uphold the basic principles of free and fair competition in trade. The EU has the market size and institutional capacity to do so, while the US–China trade war gives other countries reasons to reach out to the EU.

Unlike the US, China considers itself a champion of trade multilateralism and the WTO. The EU and China have declared their intention to collaborate on reforming it. However, China's support for multilateral-trade principles lacks depth. While it might nominally abide by the letter of WTO rules, it does not abide by their spirit. This is why the EU agrees with the US that WTO reform is necessary to firm up adherence to WTO principles, and to better gear trade rules to the specificities of the Chinese economic model and to tackling unfair competition from Chinese producers.

The EU's aim should be to preserve the multilateral trading system as a pillar of globalisation. The EU, as an open economy with a large internal market, can best leverage its global influence through a multilateral system, but alternatives may become necessary.[25] The same observation applies to other fields, from greenhouse-gas-emissions mitigation to banking regulation. Even post-Trump, the world is unlikely to return completely to the post-war multilateral architecture. Global governance is bound to be more particularised and more often based on weak mechanisms.

A solution

Europeans have responded to some of the challenges of economic sovereignty, but in a distinctly unsystematic fashion. They need a more encompassing strategy for a new context in which partners and competitors are instrumentalising economic relationships in the service of broader geostrategic goals. After decades during which the EU understandably accorded priority to internal integration – through the single market, common regulations, common policies and the creation of a common currency – it needs to refocus its attention on its relationship with the rest of the world. Building economic sovereignty, in particular, requires EU policymakers to change their mindset. The EU must learn to function like a geopolitical power, clearly defining its goals and acting strategically.

This does not imply repudiating globalisation or refraining from taking an active part in collective global action. Global competition and linkages are good for growth, innovation and consumer choice. Europe's aim should not be to reduce trade or investment links with the global economy, or, worse, to decouple with China as some in the US advocate. Rather, Europe's aim should be to strengthen the rules-based order, while maintaining its economic identity and control and staying intertwined, in different ways, with both the US and China. It has enormous potential power, but its decision-making structures are too disjointed to use it.[26] It is high time to unlock this potential. To do so, Brussels must prioritise, alongside the international economic concerns for which it has traditionally been responsible, geopolitical issues customarily consigned to EU member states.

Of course, not all EU countries have the same perception of its sovereignty and the threats it faces. Some feel simply too dependent on the US security umbrella to oppose almost any US initiative. Some have built strong economic ties with China and feel constrained from criticising it. Thus, building European economic sovereignty will involve patient negotiation among European partners on a series of specific measures, and a gradual implementation period. In this light, what makes the most sense is a three-part strategy establishing an agenda for economic sovereignty, devising the mechanisms to articulate and apply it, and allowing for flexible implementation.

Economic-sovereignty agenda

Firstly, there should be an economic-sovereignty agenda focused on European and national measures that will create opportunities and incentives to integrate economic and geopolitical considerations at the appropriate level of governance. The agenda should have four broad goals: boosting Europe's research, scientific, technology and innovation base; protecting assets critical to national security from foreign interference; enforcing a level playing field in both domestic and international competition; and strengthening European monetary and financial autonomy. This effort should be top of the policy priorities of the new European Commission. Its president should outline this economic-sovereignty agenda in her first speech to the European Parliament, and should publish a more detailed proposal by early 2020.

The agenda should include several initiatives. Firstly, it should expand EU scrutiny of state aid. In particular, the EU should vigilantly monitor distortions to international trade and investment resulting from support provided to industry by foreign governments. Direct and indirect subsidies should, if possible, be tackled in the context of the WTO. If not, the EU should review its competition-policy instruments and their possible application to state aid granted by foreign governments.

Secondly, competition decisions should take into account economic-sovereignty concerns. While economic criteria should remain paramount, such decisions should also consider whether incumbents' market power can be tamed by the threat of potential entry. To address cases in which competition-policy decisions might raise security concerns, the High Representative should be empowered to invoke a security clause and object to a decision proposed by the competition commissioner.

Thirdly, the EU should develop a broad approach for screening foreign investments. Because foreign investment affords an outside party access to the entire internal market, the EU cannot regard investment control as a purely national affair. The European Commission should be able to recommend the prohibition of a foreign investment on security grounds to the Council of the EU, which should in turn be able, by qualified majority vote, to block a foreign investment based on that recommendation. The EU should also develop financial instruments, such as a dedicated investment fund, to offer member states alternatives when foreign investments are disallowed.

Fourthly, the EU should encourage a greater international role for the euro. The euro will not become a truly international currency without EU initiatives to support it in this role, including promoting a deep and integrated capital and banking market, creating a euro-area safe asset and extending euro swap lines to partner central banks. This initiative would also prepare the EU for the possibility of a politically motivated stalemate over the provision of IMF assistance to a neighbouring country. The EU should consider how the European Stability Mechanism might assume an external role and how to strengthen EU-budget-funded balance-of-payments instruments available to third countries. At the same time, the EU should preserve and leverage its influence over the international financial institutions.

Finally, the Union should develop the capacity to respond to unilateral sanctions it opposes through appropriate and proportionate economic-retaliation measures. The creation of special vehicles to permit domestic companies to continue to trade are fine to signal protest, but they will never fully solve the problem.

Implementation mechanisms

EU governance works by managing sectoral policies separately. Currently, it has no mechanisms for implementing an overarching economic-sovereignty agenda based on geopolitical considerations. Special interests could try to justify protectionist measures on ostensibly geopolitical grounds. For example, state aid intended to maintain technological competitiveness could be spent on inefficient jobs programmes, and efforts to broaden the use of the euro could morph into subsidies for favoured banks. Accordingly, the EU needs implementation mechanisms that incorporate the broad economic-sovereignty imperatives and facilitate probing evaluations of the trade-offs between economic efficiency and national security. One possibility is a European Commission Economic Sovereignty Committee, building on the 'Global Actor' priority area already established by the commission. Under the chairmanship of the High Representative, this committee would bring together European commissioners for foreign and security policy, neighbourhood and enlargement, trade, international cooperation and development, and civil protection and humanitarian aid.

A second tier, chaired by the European Commission first vice-president, would include commissioners whose portfolios are not generally thought of as having sovereignty implications, such as those for competition policy, economic and financial affairs, and research, science and innovation. The committee would also have a dedicated staff tasked to address cross-cutting issues, monitor compliance among directorates-general and ensure coordination with similar bodies in member states. This staff should include economic experts as well as diplomats and security specialists.

In addition, a Committee on Foreign Investment in the European Union, staffed by some of the economic-sovereignty staff and including representatives of relevant directorates-general, should be set up and charged with making recommendations on the national-security implications of large foreign (that is, non-EU) investments or mergers in the EU. These recommendations would be presented to the High Representative and the College of Commissioners.

Finally, an Office of Financial Sanctions Enforcement staffed by representatives of the European External Action Service, the Directorate-General for Economic and Financial Affairs, and relevant member-state representatives would closely coordinate with banks and other financial institutions to ensure that European sanctions regulations were strictly enforced. It would also impose penalties on entities that violated sanctions.

Flexible implementation strategy

Many relevant powers would inevitably remain with EU member states. As noted, member states differ significantly in their perceptions of security threats from Russia, China and the United States, their vulnerability to external pressures and their attitudes towards the US and China. For these reasons, implementation could not be just a Brussels-based effort limited to the EU itself. Furthermore, the EU and its member states will need to coordinate closely with other non-EU European partners. These will include the post-Brexit UK, although it is likely to share many of its neighbours' priorities and concerns. Thus, while an EU-wide approach is desirable, a more flexible approach based on 'minilateral' groups of states is likely to be necessary. Any policy or action involving the functioning of the single market or the customs union, of course, would need to be agreed on by the whole EU. For other matters, a club-type approach is likely to be the best short-term option.[27]

*　　*　　*

The overarching intent of the proposed effort is to create structures that integrate economic and national-security considerations at both the European and member-state levels. This change would represent a revolution in EU governance. It could not proceed easily or without opposition. But the EU has little choice but to undertake it. If Europeans fail to organise themselves to protect Europe's economic sovereignty, they will lose the capacity to control their own destiny. Key decisions affecting the future of European citizens would not be made in either Brussels or European national capitals. They would be made in Beijing, Washington or some other distant and indifferent place.

Notes

[1] See Henry Farrell and Abraham L. Newman, 'Weaponized Interdependence: How Global Economic Networks Shape State Coercion', *International Security*, vol. 44, no. 1, Summer 2019, pp. 42–79; and Mark Leonard (ed.), *Connectivity Wars: Why Migration, Finance and Trade are the Geo-economic Battlegrounds of the Future* (London: European Council on Foreign Relations, 2016), https://www.ecfr.eu/page/-/Connectivity_Wars.pdf.

[2] European Commission, 'EU–China – A Strategic Outlook: European Commission and HR/VP Contribution to the European Council', 12 March 2019, https://ec.europa.eu/commission/publications/eu-china-strategic-outlook-commission-contribution-european-

council-21-22-march-2019_en.

3   See 'Made in China 2025',
    strategy paper, http://english.gov.
    cn/2016special/madeinchina2025/.

4   One example seems to have been
    Geely's February 2018 increase in its
    ownership stake in Daimler. Another
    is the 2015 Chinese acquisition of
    Swedish company Silex Microsystems,
    which helped the Chinese transfer a
    key technology to China. See Emily
    Feng, 'How China Acquired Mastery
    of Vital Microchip Technology',
    Financial Times, 29 January 2019.

5   Laura Zhou, 'China Pledges US$23
    Billion in Loans and Aid to Arab
    States as It Boosts Ties in Middle East',
    South China Morning Post, 10 July 2018.

6   See Robin Emmott and Angeliki
    Koutantou, 'Greece Blocks EU
    Statement on China Human Rights at
    UN', Reuters, 18 June 2017; and Robin
    Emmott, 'EU's Statement on South
    China Sea Reflects Divisions', Reuters,
    15 July 2016.

7   See Ted Piccone, 'China's Long Game
    on Human Rights at the United
    Nations', Foreign Policy at Brookings,
    Brookings Institution, September
    2018, https://www.brookings.
    edu/wp-content/uploads/2018/09/
    FP_20181009_china_human_rights.pdf.

8   The document, in Italian, is available
    at http://www.governo.it/sites/
    governo.it/files/documenti/documenti/
    Notizie-allegati/Italia-Cina_20190323/
    Memorandum_Italia-Cina_IT.pdf.

9   See Jonathan Swan, 'The White
    House's Next Iran Fight', Axios, 13
    August 2018, https://www.axios.com/
    trump-administration-iran-sanctions-
    swift-financial-messaging-8fae6cd6-
    11c9-42a8-9d5b-6d3140a7ae83.html.

10 Douglas Barrie et al., 'Protecting
    Europe: Meeting the EU's Military
    Level of Ambition in the Context of
    Brexit', International Institute for
    Strategic Studies (IISS), November
    2018.

11 Ben Barry et al., 'Defending
    Europe: Scenario-based Capability
    Requirements for NATO's
    European Members', IISS, 10
    May 2019, https://www.iiss.org/
    blogs/research-paper/2019/05/
    defending-europe.

12 Petros C. Mavroidis and André Sapir,
    'China and the WTO: Towards a
    Better Fit', Bruegel, Working Paper
    2019/06, 11 June 2019, https://bruegel.
    org/wp-content/uploads/2019/06/
    WP-2019-06-110619_.pdf.

13 See Georgios Petropoulos and
    Guntram B. Wolff, 'What Can the
    EU Do to Keep Its Firms Globally
    Relevant?', Bruegel, 15 February
    2019, https://bruegel.org/2019/02/
    what-can-the-eu-do-to-keep-its-firms-
    globally-relevant/.

14 See 'Partner and Systemic Competitor
    – How Do We Deal with China's
    State-controlled Economy?', BDI
    Policy Paper – China, January 2019,
    https://english.bdi.eu/publication/
    news/china-partner-and-systemic-
    competitor/.

15 See Budesministerium für Wirtschaft
    und Energie (BMWi), 'A Franco-
    German Manifesto for a European
    Industrial Policy Fit for the 21st
    Century', https://www.bmwi.
    de/Redaktion/DE/Downloads/F/
    franco-german-manifesto-for-a-
    european-industrial-policy.pdf.

16 See Greg Clark, Secretary of State
    for Business, Energy and Industrial

Strategy, 'National Security and Investment: A Consultation on Proposed Legislative Reforms', UK Department of Business, Energy and Industrial Strategy, July 2018, https://assets.publishing.service. gov.uk/government/uploads/ system/uploads/attachment_data/ file/728310/20180723_-_National_ security_and_investment_-_final_ version_for_printing__1_.pdf.

17 See BMWi, 'Verordnung der Bundesregierung: Neunte Verordnung zur Änderung der Außenwirtschaftsverordnung', https://www.bmwi.de/Redaktion/DE/ Downloads/V/neunte-aendvo-awv. pdf?__blob=publicationFile&v=6.

18 See 'Screening of Foreign Direct Investments Into the European Union', 2017/0224, Legislative Observatory, European Parliament, https://oeil.secure.europarl.europa.eu/ oeil/popups/ficheprocedure.do?refere nce=2017/0224(COD)&l=en.

19 See 'Union Regime for the Control of Exports, Transfer, Brokering, Technical Assistance and Transit of Dual-use Items (Recast)', 2016/0295, Legislative Observatory, European Parliament, https://oeil.secure. europarl.europa.eu/oeil/popups/ ficheprocedure.do?reference=2016/029 5(COD)&l=en.

20 See European Central Bank, 'International Role of the Euro', July 2017, https://www.ecb.europa.eu/ pub/pdf/other/ecb.euro-international- role-201707.pdf.

21 European Central Bank board member Benoît Coeuré has also highlighted the potential gains for monetary policy

from a greater international role for the euro. See Benoît Coeuré, 'C. Peter McColough Series With Benoît Coeuré', Council on Foreign Relations, 15 February 2019, https://www.cfr. org/event/c-peter-mccolough-series- benoit-coeure.

22 Ibid.

23 Quoted in, for instance, Michael Peel, 'Swift to Comply with US Sanctions on Iran in Blow to EU', Financial Times, 5 November 2018, https://www. ft.com/content/8f16f8aa-e104-11e8- 8e70-5e22a430c1ad.

24 See Karen Yeung, 'China and Russia Look to Ditch Dollar with New Payments System in Move to Avoid Sanctions', South China Morning Post, 22 November 2018, https://www.scmp.com/economy/ china-economy/article/2174453/ china-and-russia-look-ditch-dollar- new-payments-system-move.

25 See Uri Dadush and Guntram Wolff, 'The European Union's Response to the Trade Crisis', Bruegel, Policy Contribution no. 5, March 2019, https://bruegel.org/wp-content/ uploads/2019/03/PC-05_2019.pdf.

26 See, for instance, André Sapir (ed.), Fragmented Power: Europe and the Global Economy, Bruegel, July 2007, https:// bruegel.org/wp-content/uploads/ imported/publications/Fragmented_ Power_Andre_Sapir.pdf.

27 See, for example, Maria Demertzis et al., 'One Size Does Not Fit All: European Integration by Differentiation', Bruegel, Policy Brief, issue 3, September 2018, https://bruegel.org/wp-content/ uploads/2018/09/PB-2018_03_final3.pdf.

Decentralising Ukraine: Geopolitical Implications

Valentyna Romanova and Andreas Umland

Ukraine's ongoing reform of local government has become an important post-Euromaidan development.[1] This rearrangement of political power and public finances is often simply called 'decentralisation'. Owing to this prosaic label, the largely technical character of the reform and its provincial focus, what is in fact a fundamental remaking of Ukrainian state–society relations has remained below the radar of many Western journalists and analysts. But its repercussions could reach beyond the country's borders and exert considerable influence on the geopolitics of Eastern Europe.

Outside the region, Ukrainian decentralisation is sometimes seen as something imposed by the West, started by the European Union's Association Agreement with Kiev, or even triggered by the conflict with Russia and the related Minsk Agreements that incorporate the term. In fact, Ukraine's current administrative restructuring has national rather than foreign roots, and started before the ratification of the Association Agreement and signing of the first Minsk documents in summer 2014.[2] Since the 1990s, the so-called 'cities of *oblast* significance' have enjoyed a meaningful degree of self-government by virtue of collecting sufficient local taxes and maintaining direct inter-budgetary relations with the central government. Numerous cities have been able to independently

Valentyna Romanova is a Senior Consultant at the Department of Regional Policy at the National Institute for Strategic Studies in Kiev and co-editor of the *Annual Review of Regional Elections* at *Regional and Federal Studies*. **Andreas Umland** is a Senior Non-Resident Fellow at the Institute of International Relations in Prague, Principal Researcher at the Institute for Euro-Atlantic Cooperation in Kiev, and General Editor of the *ibidem*–Verlag book series 'Soviet and Post-Soviet Politics and Society' and 'Ukrainian Voices'.

Survival | vol. 61 no. 5 | October–November 2019 | pp. 99–112   DOI 10.1080/00396338.2019.1662108

foster economic growth, provide better public services, improve urban infrastructure and help local businesses. Other localities, however, have been heavily subsidised and their administrations understaffed, and thus have often been incapable of providing even basic public services to their residents.

The Euromaidan uprising in February 2014, Russia's intervention in Ukraine and the subsequent two rounds of national elections in 2014 changed the composition of the ruling elites of Ukraine. The unexpected and severe threat to Ukraine's territorial integrity demonstrated the vulnerability of the theretofore centralised yet regionally diverse state. Moreover, post-Euromaidan civil society maintained pressure on policymakers and demanded substantial reforms. Ukrainian politicians were eager to devolve power to the local level to prevent federalisation, which remained popular in Russia and the West for different reasons. Moscow sees federalisation as an instrument of weakening, subverting or even decomposing the Ukrainian state. Many Western observers, in contrast, believe that a Ukrainian federation would function as well as those of the United States, Germany or Switzerland. These countries, however, do not have long borders with a militarily far superior state with irredentist impulses. Many Ukrainians' categorical rejection of federalisation has little to do with the concept in itself, but arises from the fear that Russia would be able to split up a Ukrainian federation along regional lines.

Implementing the concept

A few days after Russia illegally annexed Crimea and a few days before the Kremlin-guided armed uprising in the Donbas started, the post-Euromaidan government published a seminal document titled 'Concept of Reforming Local Self-Government and the Territorial Division of Power'. This concept was adopted during a period when Ukraine had only an acting president – Oleksandr Turchynov – who had little to lose from devolution. Furthermore, the dispersion of central power away from Kiev to local governments seemed natural in view of the completely new political situation, especially given Ukraine's historical record of unsuccessful attempts to achieve it. According to the document, Ukraine's decentralisation seeks to strengthen local governance via the unification of weak municipalities into larger territorial communities that are able to better provide basic public services and foster local development; fundamentally reform the territorial division of the state; and increase regional and sub-regional self-government via the introduction of executive committees appointed by elected councils.

The government started its local-governance reform by inviting small neighbouring villages and towns to voluntarily merge into more sustainable and self-sufficient municipalities. For this purpose, Ukraine's national parliament – the Verkhovna Rada, or Supreme Council – passed, in early 2015, the law 'On Voluntary Amalgamation of Territorial Communities'. Shortly afterwards, the central government also approved a 'Methodology for Establishing Sustainable Territorial Communities'.[3]

These and additional regulations ensured that Ukraine's original 10,900 local communities (*hromady*) – most of which, by themselves, were unsustainable – would merge into 1,200–1,800 units known as Amalgamated Territorial Communities (ATCs). By spring 2019, 884 newly established ATCs had incorporated 4,110, or 37.5%, of the old *hromady*, comprising 38.5% of Ukraine's overall territory, where 25.8% of Ukraine's population – about 9.1 million citizens – lived. The speed of the voluntary amalgamation of local communities was remarkable.[4] Another 43.5% of the population of Ukraine lives in the cities of *oblast* significance. Thus, by spring 2019, 69.3% of Ukraine's citizens lived in municipalities with solid local self-governance. The remaining 30.7% of the population was yet to benefit from the decentralisation reform.[5] Some 6,851 old and mostly very small communities had not yet amalgamated. The government plans to move in 2019 from voluntary to administrative amalgamation, and to complete the merger process by autumn 2020.

The ATCs are relatively independent and self-sufficient in their internal political operations and policy decisions, including those regarding their external relations. As of autumn 2019, 368 collaboration agreements on inter-municipal cooperation, covering matters such as healthcare, education, energy efficiency and administrative services, were being implemented in Ukraine.[6] Unlike the governing mechanisms of the old *hromady*, which lacked competence and funding, the new ATCs have significant capability and money due to wholesale amendments to the budget and tax codes that have yielded a new fiscal model.[7] The new ATCs have established direct inter-budgetary relations with the central government and are also allowed to generate more income on their own.[8] The amalgamated communities' budgets receive 60% of the collected personal income tax, as well as 100% of the property tax, 100% of administrative-services fees, 100% of state customs tax, 10% of income tax from businesses in the respective localities and increased shares of other taxes.

In addition, the ATCs have received special subsidies from the state budget to build up their new institutional and social infrastructures. They receive separate 'block grants' to better cope with new responsibilities for healthcare, school education and administrative services. Regulations requiring 'horizontal equalisation' of ATCs' tax-collecting capacities aim to moderate inter-municipal and inter-regional disparities in local development. ATCs can seek funding for qualifying regional-development projects from a new State Fund for Regional Development.[9] And local councils now have the right to apply for ownership of agricultural land in their ATCs' territories that was previously owned by the central state.

In December 2018, the National Institute for Strategic Studies, a Kiev-based government think tank, reported:

> The most important result of budgetary decentralisation is the growth of the share of local taxes and revenues within the incomes of local budgets from 2.5% in 2012–2014 to 30% in 2014, mostly due to the transfer of certain taxes and revenues to local budgets. The share of the incomes of local budgets in the overall budget [of Ukraine] equals almost 50%; for comparison, in 2014, it was 42%. The standard relationship between the [central] state and local budgets in the majority of EU countries – 50:50 – can thus be counted as achieved. Through the local budgets of Ukraine almost 15% of its GDP is redistributed.[10]

Most of these financial resources are invested in the delivery of public services.

Decentralisation's salutary effects

So far, Ukrainian decentralisation has, as intended, mostly affected local governance, finance and development. Small local communities have been merged into larger, more sustainable and powerful self-governing units. Regional and sub-regional administrative agencies whose staffs are appointed by Kiev have given way to elected territorial and city councils. Budgetary and legal competencies have devolved from national and regional organs to the municipal level. Amalgamated self-governing communities have assumed responsibilities in such fields as education and public services. Kiev also plans to apply the existing decentralisation framework to the temporarily occupied territories of the Donetsk and Luhansk *oblast*s once they are liberated.

In theory at least, decentralisation should improve governance. Public administration stands to become more visible and interactive, and therefore more rational and flexible. As democratic accountability increases, relations between the state and society tend to strengthen. As resource allocation becomes more transparent, opportunities for corruption ought to diminish. Cities, towns and villages should be able to cooperate more easily with one another, and also to compete more fruitfully for direct investment, tourism, project funding, qualified personnel and public resources. Patriotic energy can be focused on improving real communities, civic activism channelled more directly towards the public good. Grassroots initiatives are more readily transformed into efficacious public policies. Beyond these local effects, Ukraine's decentralisation in particular could make the country more resilient and cohesive, with corresponding geopolitical consequences. Presidential and parliamentary elections in 2019 were held in a peaceful manner, and a number of young civic activists won seats in parliament without intra-elite bargaining or electoral fraud.

Ukraine is becoming a less brittle state and nation by attenuating various deleterious post-Soviet aspects of public administration and local development. After Ukraine regained independence in 1991, informal regionalisation effectively rendered it a cluster of semi-autonomous fiefdoms controlled by rent-extracting oligarchs and allied bureaucrats and politicians. They formed clientelistic networks that subverted and partially controlled governmental, some non-governmental and many commercial organisations.[11] The reach of a particular oligarchic clan could cover a specific macro-region, such as the Donets Basin (Donbas), an *oblast*, or a large city and its surroundings. In addition, linguistic, cultural and religious differences have sharpened territorial divisions within the formally centralised Ukrainian state. As a result, the rule of law has suffered, economic growth has been hindered and political development has been stunted.

The intensifying sub-regional focus of Ukraine's governance reform should help to weaken and ultimately break up these patronal pyramid structures by devolving power to communities smaller than those at which most of the structures have operated. This makes state capture by private interests considerably more difficult to accomplish. While decentralisation could to an extent shift the activity of a corrupt network from the national or regional to the local level, the more prevalent effect is to empower democratically chosen governing bodies by subjecting them to direct public scrutiny and accountability. Overall, Ukraine's ATCs are less susceptible to subversion by semi-secretive, rent-seeking networks than were the old *oblast* (regional) and *rayon* (district) administrations and councils.

Many Ukrainian politicians have come to see decentralisation as a means of countering Russia's hybrid warfare.[12] Moscow's tactic since 2014 has been to instrumentalise Russian allies, proxies and agents within Ukraine to dominate certain regions and their capitals.[13] Until 2014, in Ukraine's mainly Russophone east and south, powerful regional clans and *oblast* administrations provided entry points for Russian operations designed to fan anti-centralist autonomism, pro-Russian separatism and pan-Slavic nationalism. The ongoing devolution of power to the local level in Ukraine deprives Russia's various hybrid warriors of their customary institutional frameworks and critical entry points for provoking seditious sentiment.[14] This has complicated the targeting and planning of irredentist operations similar to those undertaken in Simferopol, Donetsk and Luhansk. As regional capitals and governments gradually lose political relevance, it is becoming more difficult for the Kremlin to clearly delineate territories in which it can strongly support secession or advance annexation.

In a thoroughly decentralised Ukraine, a successful coup in an eastern or southern *oblast* centre by a Kremlin-installed 'people's governor' would have limited effect. Any such figure in a regional capital would have to persuade all of the region's respective municipal and communal legislative and executive organs of his or her cause. In March 2014, Russia could plant Sergei Aksenov, today's prime minister of Crimea, in Simferopol, even though his Russian Unity party had received only 4% in the 2010 local elections. Had strong local self-governance been in place in Crimea in February 2014, Russia's takeover of the peninsula might have been more difficult to plan and execute.

Zbigniew Brzezinski famously noted in 1994 that 'without Ukraine, Russia ceases to be a Eurasian empire, but with Ukraine suborned and then subordinated, Russia automatically becomes an empire'.[15] Ukrainian political activists and experts see the break-up of Ukraine's still partly Soviet administrative system – that is, the disempowerment of *oblast*s and *rayon*s and the enablement of local communities – as a way of consolidating and protecting the Ukrainian state. Insofar as stronger local governance bolsters Ukrainian resilience and helps stabilise the state, it increases Ukraine's resistance to Russian co-optation.

Ukraine's decentralisation furthers its Europeanisation

Another geopolitical aspect of Ukraine's decentralisation is that it supports Ukraine's ongoing integration into the EU's political and legal space in connection with the Eastern Partnership programme started in 2009, and the Association Agreement signed in 2014. For instance, the latter encourages transborder regional cooperation, which presupposes properly empowered local and regional authorities.

More broadly, Ukraine's decentralisation both expresses and furthers Ukraine's Europeanisation. Western institutions have triggered many Ukrainian reforms through various mechanisms. These include the EU's Visa Liberalisation Action Plan, IMF standby agreements, Council of Europe opinions and decisions of the European Court of Human Rights. In contrast, the ongoing transformation of Ukraine's system of local self-governance has originated from within the country. To be sure, it uses several relevant concepts gleaned from abroad – in particular, from Poland's decentralisation, which started in the early 1990s.[16] Various Western countries, such as Switzerland, Sweden, the United States and Germany, have provided national funding to Ukraine for the preparation, discussion and formulation of reform plans.[17] And the EU supports the decentralisation reform efforts through its large Ukraine Local Empowerment, Accountability and Development (U-LEAD) Programme. Still, Ukrainian decentralisation is a national rather than a foreign product, and can be seen as a manifestation of Ukraine's sense of belonging to Europe. It supports assimilation of EU governance norms and principles, and demonstrates Ukraine's embrace of pluralist and open political principles and culture. The ongoing transition's cumulative results should make Ukraine more compatible with the Union and better prepared for accession.

Decentralisation as a model

The most speculative geopolitical aspect of the transformation of Ukrainian self-governance concerns its potential to drive and influence reform in other countries. Decentralisation in Ukraine could provide policy cues and institutional templates to other, so far highly centralised, post-Soviet states. Over time, democratisation, social modernisation and economic integration are likely to gain greater traction in most post-Soviet republics and hasten political reform. Especially for former Soviet states, Ukraine, as a founding republic of the USSR, would logically be one of the most prominent and attractive models at hand.[18] The stabilising and anti-secessionist effects of its decentralisation process would be obvious assets.[19]

In this connection, Russia is of special interest.[20] During the last 15 years, the putatively federalist Russian state has actually become more and more centralised under President Vladimir Putin. Today, although Russia consists of 85 federal units and presents itself as a federal, multi-ethnic democracy, it is a de facto unitary state. Yet history has shown that extreme centralisation is no guarantee against secession. The Soviet pseudo-federal centralised order did not prevent the Soviet Union's break-up, and in fact helped to generate the centrifugal tendencies that eventually produced that result. Strong secessionist forces, of course, may not materialise after Putin's presidency is over. Even so, Russian leaders might be tempted to consider the Ukrainian model for positive reasons – namely, to make governance more effective, efficient and responsive via decentralisation while avoiding the autonomism and separatism that might be triggered in a more federalised state.

A decentralised Russia in which strong local governments control substantive prerogatives and finances would tend to focus on the socio-economic advancement of the vast underdeveloped territory of Russia as well as education, public health, infrastructure, energy efficiency, investment and environmental protection. A decentralised state would also be more stable than the current Russian Federation. And, if Russian cities and territorial communities had greater input into Russia's political decision-making, the Russian government would probably be more focused than Putin's current government on internal socio-economic advancement and less on expanding Russian power abroad.

*　　*　　*

Local-governance reform is hardly a panacea for Ukraine or other post-Soviet states, and Ukraine itself has some distance to go before its newly decentralised system is fully operating. But the Europeanising, anti-separatist and diffusion potential of Ukraine's model makes it an especially salient dimension of the country's ongoing socio-political transformation. It could bode well for more stable Russian as well as Eastern European geopolitics in the medium and longer term.

Acknowledgement

Andreas Umland's work for this article was supported by Accommodation of Regional Diversity in Ukraine (ARDU), a research project funded by the Research Council of Norway's NORRUSS Plus Programme.

Notes

1   Among the few first analyses published in the West are Ruben Werchan, 'Dezentralisierung: Der Weg zu einer effizienteren Regierung, Wirtschaftswachstum und dem Erhalt der territorialen Integrität?', in Evgeniya Bakalova et al. (eds), *Ukraine – Krisen – Perspektiven: Interdisziplinäre Betrachtungen eines Landes im Umbruch* (Berlin: WVB, 2015), pp. 187–212; Natalia Shapovalova, 'Mühen der Ebenen: Dezentralisierung in der Ukraine', *Osteuropa*, vol. 65, no. 4, 2015, pp. 143–52; Balazs Jarabik and Yulia Yesmukhanova, 'Ukraine's Slow Struggle for Decentralization', Carnegie Endowment for International Peace, 8 March 2017, https://carnegieendowment.org/2017/03/08/ukraine-s-slow-struggle-for-decentralization-pub-68219; Oesten Baller, 'Korruptionsbekämpfung und Dezentralisierung auf dem Prüfstand des Reformbedarfs in der Ukraine', *Jahrbuch für Ostrecht*, no. 2, 2017, pp. 235–68; Anatolij Tkatschuk, 'Zur Dezentralisierung: Erfolge, Risiken und die Rolle des Parlamentes', *Ukraine–Nachrichten*, 26 January 2017, https://ukraine-nachrichten.de/dezentralisierung-erfolge-risiken-rolle-parlamentes_4568; Jurij Hanuschtschak, Oleksij Sydortschuk and Andreas Umland, 'Die ukrainische Dezentralisierungsreform nach der Euromajdan-Revolution 2014–2017: Vorgeschichte, Erfolge, Hindernisse', *Ukraine–Analysen*, no. 183, 2017, pp. 2–11, http://www.laender-analysen.de/ukraine/pdf/UkraineAnalysen183.pdf; Marian Madela, *Der Reformprozess in der Ukraine 2014-2017: Eine Fallstudie zur Reform der öffentlichen Verwaltung* (Stuttgart: *ibidem*-Verlag, 2018); and Maryna Rabinovych, Anthony Levitas and Andreas Umland, 'Revisiting Decentralization After Maidan: Achievements and Challenges of Ukraine's Local Governance Reform', *Kennan Cable*, no. 34, 2018, https://www.wilsoncenter.org/publication/kennan-cable-no-34-revisiting-decentralization-after-maidan-achievements-and-challenges. Early seminal Ukrainian-language surveys were: Anatolii Tkachuk, *Mistseve samovryaduvannya ta detsentralizatsiya: Praktychnyy posibnyk* (Kiev: Sofiia, 2012); Yuriy Hanushchak, *Reforma terytorial'noi orhanizatsii vlady* (Kiev: DESPRO, 2015); Anatolii Tkachuk, *Derzhavna rehionalna polityka: Vid asymetrii do solidarnosti (robochyi zoshyt)* (Kiev: Lehalnyi status, 2013); and Anatoliy Tkachuk, *Pro detsentralizatsiiu, federalizatsiiu, separatystiv ta ul'tymatumy: zapytannia ta vidpovidi* (Kiev: Lehalnyi status, 2014).

2   See, for example, Valentyna Romanova, 'The Role of Centre–Periphery Relations in the 2004 Constitutional Reform in Ukraine', *Regional and Federal Studies*, vol. 21, no. 3, July 2011, pp. 321–39.

3   Kabinet ministriv Ukrainy, 'Postanova vid 8 kvitnya 2015 r. No. 214, Kiev, "Pro zatverdzhennya Metodyky formuvannya spromozhnykh terytorial'nykh hromad"'. https://zakon.rada.gov.ua/laws/

show/214-2015-%D0%BF#n10.

4   Centre of Expertise for Local
     Government Reform of the Council
     of Europe, 'Report on Municipal
     Amalgamation and Possible Impact
     on Territorial Reform of Upper
     Tiers of Government (2017)', 14
     November 2017, http://www.slg-coe.
     org.ua/wp-content/uploads/2017/12/
     CoE_Report_Municipal_
     amalgamation_CELGR_2017_4__.pdf.

5   'Monitoring of Power Decentralisation
     and Local Self-government Reform
     in Ukraine', *Decentralization*,
     12 March 2019, https://storage.
     decentralization.gov.ua/uploads/
     library/file/389/10.03.2019.pdf.

6   'Reyestr dohovoriv territorialnyh
     hromad', *Minregion*, 20 March 2019,
     http://www.minregion.gov.ua/
     wp-content/uploads/2019/02/reestr-
     20.03.2019.pdf.

7   Tony Levitas and Jasmina Djikic,
     *Caught Mid-Stream: 'Decentralization',
     Local Government Finance Reform, and
     the Restructuring of Ukraine's Public
     Sector 2014 to 2016* (Kiev: SIDA-SKL,
     2017), http://sklinternational.org.
     ua/wp-content/uploads/2017/10/
     UkraineCaughtMidStream-ENG-
     FINAL-06.10.2017.pdf.

8   Angela Boci, 'Latent Capacity
     of the Budgets of Amalgamated
     Territorial Communities: How Can
     It Be Unleashed?', VoxUkraine, 30
     August 2018, https://voxukraine.org/
     en/latent-capacity-of-the-budgets-of-
     amalgamated-territorial-communities-
     how-can-it-be-unleashed/.

9   OECD, *Maintaining the Momentum
     of Decentralisation in Ukraine* (Kiev:
     OECD, 2018), http://www.oecd.org/
     countries/ukraine/maintaining-the-

momentum-of-decentralisation-in-
ukraine-9789264301436-en.htm.

10   Ya. A. Zhalilo et al., *Detsentralizatsiya
     vlady: Yak zberehty uspishnist' v umo-
     vakh novykh vyklykiv?* (Kiev: NISD,
     2018), p. 12.

11   See Henry E. Hale, *Patronal Politics:
     Eurasian Regime Dynamics in
     Comparative Perspective* (Cambridge:
     Cambridge University Press, 2015).

12   See, for instance, 'How European
     Ukraine Is Being Sewn of
     Amalgamated Hromadas',
     Decentralization, 5 December 2017,
     https://decentralization.gov.ua/en/
     news/7747.

13   Some contributions to the heated
     debate about the weight of domestic
     versus foreign factors in the
     outbreak of the Donbas war include,
     in chronological order: Nikolai
     Mitrokhin, 'Infiltration, Instruktion,
     Invasion: Russlands Krieg in der
     Ukraine', *Osteuropa*, vol. 64, no.
     8, 2014, pp. 3–16; Sergiy Kudelia,
     'Domestic Sources of the Donbas
     Insurgency', *PONARS Eurasia Policy
     Memos*, no. 351, September 2014,
     http://www.ponarseurasia.org/memo/
     domestic-sources-donbas-insurgency;
     Andreas Umland, 'In Defense of
     Conspirology: A Rejoinder to Serhiy
     Kudelia's Anti-Political Analysis of
     the Hybrid War in Eastern Ukraine',
     PONARS Eurasia, 30 September 2014,
     http://www.ponarseurasia.org/article/
     defense-conspirology-rejoinder-
     serhiy-kudelias-anti-political-
     analysis-hybrid-war-eastern; Sergiy
     Kudelia, 'Reply to Andreas Umland:
     The Donbas Insurgency Began at
     Home', *PONARS Eurasia*, 8 October
     2014, http://www.ponarseurasia.

org/article/reply-andreas-umland-donbas-insurgency-began-home; Lawrence Freedman, 'Ukraine and the Art of Limited War', *Survival*, vol. 56, no. 6, January 2014–December 2015, pp. 7–38; Nikolai Mitrokhin, 'Infiltration, Instruction, Invasion: Russia's War in the Donbass', *Journal of Soviet and Post-Soviet Politics and Society*, vol. 1, no. 1, 2015, pp. 219–50; Oleksandr Zadorozhnii, 'Hybrid War or Civil War? The Interplay of Some Methods of Russian Foreign Policy Propaganda with International Law', *Kyiv-Mohyla Law and Politics Journal*, no. 2, December 2016, pp. 117–28; Andrew Wilson, 'The Donbas in 2014: Explaining Civil Conflict Perhaps, but Not Civil War', *Europe–Asia Studies*, vol. 68, no. 4, 2016, pp. 631–52; Ivan Katchanovski, 'The Separatist War in Donbas: A Violent Break-up of Ukraine?', *European Politics and Society*, vol. 17, no. 4, 2016, pp. 473–89; Serhiy Kudelia, 'The Donbas Rift', *Russian Politics and Law*, vol. 54, no. 1, 2016, pp. 5–27; Gwendolyn Sasse and Alice Lackner, 'War and Identity: The Case of the Donbas in Ukraine', *Post-Soviet Affairs*, vol. 34, nos 2–3, 2018, pp. 139–57; Elise Giuliano, 'Who Supported Separatism in Donbas? Ethnicity and Popular Opinion at the Start of the Ukraine Crisis', *Post-Soviet Affairs*, vol. 34, nos 2–3, 2018, pp. 158–78; and Andreas Umland, 'The Glazyev Tapes, Origins of the Donbas Conflict, and Minsk Agreements', Foreign Policy Association, 13 September 2018, http://foreignpolicyblogs.com/2018/09/13/the-glazyev-tapes-origins-of-the-donbas-conflict-and-minsk-agreements/.

[14] Several years before the war started, a warning of separatism and praise for decentralisation had been published in Ukrainian. See Hennadiy Poberezhnyy, 'Detsentralizatsiya yak zasib vid separatyzmu', *Krytyka*, no. 11, 2006, pp. 3–7, http://krytyka.com/ua/articles/detsentralizatsiya-yak-zasib-vid-separatyzmu.

[15] Zbigniew Brzezinski, 'The Premature Partnership', *Foreign Affairs*, vol. 73, no. 2, March/April 1994, p. 80.

[16] See, in chronological order, World Bank, *Poland: Decentralization and Reform of the State* (Washington DC: World Bank, 1992); Anthony Levitas and Jan Herczyński, 'Decentralization, Local Governments and Education Reform and Finance in Poland: 1990–1999', in Kenneth Davey (ed.), *Balancing National and Local Responsibilities: Education Management and Finance in Four Central European Countries* (Budapest: CEU Press, 2003), pp. 113–91; Paweł Swianiewicz, 'Poland and Ukraine: Contrasting Paths of Decentralisation and Territorial Reform', *Local Government Studies*, vol. 32, no. 5, 2006, pp. 599–622; Yuriy Gorodnichenko and Donna Kim, 'Poland Local Government Reform: Division of Responsibilities', VoxUkraine, 14 July 2014, https://voxukraine.org/en/37/; Anthony Levitas, 'Local Government Reform as State Building: What the Polish Case Tells Us about "Decentralization"', *Studies in International Development*, vol. 52, no. 1, March 2017, pp. 23–44.

[17] See, for instance, Oksana Myshlovska, 'Democratising Ukraine by Promoting Decentralisation? A Study of Swiss–Ukraine Cooperation', *International*

Development Policy Working Papers, 4 May 2015, http://journals.openedition.org/poldev/2010.

18 Andreas Umland, 'Für eine neue Osteuropa-Politik: Europas Weg nach Moskau führt über Kiew', *Internationale Politik*, vol. 66, no. 4, 2011, pp. 86–92.

19 Relevant analyses of this issue include, in chronological order: Ugo Panizza, 'Decentralization as a Mechanism to Prevent Secession', *Economic Notes*, vol. 27, no. 2, 1998, pp. 263–7; Bruno S. Frey and Simon Luechinger, 'Decentralization as a Disincentive for Terror', *European Journal of Political Economy*, vol. 20, no. 2, 2004, pp. 509–15; Dawn Brancanti, 'Decentralization: Fueling the Fire or Dampening the Flames of Ethnic Conflict and Secessionism?', *International Organization*, vol. 60, no. 3, 2006, pp. 651–85; Axel Dreher and Justina A.V. Fischer, 'Government Decentralization as a Disincentive for Transnational Terror? An Empirical Analysis', *IZA Discussion Papers*, no. 4,259, 2009; François Vaillancourt, Edison Roy-Cesar and Richard Miller Bird, 'Is Decentralization "Glue" or "Solvent" for National Unity?', Andrew Young School International Studies Program Working Paper no. 3, 2010; Jürgen Ehrke, *Zur Stabilisierung fragmentierter Staaten: Dezentralisierung, Entwicklungszusammenarbeit und das Gespenst des Separatismus* (Potsdam: Universitätsverlag Potsdam, 2011); and Jörn Grävingholt and Christian von Haldenwang, 'The Promotion of Decentralization and Local Governance in Fragile Contexts', *DIE Discussion Papers*, no. 20, 2016.

20 Mykola Rjabčuk, 'Dezentralisierung und Subsidiarität: Wider die Föderalisierung à la russe', *Osteuropa*, vol. 64, nos 5–6, 2014, pp. 217–25.

Decisive Response: A New Nuclear Strategy for NATO

Hans Binnendijk and David Gompert

A declining power can be a dangerous one. Take Russia, whose president, Vladimir Putin, has been engaging in external aggression to excite the patriotism of the Russian people and thus remain popular despite an economy ravaged by low energy prices, corruption and sanctions. Yet even as Russia threatens international peace and Western interests, its weak economy has caused it to fall far behind NATO militarily. Russia's defence spending is about one-tenth of NATO's;[1] and with energy prices unlikely to rise, this disparity will persist. Moreover, Russia cannot compete with the West in digital technology, which is now the main multiplier of military strength. Knowing this, the Russians have chosen an asymmetric strategy, involving hybrid warfare, deniable intervention, cyber war and nuclear intimidation. They have preyed on neighbouring states by infiltrating paramilitary forces, using agents and proxies, holding menacing military exercises and attacking computer networks; and they have hijacked social media to undermine Western confidence and cohesion. The West has struggled to answer this Russian strategy.

Within its asymmetric strategy, Russia also maintains a preponderance of regional (non-strategic) nuclear weapons, which it is likely to increase through deployments of intermediate-range nuclear forces (INF), legalised

Hans Binnendijk is a Distinguished Fellow at the Atlantic Council. He previously served as US National Security Council Senior Director for Defense Policy, Director of the US Institute for National Strategic Studies and Editor of *Survival*. **David Gompert** is a Distinguished Visiting Professor at the US Naval Academy. He has been Acting Director of National Intelligence, Special Assistant to the US president, Deputy Undersecretary of State and Vice President of the RAND Corporation.

Survival | vol. 61 no. 5 | October–November 2019 | pp. 113–128   DOI 10.1080/00396338.2019.1662119

by US withdrawal from the INF Treaty. Nuclear weapons have always been a 'cheap' option to make up for deficiencies in conventional forces, and Russia has made them a top priority. Russian spending on nuclear weapons increased by 66% between 2010 and 2016, from $5.6 billion in 2010 to $9.3bn in 2016.[2]

The combination of Russian hybrid warfare and increased reliance on nuclear weapons is dangerous for Western interests and international security. Unlike the Cold War threat of a large-scale, mechanised Soviet offensive, lower-grade Russian aggression could confound NATO decision-making, which is already complicated by the task of finding consensus among 29 members with diverse perspectives and concerns. In contrast, Russian decisions are made by one man. Would all the allies agree that reports of slowly increasing numbers of civilian-clothed Russian paramilitary personnel in Russian-speaking districts of a member state meet the standard for invoking the Article V common-defence provision of the North Atlantic Treaty? What if social-media sources (with Russian fingerprints) were reporting that ethnic Russians in those districts were being oppressed by local security? What if Moscow declared a humanitarian crisis, speciously appealed to the UN for peacekeepers and, in the meantime, 'temporarily' augmented paramilitaries with significant numbers of regular troops, giving Russia local military advantage? Would NATO do anything more than condemn, deplore and warn?

If NATO military commanders were to advise their political superiors that the forcible removal of Russian forces from a member's territory might dictate striking critical military targets in Russia, this would raise the spectre of Russian escalation up to and including use of non-strategic nuclear weapons, in which Russia has a growing advantage. In this way, Russia could be tempted to use the threat of nuclear war as a means of extending its control over Russian-speaking regions. Though such a gambit would be risky for Russia, Moscow would have reasonable grounds to doubt NATO's unity and decisiveness. NATO must seek to erase any such doubt. For that it needs a more credible nuclear-deterrence doctrine.

The role of nuclear weapons

Russia has intimated it would use nuclear weapons first if attacked by NATO conventional forces. The spectre of NATO aggression against Russia has been concocted by Putin to seal his compact with the Russian people, whereby they accept autocracy in return for a strong and secure country. Why, if Putin invented this threat, should NATO worry about Russia responding with nuclear weapons to aggression that NATO has no intention of committing?

Were Russia to use force against a NATO member – say, one of the Baltic states – it would likely rely on air bases, weapons, sensors, command and control and back-up forces stationed *in Russia*. While it might not need to rely on these capabilities at first, it *would* need them if and when NATO began to reinforce its forward forces. Therefore, in order to fulfil its obligation to defend every member, NATO might need to strike military targets within Russia. Conversely, if the Russians believed they could operate from sanctuaries such as Kaliningrad, the Kola Peninsula or Crimea, they might be more inclined to take risks in waging hybrid or even conventional warfare against NATO. With Russia having asserted that it might use nuclear weapons if attacked, NATO must dissuade the Russians from believing that they can deter NATO from striking operationally critical military targets wherever they are located.

While it is clear that Russian doctrine entails first use of nuclear weapons if attacked by NATO, it has sent mixed signals about how severe the threat would have to be to warrant such a response. Currently, Russia's declaratory policy is that it would use nuclear weapons first if the very existence of the state depended on it.[3] At other times, it has more boldly suggested that conventional aggression against Russia on a scale critical to national security could trigger nuclear escalation. The Kremlin has adopted the euphemism 'escalate in order to de-escalate' to articulate its threat to use nuclear weapons, which could include first use even if the survival of the Russian state were not at stake. Rather than trying to read the tea leaves of Russians' changing first-use policy, NATO should take as given that striking targets on Russian territory could heighten the danger of nuclear war. It follows that deterring Russian nuclear first use is paramount for NATO's ability to deter Russian conventional aggression.

Yet NATO's nuclear-deterrent policy remains vague and puzzling. The current official formulation, first set out in the 2010 Strategic Concept adopted before the new Russian threat emerged, is that NATO needs an 'appropriate mix of nuclear and conventional weapons' to deter aggression. This policy contemplates nuclear use only in 'extremely remote' circumstances.[4] In 2012, the NATO Deterrence and Defence Posture Review reiterated this basic policy, adding a reference to negative-security assurances for adherents of the Non-Proliferation Treaty and noting the complementary role of missile defences as part of the 'appropriate mix'.[5] More recently, at its 2016 Warsaw Summit, NATO warned that Russian use of nuclear weapons would 'fundamentally alter the nature of a conflict', and stated that NATO has the 'capabilities and resolve' to impose unacceptable costs in response to threats to the 'fundamental security' of a member nation.[6] This formulation implies that NATO is hesitant to say it would retaliate with nuclear weapons and, indeed, could be indecisive about nuclear retaliation in the event – a stance that is hardly conducive to deterrence. It is high time that NATO fix this problem.

As a rule, deterrence policy should be communicated pointedly enough to alter an enemy's calculus, especially when it comes to nuclear war. Given Russia's general belligerence, its first-use threat and its nuclear-weapons modernisation programme, for NATO to say only that it needs nuclear weapons to deter aggression in 'extremely remote' circumstances is worse than inadequate: it's risky. Lack of clarity on using nuclear weapons may preserve maximum flexibility for NATO's political leaders, but it may also imply a lack of will or consensus.

NATO's nuclear strategy is the critical missing piece in its otherwise strong, step-by-step response to the danger of Russian aggression. Specifically, NATO has strengthened its resilience against hybrid threats by creating assistance teams to support states under this sort of pressure. It has ramped up cyber defence, said that a cyber strike could trigger an Article V response, created a cyber-operations centre and warned of cyber retaliation. Battalion-sized NATO 'battlegroups' are deployed on the territory of particularly exposed allies to oppose Russian paramilitary aggression and prompt a robust response should Russia send in combat forces. A highly ready joint task force has been created, and the NATO Response Force has been strengthened. Moreover, the Alliance is improving its readiness, mobility and command and control so that it can reinforce its positions, gain an advantage and defeat Russian forces if required.[7] More needs to be done in the realm of conventional defence, but NATO's deterrent posture has significantly improved during the past five years.

Though necessary, all these measures could prove insufficient if NATO is deterred by Russia's nuclear-first-use threats from striking critical Russia-based military assets with conventional forces where needed to avoid a NATO defeat. For its overall defence strategy to successfully deter Russian aggression with the potential to escalate, NATO needs a new nuclear strategy. This raises some prickly questions for the Alliance: how should it explain why it needs nuclear weapons? What doctrine should govern why, when and how these weapons could be used? How should NATO's nuclear weapons fit into its overall defence strategy? What capabilities are needed, including theatre and strategic deterrent forces, and who should possess them? How should NATO's nuclear strategy tie into global strategic stability? What, if any, arms limitations would complement NATO's nuclear strategy? This article lays out our answers.

From flexible response to decisive response

By the 1960s, NATO faced two growing threats: the Soviets' capability to mount a vast, mechanised military offensive against NATO; and their acquisition of a large, intercontinental, strategic nuclear arsenal. These threats increased the difficulty of both 'forward defence' along what was then the inter-German border and of depending on strategic nuclear 'massive retaliation' by the United States, which was NATO's response to the threat of Soviet aggression in the 1950s. Just as the Soviet conventional threat grew, the advent of Soviet intercontinental missiles undercut the US threat to resort directly to wholesale strategic nuclear warfare.

In light of this dangerous predicament, the US proposed – and, in 1967, NATO approved – a strategy of 'flexible response'. In essence, NATO warned that it would use in-theatre nuclear weapons first if conventional defence failed, and then escalate as necessary until the Soviets ended their aggression. Although this strategy would expose both the European allies and, ultimately, the United States to Soviet nuclear retaliation, that gamble was deemed worth taking for the sake of deterrence. The bet was that the Soviets would cease attacking if NATO showed a resolve to initiate nuclear war, especially if Warsaw Pact tank armies were obliterated by nuclear weapons. If the threat of flexible response was not credible enough to deter the Soviets, NATO's actual initial use of nuclear weapons would be. To create a believable option and a link between its conventional forces and strategic nuclear forces, NATO built up its battlefield nuclear forces.

Toward the end of the 1970s, West Germany and other European allies became concerned that strategic nuclear parity, as codified in US–Soviet arms-control agreements, cast doubt on whether the US threat to escalate to the use of intercontinental weapons if all else failed remained credible enough to assure deterrence. This concern was inflamed by the Soviet deployment of INF – notably, SS-20 missiles – that could strike Europe but not the United States. There were no comparable NATO systems deployed in Europe that could reach Moscow. Under the circumstances, Europeans feared 'decoupling' from America's nuclear umbrella. In order to repair this credibility gap, NATO decided to deploy its own INF missiles capable of reaching Moscow. As the Cold War wound down, the US and the Soviet Union reached an agreement banning INF missiles. The United States declared that NATO's nuclear weapons would be used only as a 'last resort'. Still, NATO did not rescind flexible response, and it has yet to clarify why it needs nuclear weapons beyond vague statements about deterrence.

NATO did not rescind flexible response

Just as NATO's nuclear doctrine needed revision in 1967 and 1979, so it needs revision now, starting with a basic question: why does NATO still need nuclear weapons? We propose that the reason is, purely and simply, to deter Russia from using nuclear weapons first. To achieve this goal, NATO should unambiguously warn of proportional nuclear retaliation for Russian first use. Provided it is clear about its response if Russia resorted to nuclear weapons, NATO need not state categorically that it would refrain from using nuclear weapons for any other reason, thus finessing the contentious no-first-use issue. A statement by NATO that it needs nuclear weapons to deter Russian first use would be clear, understandable and politically defensible. Strategically, it would disabuse the Russians of any belief that their first-use threat could make Russia itself a sanctuary from which to stage and support aggression against a NATO state.

This nuclear strategy, which would be complete and coherent, could be termed 'decisive response' in that it conveys resolve and dispels any doubts the Russians might harbour about NATO's willingness to use nuclear weapons in retaliation. Though NATO's current policy does not exclude this possibility, present conditions make it necessary to eliminate any lingering ambiguity.

A declaration by NATO explaining its need for nuclear weapons would not constitute a no-first-use pledge: it would specify what NATO would do, not what it wouldn't do.[8] Several allies, including the United States, resist a no-first-use policy to deter biological or cyber attacks – reasons having nothing to do with a Russian conventional threat.[9] But NATO need not make a no-first-use pledge in order to make plain that its nuclear weapons exist to deter Russia from using such weapons first.

The doctrinal implications of this strategy would need to be understood and addressed in advance. Waiting until conflict breaks out before confronting the meaning of 'fundamentally altering the nature' of a war is a recipe for confusion and contention at the worst possible moment. Final decisions regarding the use of nuclear weapons will of course depend on the crisis at hand and remain fundamentally political. But there should be no delay in stating the principles and implications of the strategy.

Thus, options regarding weapons and targets in the event deterrence fails must be anticipated. Strategic-deterrence theory distinguishes between 'counter-value' and 'counterforce' options, the latter comprising enemy nuclear-retaliatory capabilities and the former being essentially anything else, including other war-making capacities, industrial centres and, by implication (though never uttered), population centres. In the Cold War, NATO's battlefield nuclear weapons were targeted on massed Warsaw Pact armoured forces, a target that is no longer relevant. Under decisive response, the targets hit by NATO in a proportional response would depend greatly on the character of Russia's initial nuclear strike. If Russia chose to attack

NATO conventional forces, it would face a response that would severely damage its remaining conventional capability and guarantee its defeat.

Decisive response and NATO's overall defence strategy

NATO is making serious efforts to prevent Russia from threatening even the most exposed ally. Forces are being deployed to forward areas; readiness is being improved; and the ability to surge over-matching forces to end Russian aggressions is being enhanced.[10] Russia must know that the inevitable outcome of conventional conflict would be defeat once NATO reinforcements were brought to bear. But again, such reinforcements could be inadequate or terribly costly if NATO were inhibited from striking targets on Russian soil.

Say Russia attempted to seize eastern Estonia, with its Russian-speaking majority. Without delay, NATO would attempt to gain air control – the ability to deny enemy use of the air and to strike enemy forces on the ground at will. Russia has world-class extended-range integrated air-defence systems (IADS) with which to challenge NATO air control. Critical components of IADS are based on Russian territory. If NATO failed to suppress Russian air defence out of a fear of provoking nuclear war, its forward battlegroups could be destroyed, captured or made to retreat, and reinforcements would incur heavy losses.

It is possible that Russia would commit such low-grade aggression against a NATO member that forward-deployed local and NATO forces could handle the situation. Yet even low-grade aggression is still aggression, and NATO would still need to use sufficient force to eliminate a Russian military presence from NATO territory – possibly forcing Russia to rely on capabilities based on its own territory. In any case, imagining that there could be circumstances in which NATO would not need to strike Russian territory is hardly an argument against a nuclear strategy aimed directly at deterring Russian first use. Bluntly put, Russia must understand that NATO will not hesitate to strike targets in Russia if that is what is needed to defeat aggression. Russian hybrid warfare argues for, not against, decisive response.

NATO's overall defence strategy under decisive response would be to deploy light forces; reinforce them rapidly with enough power to defeat

Russian forces; strike critical military capabilities on Russian territory if necessary to ensure NATO forces prevail; and use the threat of nuclear retaliation to deter Russian use of nuclear weapons in response to such strikes. Decisive response would give the Russians pause before contemplating *any* aggression, including the hybrid sort, against a NATO ally in the belief that their own territory is off-limits.

Decisive response and strategic nuclear deterrence

Even the most erudite deterrence theorists had trouble reconciling flexible response with mutual assured destruction (MAD). Would the United States escalate to the use of intercontinental nuclear weapons, as flexible response could call for, knowing that assured destruction would result? The gamble, or bluff, was that the Soviets would stop hostilities against NATO rather than test US willingness to use strategic weapons. Yet MAD diminished the credibility of flexible response because the latter put the onus on the United States to decide whether to escalate to all-out nuclear war and thus risk its own destruction.

MAD, which remains the keystone of US–Russian strategic nuclear stability, is easier to square with decisive response than it was with flexible response. The onus of starting a nuclear war, of escalating and of deciding whether to risk assured destruction would fall squarely on the Russians. NATO and the United States would be using nuclear weapons only to retaliate proportionately and in kind. Strategic theory suggests that in such a spiralling conflict, the side with the highest local stakes and advantage has the upper hand – and that would be NATO.[11]

The US–Russian strategic nuclear relationship is bound to influence the efficacy of decisive response. Although MAD remains in effect, the relationship is more complicated than that formulation would suggest. Given the United States' survivable, unmatched strategic offensive forces and the paucity of Russian capabilities to counter them, the US has no cause to worry about its second-strike capability. In contrast, the Russians worry a great deal – much more than they should – about the viability and credibility of their retaliatory force. The United States is superior to Russia in ballistic-missile defence (BMD), global intelligence, surveillance and reconnaissance

(ISR), conventional prompt global strike (CPGS) and anti-satellite (ASAT) capabilities, all of which could be used to degrade Russia's retaliatory capability. The Russians worry not only about a US strategic nuclear first strike, but also about a non-nuclear one.[12] The Russians' apprehension about their strategic deterrent is apparent in their strategic-force investment and modernisation programmes, such as their transoceanic nuclear torpedo and hypersonic glide missiles, which are inherently second-strike systems.[13]

This is not the place to consider whether the United States should try to alleviate the Russians' worries about their strategic deterrent, given the risk of Russian launch-on-warning, or instead to let them squander scarce state resources to protect a deterrent which the US does not really mean to challenge. The United States remains wedded to the need for strategic nuclear stability and thus mutual deterrence. For the purposes of NATO strategy, however, if Russia has doubts about the effectiveness of its strategic deterrent, it should be that much more reluctant to initiate nuclear war in the first place. In this respect, Russian concerns about US strategic superiority reinforce decisive response.

Capabilities

Numerical equality and matching weapon types are less important than the absolute capability of NATO to retaliate on a scale that would exceed any possible Russian gain in attacking a NATO member. Conceptually, it is important for NATO to have the capability to respond at both the regional level and the intercontinental level.

NATO has stated that 'the strategic forces of the Alliance, particularly those of the United States, are the supreme guarantee of the security of the Allies'.[14] And indeed, these forces could be called on at some point as part of decisive response in the event Russia starts a nuclear war. However, because a strategic nuclear attack on Russia could lead to Russian strategic *and* regional nuclear strikes, region-level weapons might be NATO's better initial option, while it holds strategic weapons in reserve to deter Russian escalation.

Whereas flexible response required nuclear-weapons capabilities on every rung of the escalatory ladder, decisive response would not. It is only important that NATO have capabilities in theatre to respond in kind to what might be a very limited Russian first strike. The key to decisive response lies not in outsized arsenals of theatre nuclear-delivery systems, but in unhesitating decision-making and action. The few hundred B-61 gravity bombs available in Europe[15] to be delivered by allied dual-capable aircraft provide an adequate deterrent capability provided they are linked with decisive decision-making. Of course, this force must be kept modern, safe and ready to use on short notice.

In addition, if Russia deploys large numbers of ground-based INF systems, the United States can respond with nuclear air- and sea-launched cruise missiles, which are as capable as ground-launched cruise missiles and can strike targets well inside Russia with extraordinary precision. There is no need for another divisive debate over NATO land-based INF deployments like the one the Alliance experienced 40 years ago. Back then, NATO relied on the threat to use nuclear weapons first and to escalate as necessary in order to deter Soviet aggression. Now, consistent with decisive response, NATO would use nuclear weapons in retaliation for Russian first use. Because the threat to use nuclear weapons second is inherently more credible than the threat to use them first, NATO need not match Russian nuclear capabilities of every sort and on every rung, including land-based INF. Likewise, NATO battlefield nuclear weapons are unimportant because there is no threat of a Russian conventional attack too massive to defeat with conventional defence.

It is important to consider the role of missile defence in decisive response. The United States has gone the extra mile to try to assuage Russian fears that BMD has been intended all along to deny Russia's retaliatory capability and thus support a first-strike strategic posture. NATO's BMD deployment is meant to counter Iranian missiles and is not capable of intercepting a Russian missile attack on the United States, which in any case would be too large to destroy. At the same time, Russia's generally belligerent behaviour, reliance on nuclear first use and emphasis on theatre nuclear weapons raise the question of whether NATO should consider deploying missile defence against Russia to complement decisive response. Under certain circumstances, we believe it should.

It is not yet necessary to shift from NATO's current policy of deploying missile defences only against threats from the Middle East. However, if the demise of the INF Treaty encourages Russia to increase its INF capabilities directed against NATO, the Alliance could respond by developing and deploying defences specifically for this threat, with Iran becoming a 'lesser but included case'. Russia might invest in some mixture of ballistic, cruise and, once developed, hypersonic weapons. As technology advances, US regional missile defence, made available to NATO, could be effective against all three types of missiles, though ballistic ones still represent the biggest challenge because of their extraordinary speed. Such a NATO system would not negate Russia's strategic deterrent, though the Russians would insist otherwise.

Of course, Russia could respond to the development of NATO missile defences by increasing its arsenal of INF missiles, which could overwhelm these defences. Based on available technology, nuclear warfare remains 'offence dominant': it is cheaper to add missiles (or decoys) than to expand defence, and a sizeable fraction of a large missile attack would surely avoid interception. Nevertheless, by reducing the expected damage from a Russian nuclear attack, enhanced NATO missile defence could complement deterrence based on decisive response. While enhanced NATO missile defence might lead Russia to expand its nuclear forces, this could severely tax Russia's limited resources, or divert them from more useable non-nuclear offensive capabilities. At the same time, increased Russian INF – whether stimulated by NATO or not – would not undermine the credibility of decisive response, especially since Russia lacks missile-defence technology.

Lastly, NATO must decide on the role of its conventional deep-strike systems. It may be tempting to view these as an alternative to nuclear weapons – indeed, that is precisely what worries the Russians. Decisive response would require making clear that the Russians can count on nuclear retaliation by NATO if they use nuclear weapons first. The possibility of a conventional response to a Russian first nuclear strike would harm deterrence. While the United States presumably will continue to invest in and improve its conventional deep-strike capabilities for various global needs, the logic, credibility and utility of decisive response require that these are not intended for retaliation against a Russian first use of nuclear weapons.

Arms limitations and restraint

Given NATO's conventional military superiority and its concern about Russia's first-use policy, a no-first-use agreement with Russia would have merit. However, it would be difficult to achieve a consensus in NATO to propose this – starting with US and French objections. Moreover, the Russians could be counted on not to agree. A no-first-use offer would make clear to the world, including to European publics, that Russia and not NATO would be the side to start a nuclear war.

Negotiation of a post-INF Treaty agreement to limit theatre nuclear weapons up to and including INF would also make sense, though China's growing INF capabilities could not be ignored. Conceivably, NATO investment in a more robust missile-defence system would increase Russian interest in a new agreement to limit *both* offensive and defensive capabilities in Europe. In any case, the United States should not negotiate away its air- and sea-launched cruise-missile capabilities, which have vital worldwide missions, including non-nuclear ones. In sum, both a no-first-use agreement and a new INF agreement are long shots, but may be worth trying for. Decisive response could strengthen NATO's negotiating position in both, but should not be contingent on either one.

Negotiations to extend or replace the New Strategic Arms Reduction Treaty would follow their own logic. Extending it, for now, would help to maintain strategic stability, which would in turn reinforce decisive response. A replacement agreement might require the participation of China, US willingness to scrap or halt BMD, or both. Neither is likely to happen. In any case, decisive response should not – and its effectiveness would not – depend on a new US–Russian strategic deal.

One understanding that would be useful, with or without decisive response, would be to place nuclear command, control and communications off-limits for cyber war.[16] If NATO opts, for respectable political reasons, to accompany a new nuclear posture with an arms-control initiative, this would be a good candidate.

*　　　*　　　*

Lurking in the shadows of this argument is the question of whether America's European allies would endorse decisive response. Politics and diplomacy – which aim to avoid offending allied publics and Russian sensibilities – may favour continued ambiguity, which we believe is risky. Instead, we recommend expounding the need for clarity in a way that shines the spotlight on Russia's nuclear threat. (Ironically, the very fact that NATO's current nuclear strategy is uncontroversial underscores its inefficacy.) Even in the darkest days of the Cold War, NATO had its eye on public sentiment in espousing a commitment to both defence and detente. When it came time to counter the Soviet build-up of INF, NATO adopted a dual-track approach, calling for an INF ban even as it deployed missiles of its own.

Allies could insist on some sort of olive branch to accompany a clearer nuclear strategy. Alternatively, they may have seen enough of Putin's unruliness to justify decisive response on its own merits. Moreover, the doctrine is designed to deter both nuclear war and nuclear escalation. After all, it is Russia that has exhibited a proclivity to menace its neighbours, to call out NATO as an aggressor and to warn that it would use nuclear weapons first. The fact that the nuclear strategy proposed here is strictly retaliatory, is meant to prevent nuclear war and is needed to fulfil NATO's defence obligations could provide allies with sufficient political cover to accept it.

No harm would come from talking to the Russians about the role of nuclear weapons in European security – but only *after* decisive response is approved. NATO's position would be that nuclear weapons should be kept at a low level and used for retaliation. Where such a conversation would lead is hard to predict. At some point, Russia, strapped for resources, may seek accommodation. In that event, decisive response would help NATO drive a hard bargain.

Before closing, we cannot ignore the current turmoil in transatlantic relations, as well as questions that have been raised about US trustworthiness and commitment to NATO. This may or may not pass, depending on American and European politics and allies' reactions to one another. In one scenario, the European allies would pursue increasing autonomy – presumably EU-centric – from the United States in foreign and security policy, both in and beyond Europe. In turn, the United

States could become less active in European security affairs, perhaps even welcoming greater allied accountability. Where would such developments leave a NATO nuclear strategy of decisive response, given its crucial reliance on US nuclear capabilities and doctrine?

The answer depends on the viability of NATO under conditions of increasing political separation between the United States and Europe. Yet it is hard to foresee the death of NATO in the years to come even with this separation. While the Alliance's function as a venue for transatlantic consultation and collaboration on security matters in Europe and elsewhere could unfortunately decay, the North Atlantic Treaty itself, and its common-defence provision, will probably survive. Unless and until the Russian threat of aggression – hybrid or otherwise – recedes, Europeans and Americans will probably stick together to deter and defeat it. As long as any allies are exposed to this threat, NATO will need the ability to defend them. And as long as Russia relies on the threat to use nuclear weapons first to make itself a sanctuary in the event of war, NATO will have a need to make clear that it would unleash nuclear retaliation against any such Russian action. Decisive response, along with doctrine, capabilities and procedures to carry it out, would meet that continuing need.

Notes

[1] The Stockholm International Peace Research Institute (SIPRI) reports that Russia spent $61.4bn on defence in 2018. See Nan Tian et al., 'Trends in World Military Expenditure, 2018', SIPRI Fact Sheet, April 2019, https://www.sipri.org/sites/default/files/2019-04/fs_1904_milex_2018.pdf. Others place the number higher, especially when calculated using purchasing-power parity. See, for example, Michael Kofman, who gives a figure of $150–180bn in 'Russian Defense Spending Is Much Larger, and More Sustainable than It Seems', *Defense News*, 3 May 2019, https://www.defensenews.com/opinion/commentary/2019/05/03/russian-defense-spending-is-much-larger-and-more-sustainable-than-it-seems/. NATO defence spending is about $1 trillion per year and, unlike Russian defence spending, is growing. See NATO, 'Defence Expenditure of NATO Countries (2012–2019)', 25 June 2019, https://www.nato.int/nato_static_fl2014/assets/pdf/pdf_2019_06/20190625_PR2019-069-EN.pdf.

[2] Julian Cooper, 'How Much Does Russia Spend on Nuclear Weapons?', SIPRI, October 2018,

https://www.sipri.org/commentary/
topical-backgrounder/2018/how-much-
does-russia-spend-nuclear-weapons.

3 Embassy of the Russian Federation
in the United Kingdom, 'Military
Doctrine of the Russian Federation',
25 December 2014, section III, para.
27, distributed as a press release dated
29 June 2015, http://rusemb.org.uk/
press/2029.

4 NATO, 'Active Engagement, Modern
Defense', 19–20 November 2010, para.
17.

5 See NATO's 'Deterrence and Defence
Posture Review', 20 May 2012.

6 NATO, 'Warsaw Summit
Communiqué', 9 July 2016, para. 54,
https://www.nato.int/cps/en/natohq/
official_texts_133169.htm.

7 More needs to be done in regard to
conventional defence, especially long-
range strike.

8 In this sense, decisive response would
differ somewhat from the suggestion
made by US vice president Joseph
Biden in January 2017 that deterring
a nuclear strike (and if necessary
retaliating against it) should be the
'sole purpose' of nuclear weapons.
See 'Remarks by the Vice President on
Nuclear Security', Washington DC, 12
January 2017.

9 France sees no-first-use as incompatible with its rationale of having nuclear
weapons to ensure its survival.

10 See Franklin D. Kramer and Hans
Binnendijk, 'Meeting the Russian
Conventional Challenge: Effective
Deterrence by Prompt Reinforcement',
Atlantic Council, February 2018.

11 This is one of the key lessons of the
Cuban Missile Crisis. See, for example,
Graham Allison, *Essence of Decision:
Explaining the Cuban Missile Crisis*, 2nd
ed. (New York: Pearson, 1999).

12 See James M. Acton, 'Russia and
Strategic Conventional Weapons:
Concerns and Responses',
Nonproliferation Review, vol. 22,
no. 2, 2015, pp. 141–54, https://
carnegieendowment.org/2016/02/03/
russia-and-strategic-conventional-
weapons-pub-62676.

13 These Russian programmes are
designed to foil US BMD in a retaliatory attack, but they have no
first-strike utility.

14 See NATO, 'Warsaw Summit
Communiqué', para. 53.

15 For a recent estimate of the number
of B-61s in Europe, see NTI, 'Nuclear
Disarmament NATO', 28 June 2019,
https://www.nti.org/analysis/articles/
nato-nuclear-disarmament/.

16 See David C. Gompert and Martin
Libicki, 'Cyber War and Nuclear
Peace', *Survival*, vol. 61, no. 4, August–
September 2019, pp. 45–62.

Hypersonic Weapons and Strategic Stability

Dean Wilkening

Hypersonic weapons – in particular, hypersonic boost-glide vehicles and hypersonic cruise missiles – are rapidly becoming a reality. China, Russia, the United States and several other countries are pursuing these weapons. Some may carry nuclear warheads. China, in particular, has sprinted ahead in the competition to exploit the near-space domain (20 to 60 kilometres in altitude) with a large number of recent flight tests and infrastructure improvements to become a world leader in some facets of hypersonic technology.[1] The principal rationale for developing similar weapons in the United States is to hold Russian and Chinese mobile targets at risk and to improve the ability to penetrate advanced integrated air-defence systems. These weapons, especially when conventionally armed, could have a profound effect on strategic stability. So far, suggested approaches to avoiding their destabilising effects do not appear promising.

Hypersonic weapons

Hypersonic weapons travel faster than Mach 5, at a speed of approximately one mile (1.6 km) per second. They come in three classes: ballistic missiles, boost-glide vehicles and cruise missiles. Hypersonic gun-launched weapons also are being developed, but they are less relevant to strategic stability due to their relatively short range. Ballistic missiles with ranges greater than approximately 300 km re-enter the atmosphere at speeds above

Dean Wilkening is a physicist at the Johns Hopkins University Applied Physics Laboratory.

Survival | vol. 61 no. 5 | October–November 2019 | pp. 129–148   DOI 10.1080/00396338.2019.1662125

Mach 5. Ballistic missiles have been around for decades. The two new types of non-ballistic hypersonic weapons — hypersonic boost-glide vehicles and hypersonic cruise missiles — are on the threshold of becoming viable weapons systems because new technology is overcoming the challenges associated with surviving the intense aerothermal environment of extended high-speed flight in the upper atmosphere.[2]

Hypersonic boost-glide vehicles are launched by rockets in much the same way as ballistic missiles; however, instead of sending their payload into outer space on a ballistic trajectory, they boost the glide vehicle into a flatter trajectory that allows the vehicle to re-enter the upper atmosphere, whereupon it uses aerodynamic lift to glide as it slowly descends in altitude. To extend their range, boost-glide vehicles may adopt a porpoising motion in the upper atmosphere.

Hypersonic cruise missiles, on the other hand, are powered by supersonic combustion ramjet – scramjet – engines. Scramjets, as opposed to traditional ramjet engines, are required to achieve speeds above approximately Mach 5. A hypersonic cruise missile is boosted to high speeds by a rocket motor. Then the scramjet engine ignites, and the missile follows a high-altitude cruise trajectory at a more or less constant speed and altitude. While ballistic missiles spend a relatively short period inside the atmosphere – only during their boost and re-entry phases – hypersonic boost-glide vehicles and cruise

Figure 1: **Hypersonic ballistic, boost-glide and cruise-missile flight paths**

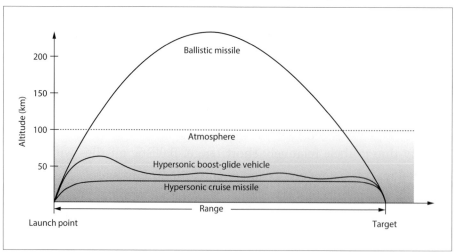

missiles spend the bulk of their flight paths within the upper atmosphere, typically at altitudes of between 20 and 60 km. Figure 1 illustrates notional flight paths for these different hypersonic vehicles.

The range of a hypersonic boost-glide vehicle depends on the speed with which it re-enters the atmosphere and the lift-to-drag ratio of the vehicle. The range of hypersonic cruise missiles depends on the ratio of the initial mass divided by the final mass after fuel exhaustion, scramjet fuel efficiency (that is, specific impulse) and the vehicle lift-to-drag ratio.[3]

Perhaps the most significant difference between hypersonic ballistic missiles and hypersonic boost-glide vehicles and cruise missiles is the latter's superior manoeuvrability. Ballistic missiles follow a relatively predictable flight path, which allows for accurate attack warning and attack assessment. Attack warning arises from detecting the large infrared signature from the rocket motors during lift-off. Attack assessment derives from tracking incoming ballistic missiles in mid-course with radar so as to predict, with reasonable accuracy, where the warheads will land and hence which targets are under attack. This information provides useful clues about the intent of the attack.

Attack warning for non-ballistic hypersonic weapons is possible because they too are launched with fairly large rocket motors. However, radar will detect these vehicles relatively late in their mid-course flight (that is, their glide phase) because they fly at low altitudes compared to ballistic missiles. Infrared sensors on satellites or high-altitude aircraft can, in principle, track non-ballistic hypersonic vehicles in mid-course from greater ranges due to their bright infrared signature (they become very hot as they fly through the upper atmosphere). Attack assessment, however, is more difficult because hypersonic boost-glide vehicles and cruise missiles can manoeuvre hundreds of kilometres in cross range during their glide phase. Therefore, even if these vehicles can be tracked, what targets are under attack will remain uncertain until late in the vehicles' trajectory. This inability to arrive at accurate attack assessments for non-ballistic hypersonic vehicles – a major difference between ballistic and non-ballistic hypersonic weapons – makes it much more difficult to determine the intent of an attack from hypersonic boost-glide vehicles and hypersonic cruise missiles.

Strategic stability

Strategic stability has been an organising concept in US nuclear-weapons policy for decades. It has been enshrined in nuclear-arms-control treaties, and Washington has used it to justify US nuclear-weapons programmes. Whether or not it should be an objective for US nuclear policy is not so much a strategic choice as an indelible feature of the nuclear balance between major nuclear powers. Much as one might desire nuclear superiority, major powers always have the option to deny it to their opponent. The term 'strategic instability' means different things to different audiences. Frequently, it refers to any action that increases the likelihood of war – an intuitively reasonable definition, but one that admits too many interpretations to be useful.[4] During the Cold War, the concept of strategic stability had two precise meanings: crisis stability and arms-race stability.[5]

Crisis stability refers to a situation between nuclear powers in which both sides believe their strategic nuclear forces are largely invulnerable, and that they can penetrate any defences the adversary might construct in sufficient numbers to deter attacks. In other words, both sides believe they can deter their opponent from attacking first in a crisis by assuring devastating retaliation.[6] The opposite, crisis instability, refers to what Thomas C. Schelling called the 'reciprocal fear of surprise attack'.[7] Two types of weapons systems were implicated in crisis instability during the Cold War: counterforce weapons that could destroy a large portion of an opponent's strategic nuclear forces or its strategic nuclear command, control and communication system in a surprise attack; and nationwide air and ballistic-missile defences (often called strategic defences or homeland defences, as opposed to theatre defences intended to protect military assets on the battlefield). Ballistic missiles with short flight times and accurate multiple independently targetable re-entry vehicles (MIRVs) are an example of the first kind of destabilising weapon. The second kind, nationwide defences, were thought to be destabilising if robust enough to intercept a large fraction of the opponent's retaliatory strikes after its retaliatory capability had been degraded by a pre-emptive counterforce attack. Thus, the Anti-Ballistic Missile Treaty did not ban nationwide ballistic-missile defences altogether but rather limited their size and technical characteristics so they could not effectively blunt a retaliatory strike.[8]

Pre-emptive counterforce options and strategic defences fall under the rubric of damage-limiting capabilities that allow a nuclear power to limit the damage an opponent's strategic nuclear forces can inflict in retaliation. Note that counterforce in this context contemplates pre-emptive attacks against an opponent's strategic (typically intercontinental-range), as opposed to non-strategic (typically theatre-range), nuclear forces because the former could strike the American and Russian homelands. Non-strategic nuclear weapons usually are associated with use on the battlefield or in a theatre campaign, and consequently are not tied directly to the survival of the homeland, although some US non-strategic nuclear weapons could reach Soviet territory during the Cold War – a point of considerable concern to Soviet leaders at the time.

If a state can limit damage through a combination of pre-emptive counterforce and defence to such a degree that striking first is no longer unthinkable, this would be destabilising. Thus, strategic instability involves a quantitative as well as a qualitative assessment. For example, if a state can reduce the damage from a retaliatory strike against its homeland by 30% through a combination of counterforce and defence, that state presumably would have little incentive to strike first in a crisis because the damage caused by the remaining 70% in a nuclear war would still be devastating. But a reduction in damage by 95% might provide such an incentive. During the Cold War, US and Russian planners worried about the vulnerability of their strategic nuclear forces under a range of different scenarios. 'Bolt out of the blue' attacks – a major US preoccupation – would occur with little strategic warning when nuclear forces were not on high alert and were relatively more vulnerable. At the other extreme, nuclear forces on high alert (for example, during a major conventional war) would be much less vulnerable. Accordingly, debates about crisis instability often turned on the credibility of different scenarios for nuclear war.

Most importantly, crisis instability depends on reciprocal fear. Only when both sides can significantly limit damage by striking first is there a strong incentive to pre-empt out of fear that, if one waits, the opponent may attack first and gain a tremendous advantage. One-sided damage-limiting options are not crisis destabilising to the same degree because there is no corresponding fear that the less capable side will attack first. It is sometimes argued that the vulnerable side might attack first because it faces a 'use them or lose them' situation; however, this would be suicidal because launching an attack under these circumstances would be met with the full force of the opponent's survivable nuclear force. Threatening to launch one's vulnerable forces on warning that a massive counterforce attack was under way might give the attacking country pause, thus contributing to deterrence, but if implemented it would lead to tragic nuclear escalation if the warning were in error. Accordingly, this tactic largely has been, and should be, avoided.

Actions that make nuclear escalation difficult to control constitute another central aspect of crisis instability. During the Cold War, the United States and the Soviet Union considered crossing the nuclear threshold first to deter various acts of aggression, especially in the context of losing a conventional battle. Strategists worried about how to control escalation once the nuclear threshold was crossed because in most scenarios the stakes involved were not commensurate with the destruction wreaked by an all-out nuclear war.[9] 'Off ramps' were sought for an escalating nuclear conflict, but few plausible ones that provided much comfort arose. By the end of the Cold War, few strategists were confident that escalation could be controlled in a rational manner, and threats to cross the nuclear threshold first were considered those that left something to chance. Controlling escalation clearly is more difficult than ensuring the survival of one's strategic nuclear forces because the former involves human behaviour *in extremis*, while the latter is more akin to a problem in engineering.

If the strategic nuclear forces of only one side are vulnerable, that side can be coerced at will by its opponent. Consequently, the vulnerable side has a strong incentive to modernise its strategic nuclear forces to reduce their vulnerability to pre-emptive attack and to improve their ability to penetrate strategic defences. This gives rise to the second common understanding of strategic instability, namely, arms-race instability. The more vulnerable side has a strong incentive to modernise its strategic nuclear forces, if not to increase their size, to re-establish the effectiveness of its strategic deterrent. Whether this leads to an action–reaction cycle depends on whether the dominant side continues to threaten the opponent's strategic nuclear forces. If so, the dominant side will invest in further damage-limiting capabilities, which then stimulate the opponent to neutralise them, and so on. However, if the threat to the opponent's strategic nuclear forces is unintentional (for example, if it results from a capability to hold at risk the opponent's conventional military forces), the action–reaction cycle might stop after one iteration.

Many examples of arms-race instability arose between the United States and the Soviet Union. Highly accurate MIRVed intercontinental ballistic missiles (ICBMs) threatened the survival of silo-based ICBMs, giving rise to programmes to harden missile silos and deploy mobile ICBMs. Submarine-launched ballistic missiles (SLBMs) and nuclear-armed cruise missiles had a theoretical capability to threaten bomber bases, submarine bases and nuclear command-and-control sites with short-warning surprise attacks, which prompted modernisation efforts. Anti-submarine warfare (ASW) against conventional submarines potentially threatened ballistic-missile submarines, stimulating the development of new generations of quieter ballistic-missile submarines that were harder to find.[10]

More recently, Russia has raised concerns about conventional counterforce capabilities – in particular, US long-range precision-guided conventional weapons. This concern is reflected in the preamble to the New Strategic Arms Reduction Treaty (New START), which states that both parties are 'mindful of the impact of conventionally armed ICBMs and SLBMs on strategic stability'. While most US analysts have cast Russian concerns as exaggerated, this may change with the advent of long-range conventionally armed hypersonic weapons.

Hypersonic weapons and crisis instability

Many countries, Russia and China in particular, ensure the survival of their military forces by making them mobile. China has amassed a large arsenal of conventionally armed short-, medium- and intermediate-range mobile land-based ballistic missiles, and many reportedly can attack targets on land as well as ships at sea.[11] The United States and Russia were banned from deploying such systems by the Intermediate-Range Nuclear Forces (INF) Treaty, which both parties have now repudiated. China is not a party to this treaty. In the future, China, which has an active hypersonic-weapons programme, will probably add mobile hypersonic boost-glide vehicles and hypersonic cruise missiles to its arsenal. Russia's conventionally armed mobile ballistic missiles, such as the *Iskander*-M, reportedly have ranges of less than 500 km in compliance with the INF Treaty, although Russia too is exploring other types of theatre-range hypersonic weapons.

Medium- and intermediate-range hypersonic weapons pose a serious threat to US forces deployed in Europe and the western Pacific, frequently called an anti-access/area-denial (A2/AD) threat. The US is seeking to neutralise this threat by developing the means to destroy these weapons before they can be used. Attacking mobile missile transporter-erector launchers (TELs) while they are moving is difficult. To launch its missile, however, the TEL must stop for a short period of time, during which it is vulnerable. Because this window of vulnerability can be short, attacking weapons either have to be very close to their target or travel at very high speeds. Destroying mobile targets while stationary, before they move, is one of the principal rationales for US hypersonic-weapons programmes.

> *Russia is exploring theatre-range hypersonic weapons*

The question naturally arises whether US conventionally armed hypersonic weapons also can threaten the survival of Russian or Chinese mobile ICBMs, the backbone of their land-based strategic nuclear forces and their respective nuclear deterrents. Mobile ICBMs operate in much the same way as mobile theatre-range ballistic missiles (TBMs), remaining garrisoned or hidden until called upon to attack, whereupon they move to remote launch locations, stop to erect and launch their missiles, then move back to hide sites. Because mobile ICBM TELs are similar to TBM TELs, holding the latter at risk may give rise to a capability to threaten the former, depending on whether hypersonic weapons have sufficient range to reach mobile ICBM sites.

Threatening the survival of mobile ICBMs is crisis destabilising, although other elements of Russia's and China's strategic nuclear forces could remain intact. For Russia, these include SLBMs and long-range bombers. For China, they currently include only SLBMs, although it may add long-range bombers in the future. Thus, if the United States could not significantly limit damage through a combination of counterforce and strategic defence, there would be very little incentive to strike first in a crisis, and the strategic nuclear balance would remain quite stable even if mobile ICBMs became vulnerable.

Threats to a portion of an opponent's strategic nuclear force are not a new phenomenon. During the Cold War, accurate MIRVed ICBMs threatened silo-based ICBMs, and ASW capability against conventional submarines could threaten some ballistic-missile submarines. Yet at no time did the strategic nuclear balance between the United States and the former Soviet Union give rise to a serious incentive to strike first in a crisis. Such an incentive would have arisen only if other US attack options could have simultaneously destroyed most of the Soviet Union's strategic nuclear forces. This was never the case. Today, US ASW may appear more threatening to China – although accurate quantitative assessments are difficult to obtain because submarine operations and ASW capability are shrouded in secrecy – because China has yet to develop a long-range bomber force and relies solely on ballistic missiles for its strategic deterrent.

Finally, Russian and Chinese conventionally armed hypersonic weapons cannot threaten the US strategic nuclear arsenal to any significant degree, so a US capability to hold mobile ICBMs at risk would be a one-sided advantage. Consequently, it would not lead to a reciprocal fear of surprise attack. However, it almost certainly would induce Russia and China to modernise their ICBM forces, which could lead to arms-race instability. More problematically, Russia or China could adopt a launch-on-warning posture to mitigate the vulnerability of their mobile ICBMs. As noted, launching a nuclear retaliatory strike based only on tactical warning would be the height of folly. What makes launch-on-warning particularly troubling in the hypersonic age is that, whereas the impact area of a ballistic missile can be determined with reasonable accuracy within a few minutes after launch, hypersonic boost-glide vehicles' and cruise missiles' substantial manoeuvrability enables them to divert to targets hundreds of kilometres to either side of their initial trajectory. Therefore, Russia and China would not know the intended targets of a US hypersonic attack until the last few minutes before impact, potentially inducing fears that their strategic nuclear forces might be under attack when they were not.

The compressed timeline associated with hypersonic attacks – whether ballistic, boost-glide or cruise – also contributes to crisis instability because there will be precious little time for careful decision-making in the midst of an attack. Hypersonic weapons, however, are only one aspect of a trend towards increasing speed in modern conventional war brought about by technical advances in new anti-satellite weapons, cyber attacks and possibly artificial intelligence. This, combined with the lack of accurate attack assessment for non-ballistic hypersonic weapons, means that misperception, misunderstanding and miscommunication in the midst of war are more likely, contributing to inadvertent escalation.

There will be little time for careful decision-making

Ultimately, conventionally armed hypersonic weapons raise a fundamental tension between the goal in conventional war – to destroy the opponent's military forces as fast as possible – and the goal of maintaining a stable nuclear balance – avoiding threats to an opponent's strategic nuclear forces, not as a strategic preference but because no state with the wherewithal to prevent this from occurring will allow it to happen. It is not clear how to resolve this dilemma. Similar concerns were raised in the early days of the Cold War, when debates arose about how best to fight conventional wars beneath the nuclear threshold given the paramount goal of avoiding a major nuclear war.[12] These debates should be revisited in the hypersonic age for insight into how limited conventional wars can be managed without risking nuclear Armageddon.

Hypersonic weapons also may create problems of warhead ambiguity.[13] An adversary may not know whether an incoming hypersonic strike is nuclear or conventional if it is possible to arm hypersonic weapons with either warhead type. This issue became salient in the US debate over the Conventional Trident Modification programme, a plan to place conventional warheads on *Trident* SLBMs, customarily used only to deliver nuclear weapons, and was in part responsible for the cancellation of the programme. Analogous concerns came up during the Cold War when NATO deployed aircraft that could deliver both conventional and nuclear ordnance, but because dual-capable aircraft were essentially tactical, the intent behind the use of such weapons was assumed to be conventional until proven otherwise – a not unreasonable assumption, because assuming otherwise could trigger unnecessary nuclear escalation.

None of the hypersonic weapons the US is currently pursuing use delivery systems previously associated with nuclear weapons, so warhead ambiguity should be less of a problem. Nor are there any current plans to place nuclear payloads on US hypersonic weapons.[14] As of now, they will be conventionally armed tactical systems forward-deployed during a crisis and used in a conventional military conflict. In addition, the trajectory of non-ballistic hypersonic weapons is quite distinct from a ballistic trajectory (see Figure 1). Accordingly, although Russia and China may not believe US claims that its theatre-range hypersonic systems are entirely non-nuclear without some form of verification, mistaking a conventional attack for a nuclear one is considerably less likely than it would have been with, say, a conventionally armed *Trident* SLBM. It is less clear whether Russia and China will eschew hypersonic weapons with nuclear warheads. China reportedly has deployed some mobile TBM variants with nuclear warheads, and Russia may have done likewise.[15] If so, such systems would create warhead-ambiguity problems.

Ultimately, arms-control measures designed to verify the presence of nuclear warheads on different hypersonic weapons could be devised. Arms-control treaties have met the challenge of distinguishing nuclear from non-nuclear warheads in the past. For example, New START authorises technical means of verifying the actual number of nuclear warheads deployed on a given ballistic missile. These include radiation-monitoring techniques, requiring only limited physical access to the payload, to detect the presence of nuclear warheads without revealing sensitive nuclear-design information.[16] Thus, verifying that hypersonic weapons are not deployed with nuclear warheads is, in principle, possible with current techniques.

In addition, a problem with target ambiguity arises when conventional- and nuclear-delivery systems or command-and-control systems are commingled at the same site. Attacking such sites could blur the distinction between conventional and nuclear war. This increases the chance that the attack will be misperceived as an attempt to degrade a country's nuclear, as opposed to conventional, military forces. Commingling, however, typically occurs only with non-strategic nuclear forces. Threats to the survival of these forces are not as destabilising as threats to strategic nuclear forces. More importantly, it is the target side rather than the attacking side that would create this problem. If an adversary chooses to commingle conventional and non-strategic nuclear forces, it should understand that these assets likely will come under attack in the event of a conventional war because it may not be possible to distinguish between the two. Obviously, to minimise the chance that such attacks would be misinterpreted as a prelude to nuclear war, the United States should communicate clearly in advance that commingling nuclear and conventional weapons will not establish a sanctuary for conventional forces.

Unfortunately, avoiding commingling will not entirely solve this problem because the exceptional manoeuvrability of hypersonic boost-glide vehicles and hypersonic cruise missiles makes their targets difficult to discern until the last few minutes before impact. While timely warning of non-ballistic hypersonic attacks should be possible, timely attack assessment may not be. Hardened dual-purpose command-and-control sites are less vulnerable to attack by non-ballistic hypersonic weapons because these weapons have relatively small conventional warheads. But leaders may not know if ICBM silos, mobile ICBM garrisons, bomber bases or submarine bases are under attack until it is too late to guarantee their survival, even if they are not co-located with conventional systems.

Finally, concerns may arise about the signal sent when an intercontinental-range hypersonic weapon, as opposed to a tactical hypersonic weapon, is launched. Tactical or theatre hypersonic weapons will be deployed forward in a crisis in larger numbers, and their use authorised by theatre commanders as part of a conventional conflict that is likely to appear less escalatory. Intercontinental-range weapons will necessarily be fewer in number due to their high cost, and likely will require national command authorisation for release. Therefore, an adversary who detects the launch of such a weapon may infer that the attack is strategic in nature and, hence, escalatory.[17]

Hypersonic weapons and arms-race instability

Threatening Russian or Chinese mobile ICBMs with US conventionally armed hypersonic weapons will exacerbate arms-race instability because Russia and China will need to modernise their mobile ICBM forces to make them less vulnerable. This should not worry the United States if it is merely the collateral effect of holding mobile TBMs at risk, and the United States need not respond to Russian and Chinese modernisation efforts. Any action–reaction cycle would stop after the first step, and only a mild form of arms-race instability would result. However, if the same technique used to reduce the vulnerability of mobile ICBMs is employed to ensure the survival of mobile TBMs, this could stimulate an action–reaction cycle as the United States continues to pursue the capability to hold Russian and Chinese A2/AD capabilities at risk.

Penetrating advanced integrated air-defence systems is another key rationale for developing US hypersonic weapons. Currently, the United States relies on stealth, electronic attack, saturation and low-altitude penetration tactics to defeat such systems. While these means are effective, their utility may be eroding. Hypersonic weapons, by virtue of their high speed, high altitude and substantial manoeuvrability, stress air defences in fundamentally different ways and represent an attractive option for penetrating defences well into the future. High speeds compress the battlespace for defensive systems and challenge the performance of interceptors. Their high altitude keeps hypersonic weapons out of reach from most air-defence systems.

The manoeuvre capability of hypersonic weapons, however, differs by type. Ballistic missiles have virtually no manoeuvre capability in outer space, but have substantial manoeuvrability in the terminal phase if they possess manoeuvrable re-entry vehicles. Hence, ballistic missiles are a readily available means for defeating Russian and Chinese integrated air-defence systems, barring any constraints imposed by treaty on the kinds and numbers of allowed US ballistic missiles, which appear less salient given the Trump administration's withdrawal from the INF Treaty.[18] Russia and China are developing ballistic-missile defences to some extent, which implies that US ballistic missiles might become vulnerable to mid-course defences at some point in the future. Hypersonic boost-glide vehicles and cruise missiles, on the other hand, fly beneath mid-course ballistic-missile defences and can fly above or around most integrated air-defence systems. The manoeuvrability of non-ballistic hypersonic weapons makes it difficult to track them with sufficient precision to launch interceptors against them should they enter the envelope of advanced surface-to-air missile (SAM) systems. In addition, the acceleration overmatch required for successful intercepts against manoeuvring hypersonic vehicles stresses SAM agility. Consequently, hypersonic boost-glide vehicles and cruise missiles are a better long-term option for defeating Russian and Chinese air and ballistic-missile defence systems. Moreover, defences against hypersonic weapons of any type likely will be more expensive than offensive hypersonic weapons, implying that defences will not be cost-effective at the margin. In fact, hypersonic weapons, especially boost-glide and cruise missiles, may be so difficult to intercept that they may usher in an era of offence dominance in conventional-strike warfare.

The upshot is that hypersonic weapons of all types will stimulate an intense offence–defence competition – a classic form of arms-race instability. This is already occurring with US efforts to improve its ballistic-missile defences in response to Russian and Chinese hypersonic weapons. This response raises the important question of the extent to which the United States should engage in this competition given its cost, with the understanding that limited defences still have a legitimate role in blocking less sophisticated attacks, whether intentional or accidental. From another perspective, the United States could invite an offence–defence competition between US hypersonic weapons and Russian and Chinese advanced air-defence systems as a cost-imposing strategy that would force them to spend disproportionate sums to improve their air defences. To the extent hypersonic weapons – ballistic missiles, boost-glide vehicles and cruise missiles – introduce offence dominance in conventional-strike warfare, reliance on conventional deterrence will be the least unattractive strategy to adopt.

Avoiding strategic instability

The problems of crisis instability and arms-race instability that hypersonic weapons create do not imply that the United States should forgo developing these weapons. The US has sound strategic reasons – in particular, holding mobile targets at risk and penetrating advanced integrated air-defence systems – for pursuing them. The fact remains that large numbers of conventionally armed hypersonic weapons may create a less stable strategic environment. Consequently, it behoves the major nuclear powers to think carefully about how to mitigate potential instabilities before they become truly unmanageable.

There are no ready solutions. It is difficult to see how the United States can avoid increasing the threat to mobile ICBMs while holding at risk conventionally armed mobile TBMs. But Russian and Chinese efforts to modernise their mobile ICBMs need not lead to endless action–reaction cycles unless the same means of ensuring the survival of ICBMs is used to ensure the survival of TBMs. For example, one might deploy ICBMs deep underground so they survive attack while providing for their egress in the event of nuclear war, indicating to the adversary that retaliation is assured even if not immediate. Such a basing mode would not be appropriate for conventional TBMs due to the need to have hundreds of them at the ready to launch on short notice against forward-deployed US forces in a conventional war. Eventually, Russia and China will have to decide if land mobility remains a viable means of ensuring the survival of critical military assets. For the past several decades, it has worked. Although camouflage, concealment and deception techniques improve the survival of mobile systems, the advent of hypersonic weapons guided by off-board sensors or advanced seekers still may render mobile systems vulnerable.

The speed with which conventional hypersonic attacks may unfold is cause for concern. It is arguable that the United States should avoid developing offensive hypersonic weapons altogether and rely instead on defences. However, defences against hypersonic weapons will be difficult to develop, expensive to deploy and of uncertain effectiveness. Point defences might be an option for protecting some critical military assets. More importantly, the offence–defence competition stimulated by hypersonic weapons may provide the United States with attractive asymmetric leverage against any state with advanced integrated air-defence systems, especially China. If so, conventional arms competitions will be an enduring feature of the future, much as they have been in the past.

Arms control is the traditional approach to ameliorating the destabilising consequences of novel weapons. That was the motivation for banning MIRVed ICBMs by way of START II. Expanding the INF Treaty to include China probably has little appeal to Beijing and, in any case, would only ban ground-launched ballistic missiles and cruise missiles, not other types of hypersonic weapons. This approach appears moribund in any case with the imminent demise of the INF Treaty. Banning new classes of hypersonic weapons – hypersonic boost-glide vehicles and hypersonic cruise missiles – might appear attractive. But ballistic missiles also are hypersonic weapons. Although leaving ballistic missiles unconstrained would improve the ability to obtain accurate attack assessment, it would not remove the problems of conventional counterforce and the rapid speed of conventional warfare. Furthermore, banning non-ballistic hypersonic weapons would reduce the US opportunity to impose asymmetric costs on Russian and Chinese integrated air-defence systems, in the event they deploy effective mid-course ballistic-missile defences.

If strategic stability is the paramount goal, then banning all short-time-of-flight counterforce weapons, including ballistic missiles, would make sense. A world with only subsonic aircraft and cruise missiles is much more stable than one with hypersonic weapons because, owing to the former's long flight times, counterforce attacks are virtually impossible. Escalation also would be easier to control given the relatively slow pace at which conventional and nuclear attacks would unfold. The existence of stealth aircraft does not change this conclusion because they cannot hide from detection by some types of early-warning radar, thus allowing most strategic nuclear forces to survive through dispersal. In such a world, concerns about the effectiveness of strategic air defences in blunting retaliatory capability would still exist, so they too might have to be constrained. Nevertheless, banning 'fast flyers' is unlikely to gain much traction because Russia and China would have to abandon ICBMs, the backbone of their strategic nuclear forces, and the

United States would have to abandon SLBMs, the most survivable component of its strategic nuclear triad. Nor would France or Great Britain have much enthusiasm for this proposal, as their respective nuclear deterrents depend heavily on ballistic missiles.

Confidence-building measures – reciprocal actions taken to reduce the dangerous consequences of particular weapons systems without formal treaties – constitute another possible way to improve strategic stability. For example, keep-out zones for hypersonic weapons could increase their flight times. However, given the multiplicity of possible hypersonic launch platforms – land-based mobile missiles, aircraft, surface ships and submarines – it is difficult to imagine how keep-out zones could be enforced. The problem of warhead ambiguity would be reduced, but not eliminated entirely, if conventional hypersonic weapons were not launched by rockets previously associated with nuclear weapons, and if verification mechanisms could be employed to ensure that hypersonic weapons were not armed with nuclear warheads. This would require a level of trust and an acceptance of on-site inspections that do not exist in the current political environment. Target ambiguity can be avoided by not co-locating nuclear and conventional forces at the same site. Finally, 'hotlines' often are invoked as a way to avoid inadvertent escalation, the idea being that rapid communication between heads of state may avert misunderstandings. But they could also be used to convey disinformation, thereby obfuscating the intent of an attack.

*   *   *

Near-space is becoming a critical new domain for military competition. Moreover, the speed and manoeuvrability of hypersonic weapons make defending against them difficult to accomplish at an affordable cost, potentially ushering in an era of offence dominance in conventional-strike warfare. If this materialises, these weapons may stimulate an intense offence–defence competition that favours the offence. From this perspective, US hypersonic weapons could be an effective asymmetric strategy for defeating Russian and Chinese integrated air-defence systems. Fundamental to the problem of maintaining strategic stability will be balancing the demands of conventional warfare with the need to maintain a stable strategic nuclear balance with Russia and China. This quandary will demand much more careful thought lest the major powers find themselves in a situation in which escalation, perhaps across the nuclear threshold, becomes difficult to control. Other destabilising considerations – in particular, warhead ambiguity and target ambiguity – are less relevant to US hypersonic-weapons programmes but should be considered carefully by Russia and China.

At this juncture, unilaterally curtailing US hypersonic-weapons programmes owing to concerns about strategic stability will not impede Russian and Chinese hypersonic-weapons programmes. In fact, deploying such weapons might be required for Russia and China to take seriously attempts to limit the weapons' destabilising effects, much as NATO's two-track decision to deploy ground-launched ballistic and cruise missiles in Europe in the 1980s led to efforts to eliminate these weapons by way of the INF Treaty. Accordingly, the time is right for the United States, Russia and China to begin discussing together the destabilising implications of hypersonic weapons in an effort to avoid potential misunderstandings, misperceptions and miscommunications in the event that they are ever used in war.

Acknowledgements and distribution statement

The author would like to thank Jerry Carson, Larry Jones, Russell Popkin, Brad Roberts and David Van Wie for helpful conversations and comments relating to this paper. Responsibility for any final confusion remains, of course, entirely with the author. Distribution Statement A for US Department of Defense contractors: this article has been approved for public release; distribution is unlimited.

Notes

1   See, for example, James Acton, *Silver Bullet: Asking the Right Questions About Conventional Prompt Global Strike* (Washington DC: Carnegie Endowment for International Peace, 2013); Guy Norris, 'Hyper Threat', *Aviation Week and Space Technology*, 20 February–5 March 2017; Mark Stokes, 'China's Evolving Conventional Strategic Strike Capability', Project 2019 Institute, 14 September 2009; and John Tirpak, 'The Great Hypersonic Race', *Air Force Magazine*, August 2018.

2   Ivett A. Leyva, 'The Relentless Pursuit of Hypersonic Flight', *Physics Today*,

vol. 70, no. 11, November 2017, pp.
30–6.

3   For a more detailed treatment of
     hypersonic-vehicle ranges, see James
     Acton, 'Hypersonic Boost-Glide
     Weapons', *Science & Global Security*,
     vol. 23, no. 5, October 2015, pp.
     191–219; Preston H. Carter, II, Darryll
     J. Pinest and Lael von Eggers Rudd,
     'Approximate Performance of Periodic
     Hypersonic Cruise Trajectories
     for Global Reach', *IBM Journal of
     Research and Development*, vol. 44, no.
     5, September 2000, pp. 703–14; and
     Alfred J. Eggers, Jr, H. Julian Allen
     and Stanford E. Neice, 'A Comparative
     Analysis of the Performance of Long-
     Range Hypervelocity Vehicles', NACA
     Technical Report 1382, 1957.

4   Many actions arguably increase the
     likelihood of war and therefore could
     be destabilising under this definition.
     Such debates rapidly degenerate into
     criticisms of any undesirable action
     by one's opponent. Russia's annexa-
     tion of Crimea and intervention in
     eastern Ukraine; Russian and Chinese
     cyber activities against the United
     States; and China's construction of
     human-made military outposts in the
     South China Sea in violation of the
     UN Convention on the Law of the Sea
     all arguably increase the likelihood of
     war and, therefore, according to this
     definition, could upset strategic stabil-
     ity. This is not the meaning given to
     this term in this article.

5   See Thomas C. Schelling, *Arms and
     Influence* (New Haven, CT: Yale
     University Press, 1966); and Thomas
     C. Schelling and Morton H. Halperin,
     Strategy and Arms Control (Washington
     DC: Pergamon-Brassey, 1975).

6   See, for instance, Bernard Brodie, 'The
     Development of Nuclear Strategy',
     International Security, vol. 2, no. 4,
     Spring 1978, pp. 65–83.

7   Thomas C. Schelling, *The Strategy of
     Conflict* (Cambridge, MA: Harvard
     University Press, 1960).

8   The Anti-Ballistic Missile Treaty
     specifically limited nationwide
     ballistic-missile defences to no more
     than 100 interceptors at a single
     launch site. This treaty no longer is
     in force because the United States
     withdrew in 2002. New START, signed
     in April 2010, also draws attention
     to the impact of strategic defences
     on strategic stability in its preamble,
     wherein it states that the United States
     and Russia recognise 'the existence of
     the interrelationship between strategic
     offensive arms and strategic defensive
     arms … and that current strategic
     defensive arms do not undermine
     the viability and effectiveness of the
     strategic offensive arms of the Parties'.

9   See, for example, Desmond Ball, *Can
     Nuclear War Be Controlled?*, IISS *Adelphi
     Paper* 169 (London: International
     Institute for Strategic Studies, 1981);
     and Morton H. Halperin, *Limited
     War in the Nuclear Age* (Westport, CT:
     Greenwood Press, 1963).

10   The dynamics of arms-race insta-
     bility during the Cold War were
     not confined to threats against the
     opponent's nuclear forces alone. For
     example, simply increasing the size
     of one's nuclear arsenal often made
     the other side feel disadvantaged, not
     because its deterrent was vulnerable
     but because parity was considered
     necessary to prevent intimidation in
     the midst of a crisis. The large Warsaw

Pact conventional armies facing NATO also gave rise to pressures to modernise US strategic and non-strategic nuclear forces to buttress extended deterrence, giving rise to nuclear arsenals with tens of thousands of nuclear weapons on both sides at considerable cost, and with questionable benefits for each side's security.

[11] Office of the Secretary of Defense, 'Annual Report to Congress: Military and Security Developments Involving the People's Republic of China 2018', US Department of Defense, May 2018, pp. 36, 60, 71.

[12] See Barry R. Posen, *Inadvertent Escalation: Conventional War and Nuclear Risks* (Ithaca, NY: Cornell University Press, 1992).

[13] See Acton, *Silver Bullet*.

[14] Amy F. Woolf, 'Conventional Prompt Global Strike and Long-Range Ballistic Missiles: Background and Issues', Congressional Research Service, 8 January 2019, https://fas.org/sgp/crs/nuke/R41464.pdf.

[15] Office of the Secretary of Defense, 'Annual Report to Congress', p. 76.

[16] Jonathan Medalia, 'Detection of Nuclear Weapons and Materials: Science, Technologies, Observations',

Congressional Research Service, 4 June 2010, https://fas.org/sgp/crs/nuke/R40154.pdf; and Steve Fetter et al., 'Detecting Nuclear Warheads', *Science and Global Security*, vol. 1, nos 3–4, December 2007, pp. 225–302.

[17] The preference for intercontinental-range weapons over theatre-range weapons arises, in part, from a debate about how much strategic warning is prudent to assume for conflicts with Russia and China. If the assumption is that less warning time will be available, systems based in the continental United States will be favoured because they can be available for use on a moment's notice. However, if the assumption is that strategic warning is available so that theatre systems can be forward-deployed in a crisis, the preference shifts to less expensive theatre-range hypersonic weapons that can be deployed in larger numbers.

[18] For a discussion of arms-control constraints on hypersonic weapons, see Dean Wilkening, 'Hypersonic Arms Control: Treaty Constraints on Development and Deployment', Johns Hopkins University Applied Physics Laboratory, FPS-R-19-0216, April 2019.

Chernobyl: A 'Normal' Accident?

Rodric Braithwaite

Chernobyl (TV miniseries)
Craig Mazin, writer. Johan Renck, director. Distributed by HBO
(US) and Sky (UK), 2019.

As the radiation drifted westwards, Western governments deduced that a disastrous explosion had occurred at the nuclear power station at Chernobyl in Ukraine early in the morning of 26 April 1986. The Soviet authorities were saying nothing. Arriving at the annual G7 summit in Tokyo with the other leaders of the world's seven largest economies, US president Ronald Reagan was blistering: 'The contrast between the leaders of free nations meeting at the summit to deal openly with common concerns and the Soviet government, with its secrecy and stubborn refusal to inform the international community of the common danger from this disaster, is stark and clear.'[1]

Reagan and his colleagues did understand, though, that there was a downside. After all, the Americans had had their own nuclear accident at Three Mile Island in 1979. The British reactor at Windscale used a graphite moderator similar to the one at Chernobyl; official attempts to play down the fire there in 1957 were unconvincing. No one could be sure that nothing like that would happen again.

Rodric Braithwaite was British ambassador in Moscow (1988–92) and Chairman of the Joint Intelligence Committee (1992–93). Now a writer, his most recent book was *Armageddon and Paranoia: The Nuclear Confrontation* (Profile Books, 2017).

Survival | vol. 61 no. 5 | October–November 2019 | pp. 149–158   DOI 10.1080/00396338.2019.1662152

On 5 May the G7 leaders wisely chose to express deep sympathy for those affected by the explosion, offering medical and technical help, reaffirming their belief that nuclear power was safe, and calling on the Soviet Union to report fully to the International Atomic Energy Agency (IAEA) in Vienna.

A flawed system

By then it was already becoming a settled view in the West that the disaster stemmed from the technical and organisational inadequacies of the Soviet system, exacerbated by the ingrained mendacity of the regime and its pathological devotion to secrecy. In dealing with the disaster, the Soviet authorities were hampered by a number of factors. Soviet professionals were proud of the RBMK reactor they had designed and built. They believed that it was entirely safe, and that it demonstrated how capable their country was of matching and indeed exceeding the West. They were reluctant to recognise its weaknesses.

Soviet construction teams regularly cut corners to meet planned targets. Many people knew about the resulting flaws in the Chernobyl reactors, but once the reactors started to produce electricity, their managers were under pressure to satisfy the energy requirements of their local clients, industry and ordinary people alike. That led to operators taking short cuts.

These were systemic flaws. But some of the reactor's technical weaknesses were also known. Some years earlier, there had been a problem in a reactor in the Leningrad region similar to what later happened at Chernobyl. There had been no accident, and information about the flaw was not distributed throughout the industry as it should have been.[2] Academician Valery Legasov, the distinguished scientist who played a major role in the clean-up, knew that. He spent years complaining that the RBMK reactor, unlike Western reactors, lacked a structure to contain the fallout should there be an explosion. He was told that the reactors were safe enough and that covers would be too expensive to install.[3]

The authorities reacted quickly after the Chernobyl reactor exploded at 1.23am on 26 April. Firefighters were called in five minutes later and Moscow was alerted. An hour later, the Soviet prime minister, Nikolai Ryzhkov, had already taken charge, supported by other senior officials. Their boss, Mikhail Gorbachev, was awakened at 5am. A commission of investigation was set up under an experienced deputy prime minister, Boris Shcherbina. Its first members were on their way to Chernobyl by 9am.

Despite all this activity, the men on the spot and their superiors in Moscow were in a state of shock, unable to understand how it had happened.[4] Their response to the accident was hobbled by a lack of clarity in the chain of responsibility, and a desire at all levels to avoid blame. Even the scientists could not be sure what remedial methods would work, or that there would not be another, much more catastrophic explosion.

The authorities were impeded too by their determination to control the spread of information. Right at the start, the local KGB ordered that telephone connections between Pripyat, the Chernobyl company town, and the outside world be severed. Secrecy had always surrounded anything to do with nuclear power in the Soviet Union because of its military associations. Some of the nuclear disasters associated with the development of Soviet nuclear weapons were kept secret for decades. But it went wider: there was always a deep-rooted instinct to keep news of *any* disaster hidden. Major accidents to aircraft or trains were rarely reported in the press.

Gorbachev, unlike his prime minister, never visited Chernobyl. His TV address to the people was too long delayed. It was quite well judged, but there was still too much ideological jargon, and he attempted to divert blame to the West for its allegedly 'unrestrained anti-Soviet campaign' (the first Western news reports had exaggerated the casualties).[5] But he and his successor, Boris Yeltsin, realised thereafter that it was no longer possible to keep disasters secret, and that the best way to allay popular concern was to explain what had happened as quickly as you could. President Vladimir Putin appeared to forget the lesson: his handling of disasters such as the sinking of the submarine *Kursk* in 2000 was often belated, callous and counterproductive.

But Gorbachev and his colleagues feared panic, and with reason. There had been serious panic at Three Mile Island. The deaths suffered when the reactor at Fukushima in Japan was damaged by a tsunami in 2011 were caused by panic, psychological trauma and accidents, not by radiation.[6] The

Soviet authorities worried about what might happen if news of the accident, exaggerated and distorted by the rumour mill, set the population afire before appropriate measures had been set in place. Preparations to evacuate people from Pripyat began on the first day, but were not implemented until the following afternoon.

Nor were coherent measures ever taken to evacuate the 2.5 million people who lived in Ukraine's capital, Kiev, less than 100 kilometres from the damaged reactor. Indeed, Gorbachev ordered that the annual parade should take place there on May Day, despite the worries of the Ukrainian authorities. He later argued that he had had insufficient information to take a proper decision. Nevertheless, his reputation was permanently damaged among the people of Ukraine.

The Soviet state, and the Russian state before it, had always been masters at moving large amounts of material and great numbers of people around the country, though this often resulted in great loss, hardship and even death for those involved. This logistical mastery was now brought into play. By the time the consequences of the explosion had been largely overcome, more than 600,000 people had worked as 'liquidators' cleaning up the site around the reactor.[7] Half were soldiers and airmen, the rest officials, scientists, engineers and ordinary local people. Their courage and dedication have rightly been celebrated.

Fallout

The explosion generated far more radioactivity than the Hiroshima bomb because it took place at ground level. The figures for death and illness have since been much debated. There is general agreement that between 31 and 54 people died directly from the blast or from radiation. Estimates for deaths in the longer term rise as high as 93,000 or even much more.[8] In 2005, the United Nations, on the other hand, estimated that the total number of deaths, including future deaths among emergency workers and local residents, was about 4,000.[9] The long-term effects, said the UN, were psychological and economic, rather than medical. Some use such figures to argue that the danger of nuclear accidents has been grossly exaggerated by those opposed to nuclear power.[10]

Twenty years later, Gorbachev remarked that the catastrophe at Chernobyl, even more than his launch of perestroika, was the real cause of the collapse of the Soviet Union five years later.[11] His judgement has been repeated by historians and commentators. Two years later he launched his radical programme of reform, and Russia began to resemble an open democracy, where no leader would have tried to suppress news of a catastrophe like Chernobyl. But many things besides Chernobyl brought the Soviet Union to collapse: the war in Afghanistan, American policy, growing public discontent, and above all the unviability of the Soviet political and economic system itself.

The disaster does seem to have had a significant impact on Soviet military thinking. The Soviet generals were always more sophisticated than foreigners and many of their fellow countrymen believed. Now they began to look again at their ideas about nuclear war. Gorbachev himself remarked, 'In one moment we all felt what nuclear war is.'[12] General Sergei Akhromeyev, the Soviet chief of staff, called the accident a tragedy on the level of the German invasion of 22 June 1941: both, he said, brought about a revolution in the hearts and minds of the Soviet people.[13] It is a remarkable comparison, given the mythical quality the 'Fatherland War' holds in the imagination of Russian people. 'After Chernobyl,' Akhromeyev wrote later, 'the nuclear danger for our people ceased to be an abstraction. It became a palpable reality.'[14] A deputy defence minister warned that even a conventional war in Europe could lead to the accidental or deliberate destruction of nuclear power stations, with incalculable consequences. The effect could be 'similar to that of a nuclear attack, and the after-effects more serious than those of Chernobyl'.[15] When they met in June 1990, Marshal Dmitry Yazov, the Soviet defence minister, used the argument in an attempt to persuade Margaret Thatcher out of her enthusiasm for nuclear weapons. She was unmoved.[16]

The catastrophe soon began to figure in Russian literature. Vladimir Gubarev, the science correspondent of *Pravda*, was one of the first journalists to visit the scene. A year later he wrote a play called *Sarcophagus*, after the immense concrete structure within which the stricken reactor was entombed.[17] It was performed across the world and ran for nearly a year in

London. It was set in a small radiology clinic outside Moscow which received some of the victims. The three young doctors at the clinic were called Vera, Nadezhda and Liubov – Faith, Hope and Charity. Overwhelmed by the scale of the disaster, Faith leaves first, followed by Hope. Only Charity remains until the end.

Recreating disaster

In 2019 the Americans made a five-part television series about the catastrophe. It is the highest-rated TV show of all time.[18] *Chernobyl* was wholly engrossing, unsentimental, sympathetic, and it spoke to everyone's deepest fears. The scale was spectacular, but as you watched, it was driven in on you: this is not a disaster movie, this is what actually happened. And you could identify with the people too: the soldiers, the firefighters, the women and children, the wives whose husbands were dying horribly of radiation, the scientists, the reactor operators, even the officials and the party men – all people like us.

The makers took the greatest possible care to get the physical details right. The action was filmed around the decommissioned RBMK reactor at Ignalina in Lithuania, the spitting image of Chernobyl. The buildings, the domestic interiors and the clothing all dated from the Soviet Union of the 1980s, or were meticulously recreated. One could almost smell the cabbage soup and the stale tobacco smoke. Only a hypercritical reviewer would find fault with the setting.

The series was less certain in its gallant attempt to portray Soviet political and social reality. By 1986, the power of the Communist Party was no longer exercised as crudely as it had been under Joseph Stalin. Stepping too far out of line, as Legasov did, could damage your career. You could end up in prison, as some senior plant operators did, if you screwed up on the job or if the authorities needed a scapegoat. But by 1986 you would not end up with a bullet in the back of the neck, as both Shcherbina and Legasov seem to fear at various points in the series.

Everyday power relationships are not shown in a convincing way either. The first principle of Soviet, indeed Russian, management is, 'I'm the boss, and you're an idiot' ('*Ya khozyain, a ty durak*'). But there are good managers in Russia, just as there are anywhere else. A scene in which Shcherbina threatens to throw Legasov out of a helicopter unless he explains how reactors work is absurd. So too is a scene in which a (fictional) scientist named Ulana Khomyuk castigates a local party official.

The most egregious departure from reality is the trial scene at the end. There are some neat touches about the way Soviet courts worked. Legasov is given a useful (though slightly improbable) opportunity to explain to the court – and the viewers – the technicalities of the reactor and the reason why it blew up. But he then delivers a wholly implausible political diatribe about 'the Lie' which, he thunders, fatally undermines the whole Soviet system. There is no evidence that he said anything like that.

The film-makers have excused themselves by pleading that they were making a drama, not a documentary.[19] It is a fair point. But one must take great care in dealing with a major event involving real people. Departures from the truth may be a convenient way of getting points across to a Western audience, but they grate on Russians who know what it was really like.

Jared Harris plays Valery Legasov in *Chernobyl*

These are largely matters of tone, and are so described by sympathetic Russian critics.[20] Ordinary Russians say much the same on the web.[21] Whatever weaknesses they detect, the series has been nearly as popular in Russia as elsewhere. Russian viewers appreciate the obvious respect that the film-makers have shown for the heroism of ordinary Russian people. One said it was just as well that no Russian equivalent had been made (though some are planned) because it would be a sensationalist blockbuster full of boringly well-known stars.[22] Of course, the usual suspects were furious that Westerners had the temerity to make a film about a Russian tragedy, and believed that the whole thing was got up by the CIA anyway.[23]

By any reasonable yardstick, *Chernobyl* is a triumph.

*   *   *

A month after the catastrophe, the Soviet Union came pretty clean. Legasov delivered such a frank report to the IAEA in Vienna that he was greeted with an ovation. The upshot of his report was that the disaster had been primarily caused by human error. A year later, a Soviet court sentenced three of the operators to prison, though one rejected the verdict until the end of his days. Suggestions that there was a flaw in the technology were glossed over. In 1992, however, an updated report from the IAEA concluded that the accident was a consequence of flawed design, inadequate safety procedures and serious errors by the operators.[24]

The real question was more general. Two years before Chernobyl, Charles Perrow, a sociologist from Yale, wrote a book called *Normal Accidents: Living with High-Risk Technologies*. Inspired by the 'unexpected', 'incomprehensible', 'uncontrollable' and 'unavoidable' accident at Three Mile Island, Perrow argued that technology is never solely to blame for disasters. Flawed organisation, bad management and human error combine to ensure that accidents escalate and that complex modern systems, such as air and marine traffic, chemical plants, dams and nuclear reactors, eventually suffer what Perrow calls a 'normal accident'.[25]

By this reckoning, the disaster at Chernobyl was not an aberration. Something like it will happen again, if not in a power station, then in one of the nuclear-weapons systems that are stacked up around the world.

That is a nightmare from which we can never entirely escape.

Notes

1 In this piece, I draw on Serhii Plokhy's deeply researched and beautifully written *Chernobyl: History of a Tragedy* (London: Allen Lane, 2019); on Svetlana Alexievich's equally impressive *Chernobyl Prayer* (London: Penguin Classics, 2016); and on my own *Armageddon and Paranoia: The Nuclear Confrontation* (London: Profile Books, 2017). The Reagan quotation comes from Abbie Llewelyn, 'Chernobyl: US President's Furious Reaction to Nuclear Disaster "Forced Soviets to Change"', *Express*, 19 May 2019.

2 See 'Windscale Fire', Wikipedia, https://en.wikipedia.org/wiki/Windscale_fire .

3 Legasov spelled this out in interviews after the accident, and in the memoir he is shown dictating in the series, which is available at Valery Legasov, 'Vospominania o khode likvidatsii posledsvii avarii na ChAES v 1986

godu. *Nauchno-prosvetitelski zhurnal "Skepsis"'*, http://scepsis.net/library/id_3205.html.

4   Margaret Thatcher was unhappy with the muddled way in which her own people reacted to the nuclear cloud approaching Britain. See 'Thatcher's Dismay over Chernobyl Chaos', *Daily Mail*, 29 December 2017, https://www.dailymail.co.uk/news/article-5219281/Thatchers-dismay-Chernobyl-chaos.html.

5   Serge Schemann, 'Gorbachev, on TV, Defends His Handling of Atom Disaster', *New York Times*, 15 May 1986, https://www.nytimes.com/1986/05/15/world/gorbachev-on-tv-defends-handling-of-atom-disaster.html.

6   Robin Harding, 'Fukushima Nuclear Disaster: Did the Evacuation Raise the Death Toll?', *Financial Times*, 11 March 2018, https://www.ft.com/content/000f864e-22ba-11e8-add1-0e8958b189ea.

7   Richard Gray, 'The True Toll of the Chernobyl Disaster', BBC, 26 July 2019, http://www.bbc.com/future/story/20190725-will-we-ever-know-chernobyls-true-death-toll.

8   See, for example, Greenpeace, 'Chernobyl Death Toll Grossly Underestimated', 24 April 2006, http://www.greenpeace.org/eastasia/news/stories/climate-energy/2006/chernobyl-death-toll-grossly-u/.

9   World Health Organization, 'Chernobyl: The True Scale of the Accident', 5 September 2005, https://www.who.int/mediacentre/news/releases/2005/pr38/en/.

10 See, for example, James Conca, 'Chernobyl Truth Drowns in Dramatized Movie', *Forbes*, 25 April 2019, https://www.forbes.com/sites/jamesconca/2019/04/25/chernobyl-truth-drowns-in-dramatized-movie/.

11 Mikhail Gorbachev, 'Turning Point at Chernobyl', *Japan Times*, 21 April 2006, https://www.japantimes.co.jp/opinion/2006/04/21/commentary/world-commentary/turning-point-at-chernobyl/#.XVqernvTW70.

12 Quoted in Braithwaite, *Armageddon and Paranoia*, p. 366.

13 For the small former Soviet republic of Belarus, this was almost literally true. Belarus lost 619 villages during the Second World War. One in four of its inhabitants died. After Chernobyl, the country lost 485 villages and hamlets, and one in five of its people – 2.1 million, of whom 700,000 were children – continued to live in contaminated territory. See Aleksievich, *Chernobylskaya Molitva* [Chernobyl Prayer] (Moscow: Ostozhye, 2015), Introduction and Historical Note.

14 S. Akhromeyev and G. Kornienko, *Glazami Marshala i Diplomata* [Through the Eyes of a Marshal and a Diplomat] (Moscow: Mezhdunarodnye otnosheniya, 1992), p. 98.

15 A. Kokoshin, *Soviet Strategic Thought, 1917–91* (Cambridge, MA: MIT Press, 1998), p. 140, quoting V. Shabanov, 'Obychnaya Voina: Novye Opasnosti' [Conventional War: New Dangers], *Novoe Vremya*, 14 January 1986.

16 R. Braithwaite, unpublished Moscow diary, 8 June 1990.

17 Vladimir Gubarev, *Sarcophagus: A Tragedy* (London: Penguin, 1987).

18 '"Chernobyl" Is the Highest-Rated TV Series Ever', *The Economist*, 4 June 2019, https://www.economist.com/

graphic-detail/2019/06/04/chernobyl-is-the-highest-rated-tv-series-ever.

19 For a good discussion of the series' departure from facts, see Aaron Bady, 'Is *Chernobyl* Historically Accurate About the Things that Matter?', *Week*, 3 June 2019, https://theweek.com/articles/844566/chernobyl-historically-accurate-about-things-that-matter.

20 See, for example, Alla Yaroshinskaya, 'Amerikanskaya Pravda na Vesakh Chernobylia' [American Truth Weighed in the Chernobyl Balance], *Rosbalt*, 14 June 2019; Masha Gessen, 'What HBO's "Chernobyl" Got Right, and What It Got Terribly Wrong', *New Yorker*, 4 June 2019; and Leonid Bershidsky, 'Russia Should Have Made HBO's "Chernobyl"', *Moscow Times*, 31 May 2019.

21 See, for example, the collection of comments on the 'Chernobyl' page of Kinopoisk.ru at https://www.kinopoisk.ru/film/1227803/reviews/.

22 See '"Communists of Russia" Demand that Makers of "Chernobyl" Be Prosecuted', *Novosti*, 14 June 2019, https://www.film.ru/news/kommunisty-vs-chernobyl. Oleg Solomenin, himself a 'liquidator', scoffed at the idea of a Russian version of *Chernobyl*. See Lucy Hale, 'What the Real Liquidators Say About the Series "Chernobyl"', Spletnik, 30 May 2019, http://www.spletnik.ru/blogs/govoryat_chto/169733_chto-pro-serial-chernobyl-govoryat-realnye-likvidatory.

23 See 'The "Goblin" Puchkov Accused the "Chernobyl" Series of Russophobia', Federal News Agency, 13 June 2019, https://riafan.ru/1186959-goblin-puchkov-nazval-serial-chernobyl-rusofobskim-i-ocenil-versiyu-o-prichastnosti-cru. A Russian film is allegedly in the making, showing that CIA agents were behind the disaster. See, for example, 'A Film About the CIA Support by the Ministry of Culture: What Is Known About the Russian Version of "Chernobyl", Which Will Appear in 2019', Tjounral.ru, 5 June 2019, https://tjournal.ru/tv/100322-syuzhet-pro-cru-i-podderzhka-minkulta-chto-izvestno-o-rossiyskom-chernobyle-ot-ntv-kotoryy-vyydet-v-2019-godu.

24 International Nuclear Safety Advisory Group, 'The Chernobyl Accident: Updating of INSAG-1', INSAG-7, International Atomic Energy Agency, Vienna, 1992.

25 See Charles Perrow, *Normal Accidents: Living with High-Risk Technologies* (New York: Basic Books, 1984).

Review Essay

American Nihilist

Jonathan Stevenson

The Volunteer: A Novel
Salvatore Scibona. New York: Penguin, 2019. $28.00. 419 pp.

Starting with *The Quiet American*, Graham Greene's uncannily prescient 1955 novel of American folly, and extending through books like Philip Caputo's *A Rumor of War*, Michael Herr's *Dispatches*, Tim O'Brien's *The Things They Carried* and *Going After Cacciato*, John Del Vecchio's *The 13th Valley*, and, pre-eminently, Robert Stone's *Dog Soldiers* and two of his subsequent novels, the thematic currency of Vietnam War fiction and narrative non-fiction has been cynicism and irony about the tyranny of good intentions badly served. Yet the goodness of the intentions held redemptive power. If only the United States and its liberal-democratic followers could get the gritty details right, its quasi-evangelical expansion of the American way would be vindicated. On that score, Stone's book is perhaps the most searing and penetrating of the first wave of Vietnam literature. Even after drugs and the scourge of a disowned war have reduced Ray Hicks, the unforgettable ex-marine protagonist of *Dog Soldiers*, to a doomed and shattered fugitive, he proclaims, savagely injecting a flabby heroin dabbler from the California counterculture with a near-fatal hotshot, 'I'm a Christian American who fought for my flag. I don't take shit from Martians.'[1] He

Jonathan Stevenson is IISS Senior Fellow for US Defence and Managing Editor of *Survival*. He is writing a biography of CIA turncoat Philip Agee.

Survival | vol. 61 no. 5 | October–November 2019 | pp. 159–170   DOI 10.1080/00396338.2019.1662151

still has hope, however remote and vain, that his war service in uniform distinguishes him and will somehow save him.

It remained implicit that the United States had meant well, and retained the principles and idealism required to do better the next time. And given its geopolitical success, the conceit was that there would be a next time. America was an object of redemption, not disavowal. In Stone's 1981 novel *A Flag for Sunrise*, Frank Holliwell, a disenchanted former CIA operative in Vietnam, is sent by the agency to assess the volatile situation in a Central American client state of the United States whose ruling regime suspects that American missionaries are aiding left-wing revolutionaries. Holliwell

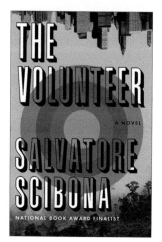

makes contact with a CIA operations officer, similarly scarred by his Vietnam years. He brags drunkenly that in Vietnam he never murdered civilians, dismembered corpses, tortured Vietcong suspects or burned villages. 'I don't claim virtue', he says. 'I don't claim to be a kindly man. I claim to be capable of honor.'[2] Like Owen Browne, the tragic protagonist – again a Vietnam vet – of his 1992 work *Outerbridge Reach*, Stone himself was 'romantic in the postwar modernist style', which is to say 'salted in stoicism and ennobled by alienation'.[3]

All was not lost. What was characterised as the West's Cold War victory, and the military cakewalk of the First Gulf War during America's fatedly short unipolar moment, provided some provisional validation of this faith. But that powered the profoundly misguided invasion and occupation of Iraq in 2003. Additions to the Vietnam canon written after that intervention – most notably Denis Johnson's *Tree of Smoke* and Karl Marlantes's *Matterhorn* – largely purged their consideration of any defensible idealistic core. Their visions were, respectively, of grand and self-perpetuating delusion and of heroic virtue confined to the battlefield unit. Another recent novel, David Means's nearly incomprehensible *Hystopia*, reductively casts the war as an aberrational but immersive episode of mass insanity. With these Vietnam books, Americans seemed to be catching up with Europeans, whose cynicism about the discrepancy between war's promised glory and its actual horror the First World War had established and the Second World War had reinforced.[4] The appealingly patriotic notion of an honourable vocation in the service of a superior state as an existential solution – a ready-made philosophy and *raison d'être* – atrophied.

Salvatore Scibona's *The Volunteer*, the latest contribution to the Vietnam canon, sounds its death knell. This extraordinary novel also transcends the category by placing the war in the context of late-twentieth-century European existentialism and that of the post-9/11 decline of American power and idealism, which may now be reaching its nadir with Donald Trump's abominable presidency and the pitiless, unrepentant and unreflective America that goes with it. In contrast to many of his introverted, post-modern peers, Scibona is possessed of the modernist's irrepressible urge to take on the whole world and make sense of it. A few American writers, such as Philipp Meyer in *American Rust* and *The Son*, have tried hard to domesticate and rationalise America's persistent bloody-mindedness. But that was before Trump. Scibona is confronted by a fallen (or at least falling) country and an increasingly deracinated West.[5] His Americans are cumulatively betrayed by the ideas and institutions they were raised to trust and respect and, unlike even the damaged Vietnam veterans conjured by earlier writers, find no saving grace in their status as scarred patriots.

Seductions of service

The book spans four generations of a chequered Middle American family, from 1949 to 2029, and features five principal characters. Potter and Annie Frade of Iowa start the line when they marry, late in life, in 1949. A year later, she gives birth to a boy, Eugene, on top of newspapers in the parlour of their farmhouse. Owing to his improbable emergence from a 46-year-old womb, they call him 'The Volunteer', Vollie for short. In the early 1970s, he becomes the guardian of a young boy, Elroy Heflin. Elroy, in turn, has a son, Janis. Both Vollie and Elroy serve in the US armed forces – Vollie as an underage marine in Vietnam, Elroy as a late army enlistee in Afghanistan – and effectively abandon their respective children. It is almost immaterial, and certainly only incidental, whether the source of this relinquishment of conventional responsibility is self-loathing or some other mental affliction or circumstantial exigency. To Scibona, it simply is what it is: a product of white American humanity as it has evolved and, at this point, regressed.

The Volunteer opens with a small boy unattended and crying in front of a gate at Hamburg–Fuhlsbüttel Airport, trying to explain himself to airport personnel in an exotic language that none of them understand. The boy would be Janis and the language turns out to be Latvian. He is the issue of Elroy and the local waitress he hooked up with while assigned to Riga, who was moving to Spain without the child and asked Elroy, then deployed in Afghanistan, to take custody of him. He does so in Riga, but bails in Hamburg, leaving the kid in a bathroom stall with a watch, a pack of gum and $263. Waiting tremulously to receive both Elroy and Janis, Vollie – now 60 and fragile but defiantly ascetic – is hunkered down in New Mexico. How he got there is the key to the novel.

In two tours in Vietnam, Vollie sees heavy combat in 1968 at the Battle of Khe Sanh, the epitome of US strategic incoherence and futility in which US forces, mainly marines, famously withstood a vicious 77-day siege of their base by the North Vietnamese Army (NVA) and the Vietcong, holding their ground at a cost of more than 200 dead and ten times as many wounded only to withdraw and relinquish it to the NVA within months.[6] His job is to ferry kit from a rear-echelon supply depot to forward combat bases, manning a truck-mounted Browning .50-caliber machine gun he has nick-named the Hog Butcher, and his standing order is 'do not stop the convoy' (p. 45).[7] He performs well, 'unaccountably not getting killed' (p. 59) and making sergeant. While he is in-country, Vollie's father, who was 53 when he was born and whom he loved, dies of a cerebral embolism. Vollie re-ups and participates in the desperately escalatory, semi-secret and arguably illegal US invasion of Cambodia in 1970. Vollie winds up a prisoner of war, sequestered in a tunnel, half-starved and turned ruthlessly survivalist, for 412 days, and then, rescued and hospitalised in Saigon, a captive audience for a jauntily predatory spy recruiter named Percy Lorch. He uses no acronym or quasi-official designation for his organisation, instead calling it 'the outfit' or 'the shop'.

If Scibona's chapter on the fighting is to some degree votive – he channels O'Brien's sombre celebrations of webgear and other equipment, and

Del Vecchio's stoically resigned refrain of 'don't mean nothin'' – the subsequent CIA-recruitment chapter is a tour de force: a thoroughly integrated, and caustically funny, synthesis of John le Carré, Abbott and Costello, and the Coen brothers. Lorch proceeds to explain that Vollie not only was never in Cambodia – 'Congress in its wisdom prohibited you from setting foot in Cambodia' (p. 94) – but deserted. He proposes cleansing Vollie's now-tainted military record to keep him out of Leavenworth and provide him with a nest egg, in exchange for services to be provided. Over a meal, Vollie asks whether his 'reintegration' would be 'voluntary'. With the casual diversionary tricks and sophistry of a practised criminal, Lorch disabuses him of any conventional mode of inference, factual or moral.

> Lorch's tongue discovered something disagreeable amid the casserole in his mouth, and he spat it in a paper napkin. 'Either there's a pebble in here or a piece of bone,' he said to the wad in his palm. 'Are you listening? That was some serious money I just quoted you. What do you mean, voluntary? You misunderstand.'

> 'Nossir, I don't. It's not my behind you're covering, it's yours. I'm a mistake you made. You want me out of the way until I can't cause you any trouble. I want me out of the way too.'

> 'You misunderstand completely. We paid a lot to get you out of where you were. We're proud of you, I mean it. We don't want you to go out. We want you to come in.' (p. 100)

Cumulative betrayal

The combat that traditionally forges the steel of soldiers is thus erased. The stuff of the superseding brotherhood is co-optation and deception. The volunteer as such, coercively drafted, is no longer. Now known as Dwight Tilly – 'nobody from nowhere' and 'a man of perfect inconsequence' (pp. 123, 125) – Vollie is planted in a mixed working-class neighbourhood of the borough of Queens, in New York City, as a deliveryman for an ice-cream warehouse – together with his 'unyielding looks', this vocation prompts the neighbourhood kids to call him 'the Iceman' (p. 137) – and assigned to locate and monitor an illegal immigrant named Hausmann. Hausmann is almost 80, decrepit and blind. Trisha, the teenage black girl hired to feed and bathe him, treats him with care and kindness. Scibona makes sure his readers know she has a life.

Hausmann speaks Greek but may be a Nazi war criminal. As Tilly, Vollie suspects the agency means Hausmann harm and, ethically constrained, withholds his location, asking Lorch to first tell him the old man's story. Lorch provides fatuous, portentously patriotic excuses for the need-to-know protocol: 'You're in the bowels of your country, Sergeant. You're part of something bigger than yourself. All you have to be is your one part. If the whole body were an eye, where were the hearing?' (pp. 174–5). Tilly holds out, dreaming of dead marine comrades, hearing from one live one, and servicing a post-office box he has secretly secured in his original name without authorisation. Lorch has mail sent to him there to let him know he knows about the box, and Tilly discerns his lack of control. Van Aken, Lorch's laconic second and an older Vietnam veteran, tails Tilly to Hausmann and kills the old man and Trisha, shooting Tilly in the foot when he intercedes and costing him three toes.

Even Johnson, in *Tree of Smoke*, saw the US government's willingness to perpetuate its mistakes and buy off the disaffected as an effectively pragmatic means of kicking the moral can down the road. (Lorch bears a passing resemblance to Johnson's Colonel Francis X. Sands, another self-appointed CIA prophet.) With *The Volunteer*, that road comes to an end. Tilly never finds out why Hausmann was killed, and Scibona never tells the reader. Tilly ditches the agency and seeks out Bobby Heflin, the Vietnam buddy he'd heard from, only to discover that he has disappeared and abandoned his boy Elroy, then just a tot, who becomes Tilly's ward when he settles down with and marries Bobby's old girlfriend Louisa. Scibona's deadpan but slyly suggestive descriptions function as oblique, oracular metaphors: 'a pot of meat simmered on the stove in a foreign green sauce' (p. 247). Unwilling to spend the US government's blood money, Tilly works as a driver for an oil wildcatter and then as a technician for the Bureau of

Land Management. They live in New Mexico. Eventually he leaves Louisa but half-heartedly helps raise a troubled Elroy, sending him to a Catholic boarding school.

The boy grows up to be a steroid-gulping ne'er-do-well. He joins the army at 31, in 2003, after spending six years in Maine State Prison for a range of violent offences. He does six deployments but, a staff sergeant at 40 in 2012, he is looking for 'a way out of the army, an escape before his brains burned down, before his body failed him or he failed his body, a route that led him not into temptation, but delivered him from evil, a way and a place to live and eat, and finding them nowhere' (p. 302). On leave, having stranded Janis a year earlier to Tilly's muted disgust, he tries to get Tilly to take veterans' benefits on account of Agent Orange exposure, but, no doubt attuned to possible ulterior motives, Tilly refuses. Elroy says it's just money. 'Nothing's just money', Tilly replies (p. 304). The Department of Veterans Affairs officer can't convince him either. But the visit is not for nothing. Dwight Tilly's records are co-located with one Eugene Frade's. Tilly learns from the administrator that, officially, Frade was killed in action by an explosive device in Vietnam in 1971. Lorch had told him only that he had secured him an honourable discharge via the vaunted CIA-rendered records purge. Now Tilly sees that the US government, with this crowning bait-and-switch, has comprehensively taken his life, on paper as well as psychically. He still takes faint solace in Elroy's apparent gains from service to country. Tilly is unaware that his ward has kicked his beloved dog Mavis and broken her ribs out of nothing more than jealousy.

America's wrath

In a plot summary, the thematic bridge between war folly and domestic desolation may seem pat or heavy-handed. In the book itself, though, it is decidedly hard-earned. Dwight Tilly seems to have even less than Ray Hicks did, but he rallies. Free of Elroy, who has returned to Afghanistan, Tilly waxes confessional to all of those he has mistreated, but, in his mental stock-taking, asks no forgiveness and is given none. Lorch tracks him down and asks him to at least name a beneficiary of the assets the government holds in trust if he doesn't want the money. Tilly finally gets it: 'I think I understand now. Your code says if we're all getting paid then there's no blood on your hands. The money cleans it all by magic' (p. 337). He rejects Lorch's pleas for financial resolution and asks him why Hausmann and Trisha had to die. Across several paragraphs of obdurate bureaucratic euphemism, Lorch implies that Hausmann was a bad actor whose utility to Uncle Sam had expired and that his termination 'was probably compelled by understandings of moral balance' (p. 338). Trisha was collateral damage.

A letter Tilly receives from a German priest who is taking care of Janis, now called Willy, confirms that Elroy has permanently abandoned him, drives home Elroy's hollowness and drains Tilly's appetite. Forlorn and emaciated, he reunites with Louisa, resolves to take Lorch's pay-off after all, and buys them some land for a new house in the foothills of the Sangre de Cristo Mountains. The planned house is dreamily described from the unabashedly materialistic – ergo American – viewpoint of Louisa, who heartbreakingly drives to the construction site every weekday.

> She liked to watch the house taking shape. A shelter made on a place that was theirs. It was a true adobe house with bricks made from mud and straw, and a *portal*, and vigas in the principal rooms that extended outside beyond the edges of the roof, and kiva fireplaces in the bedrooms, and long canales to keep the rain from undermining the foundation as had happened to the Heflin place. She wanted this house to last a thousand years. (p. 370)

That's about as far as the American Dream gets in *The Volunteer*. Pending the house's construction, they stay in what had once been a warehouse for logging equipment. Tilly travels to Hamburg to meet the priest and Janis, with a notion of adopting him, and leaves Germany with the legalities pending. Louisa, having hung back owing to 'his dark proclivities, his taste for mayhem, his willingness to lead us into wildernesses and into further wildernesses inside them' (p. 371), waits for him in Newark. They spend the night in an airport hotel. It's an improbable place for an existential reckoning. Nevertheless:

He thought about every part of her as he touched it, calling it by its right name and attaching it to the corresponding place in his mind. The deep mind that knows the elementary things before learning. Water and feet, sunlight and food. The mind that knows the time of our going out of being, and bears the record of our coming in. Memorizing her once and for all. There was a rock at the center of him, and he carved her name in it. (p. 386)

Forget about God, Scibona seems to be saying. Forget about country. Intimacy is the best you can do past solitude. Fittingly, the author interjects, as Tilly's (or rather Vollie's) personal origin myth, another awkward, and austerely beautiful, sex scene – this one involving his parents. It culminates, from the point of view of Annie Frade, in this moment: 'At first she didn't feel it. And then she did. But between not feeling the pain and feeling it, between fearing she would die and knowing her long death had started, she had time to say to herself, Time will tell' (p. 392). Rarely has indeterminacy read as so true or so sad. They raise Vollie with love but also a kind of folk toughness – for instance, dunking him repeatedly in frigid creek water to stave off meningitis – and these qualities apparently impart to him the acceptability of abandonment. In February 2014, Elroy musters out of the army only to discover that Tilly has moved and left no address. Elroy tracks him down. In the warehouse, Tilly initially denies that he intended to rid himself of Elroy, but finally comes clean, declaring flatly that he 'can't have' Elroy in his house. Elroy cuts Tilly's throat and sends him 'into the world of souls, where he had sent the dangling hajis' (p. 406). Any myth of exceptional American rectitude dies with him. Tilly never gets to live in the house he was building.

Like Stone, Scibona is concerned with the undertow of history and how it sweeps up individuals. When Vollie decides to leave his parents' farm and enlist in the Marine Corps, he understands 'that nature had found its way of casting him out of the home he had never hoped to leave, and that a force more powerful than his will had employed him as his instrument' (p. 36). Ultimately, when that force proves too dark, Vollie's will prevails. But Elroy Heflin is a different matter. He embodies America's wrath, first turned loose on the rest of the world and then twisted inwardly, patricidally, against itself. Rejected by the rejected, he chooses murder.

Willy stands in counterpoint. He will never know Heflin or Tilly, and, when the priest dies 15 years later, he is left completely alone at 24. Orphaned at least twice over, 'the boundary that separated him from everyone' (p. 417) is uniquely visible to him. He knows his real name, but it is 'a foreign object snagged in his lungs' (p. 418). For Scibona, that adjective invariably has a pejorative cast, but at this point it is applied, with precisely rendered irony, to something American, and to indicate severance. Willy remains capable of love, and of having a decent life. He never needed America or its pretensions to greatness; it was not indispensable. The realisation that the greatness was illusory had eviscerated Tilly. For Willy, in the end, it may be a relief. If Scibona is a nihilist, he is an irreverently hopeful one. He projects the end of the American myth, but also, perforce, the end of America's delusion. Should its citizens be purged of the supposed entitlements that poison their morals – in Scibona's world, people are really entitled to very little – the country may be salvageable.

*   *   *

Narrative momentum is not Scibona's métier, nor does he want it to be. Like Don De Lillo in *Underworld*, he darts backwards and forwards in a long overarching chronology, in *The Volunteer*'s case some 80 years, challenging the reader to consider and reassess his characters in light of strategically deployed back stories, and thus to operate more as a historian or a detective than a casual consumer of tidy, linear fiction.

As for its substance, well beyond the battlefield, *The Volunteer* is violent and remorseless, and some might rue the relentless grimness that Scibona brings to bear.[8] But Cormac McCarthy once said: 'Death is the major issue in the world. For you, for me, for all of us. It just is. To not be able to talk about it is very odd.'[9] Scibona's sensibilities are akin to McCarthy's. The two would likely agree that the world as it is establishes the realistic novelist's only valid frame of reference, and that the present world is indisputably bereft of forgiveness and peace. He cannot credibly write of these things without also dealing with their real-life opposites. Nasty and brutish as the book may be, Scibona toils for those features, and the story warrants them. Loathing arises in aching proximity to love, cruelty to mercy, fate to chance.

Stone died in 2015, Johnson in 2017. McCarthy, who has never tackled Vietnam, is 86. Most other contemporary writers are Martians, as it were. *The Volunteer*, of course, is far more than an astute novel of a now distant war; it is also a great novel acutely and brutally of our time, long in its reach and sure in its grasp. It amounts to a gloomy one-volume revival of defiantly modernist prose when gloomy, defiant modernists are in both short supply and dire demand.

Notes

1   Robert Stone, *Dog Soldiers* (Boston, MA: Houghton Mifflin, 1974), p. 202.

2   Robert Stone, *A Flag for Sunrise* (New York: Alfred A. Knopf, 1981), p. 170.

3   Robert Stone, *Outerbridge Reach* (New York: Ticknor & Fields, 1992), p. 12. For a critical overview of Stone's oeuvre, see Jonathan Stevenson, 'Battered Souls: The Fiction of Robert Stone', *Commonweal*, 15 October 2015, https://www.commonwealmagazine.org/battered-souls.

4   The classic study on this subject is Paul Fussell, *The Great War and Modern Memory* (New York and London: Oxford University Press, 1975).

5   For a chilling historical analogy between the present-day United States and a crumbling Roman Republic, less far-fetched than it sounds, see Andrew Sullivan, 'Our Caesar: Can the Country Come Back From Trump? The Republic Already Looks Like Rome in Ruins', *New York Magazine*, 5–18 August 2019, pp. 20–5, 76–7, http://nymag.com/intelligencer/2019/08/is-there-hope-for-the-american-republic-after-trump.html.

6   See, for instance, Matthew M. Burke, 'The Bloody Battle of Khe Sanh: 77 Days Under Siege', *Stars & Stripes*, 17 November 2014, https://www.stripes.com/news/special-reports/vietnam-at-50-legacy/the-bloody-battle-of-khe-sanh-77-days-under-siege-1.314627.

7   That chapter of *The Volunteer* was adapted and published as a short story. See Salvatore Scibona, 'Do Not Stop', *New Yorker*, 21 January 2019.

8   See, for example, Joan Acocella, '"The Work of Becoming No One"', *New York Review of Books*, vol. 66, no. 12, 18 July 2019, pp. 30–1.

9   Quoted in Richard B. Woodward, 'Cormac Country', *Vanity Fair*, August 2005, https://www.vanityfair.com/culture/2005/08/cormac-mccarthy-interview. McCarthy also famously said that 'if it doesn't concern life and death, it's not interesting'. Quoted in David Kushner, 'Cormac McCarthy's Apocalypse', *Rolling Stone*, 27 December 2007–10 January 2008, pp. 43–53.

Book Reviews

South Asia
Teresita C. Schaffer

Pakistan Under Siege: Extremism, Society, and the State
Madiha Afzal. Washington DC: Brookings Institution Press,
2018. $36.99. 192 pp.

Madiha Afzal applies a political scientist's scalpel to the vexed question of Pakistan's relationship with extremism. Using survey data, she unpacks trends and current attitudes toward extremist violence, hardline Islamist organisations and the United States, and comes up with a contradictory picture. A large percentage of Pakistanis oppose extremist violence, especially following the 2014 attack on a school for military dependants in Peshawar. A large percentage are deeply suspicious of the United States and perceive elaborate conspiracies to explain their sinister view of what the US is or might be doing.

None of these findings is very surprising taken by itself. What makes Afzal's analysis stand out from the conventional wisdom is her discussion of how the state and the military have used the 'Pakistan ideology' – the phrase is in regular use in Pakistan – to create a legal and educational underpinning that excuses extremist violence and institutionalises an especially harsh interpretation of Islam. The results have been on public display on many occasions, notably the assassination of Punjab governor Salmaan Taseer by one of his bodyguards and the garlanding of the assassin by admirers in Lahore. What Afzal has now explained is the way Pakistan's legal structure and educational materials have influenced the way people think and, just as importantly, what is considered to be proper public discourse. The issue at the root of Taseer's assassination – the charge of blasphemy and consequent death sentence passed on a Pakistani Christian woman, Asia Bibi, whose innocence Taseer had defended and whose

     DOI 10.1080/00396338.2019.1662154

sentence has since been overturned by Pakistan's supreme court – is still a hot-button public issue.

Pakistan was founded to provide a homeland for the subcontinent's Muslims, and Islam has always been at the heart of its collective identity. But the drive to excuse extremism results from another aspect of Pakistan's founding narrative: the fear that India is and always will be determined to undermine Pakistan. Afzal writes, 'The army justifies its wars as jihad and uses the jihadi narrative to support militants behind the scenes', which 'extends to a pass for ordinary citizens who respond violently' (p. 149). This sense of victimhood is part of the country's 'founding narrative' (p. 151).

Afzal argues that Pakistan still has time to change, to align prevailing policy views with the less extremist perspective that she believes better reflects how Pakistanis actually think. She argues for a major overhaul of educational materials and, more broadly, for a revamping of the country's official ideology.

Pakistan Under Siege is fascinating, and a tremendously valuable contribution to the literature. I would like to believe that the author's solution might work. However, as Afzal notes, the ideology that now prevails is deeply embedded in the army. More importantly, changing a guiding philosophy so tightly woven into the state is more easily said than done.

Fierce Enigmas: A History of the United States in South Asia
Srinath Raghavan. New York: Basic Books, 2018.
£30.00/$40.00. 486 pp.

Srinath Raghavan is one of India's most prominent historians, with a gift for combining meticulous scholarship with a delightful grace of expression. He has a dazzling list of historical works to his credit, covering many facets of India's foreign and military policy. In *Fierce Enigmas*, he sets out to synthesise the American approach to South Asia, and specifically to India, Pakistan and Afghanistan. He takes the long view, and develops his story along three axes: power, both military and economic; ideology, which he defines to mean both American exceptionalism and democracy; and culture, meaning the social assumptions of racial and cultural superiority that he believes shaped the encounter in fundamental ways. This is a masterful book, though I do not altogether agree with his argument.

The cultural dimension looms largest in the period up to India's independence. His description of the role of missionaries and aid officials in laying the foundation for relations between the people of India and of the United States is a part of their shared history that is too little known. The racial attitudes he describes are certainly accurately depicted, though I believe that he gives them more policy influence than they deserve. India became independent at about the same time that the United States was emerging as a major global power, so the power and ideological dimensions became more salient from 1947 onward.

As Raghavan recognises, US policy interest in South Asia was largely driven by the Cold War until the collapse of the Soviet Union upended the international chessboard. Because Pakistan signed on to the US-led alliance system whereas India pursued a non-aligned policy with an important relationship with the Soviet Union, Pakistan had an importance for Washington that was out of proportion to its relatively small size in the South Asian firmament. The story of the past three decades has been the growing US interest in India – and vice versa.

Raghavan considers the argument that Washington and New Delhi were brought together by their shared wariness of China insufficient to explain their rapprochement. He is right in this: important as the countries' shared security interests are, they aren't the whole story. But I believe his account gives too little weight to India's own economic expansion after 1990, and the attraction this provided to both American policymakers and US businesses.

As with Raghavan's other books, this one relies heavily on documentary evidence. Published documents from the past 20 years are scarce, which makes recent history harder to write. Despite the widely shared view that the US is now India's most important relationship, relatively few Indian scholars have immersed themselves in studying the United States the way Raghavan has. His carefully drawn account fills an important gap.

Emergency Chronicles: Indira Gandhi and Democracy's Turning Point
Gyan Prakash. Princeton, NJ: Princeton University Press, 2019.
£24.00/$29.95. 439 pp.

Gyan Prakash, Dayton-Stockton Professor of History at Princeton University, has taken a deep dive into the history of Indira Gandhi's two-year 'Emergency', modern India's experiment with autocratic government. The key driver of the Emergency, in Prakash's view, was the disconnect between India's soaring promises of democracy and prosperity and the flawed results available to the country's poor. Added to this was Gandhi's determination to do anything to avoid being driven from power, and in the first instance to stamp out the protest campaign led by Jayaprakash Narayan, then in his 70s. Colonial-era laws and India's constitutional deliberations had been built into independent India's legal-structure provisions designed to give governments freedom of action during turbulent times, making possible the mechanics of the Emergency. And with an autocratic government in place and wide powers available to the police, it was an easy step to giving extra-legal power to Gandhi's son Sanjay and his friends to implement the projects they held dear, from sterilisation campaigns to 'urban renewal'.

The themes that recur throughout Prakash's narrative are the arbitrariness of decisions during that period; the brutality visited upon those caught up in the crackdowns that punctuated the Emergency; and, especially, the toxic quality of disappointed hopes for democracy.

The Emergency ended in 1977 with a democratic election that Gandhi lost. India's battered institutions had the inner strength to run a fair election, and the circle around Gandhi seems to have told her she was sure to win. The government that followed was a hastily assembled collection of 'anything but Congress', and fell apart in two years, bringing Gandhi back to the helm. The end of the story was deeply ironic: Gandhi was assassinated in 1984; 30 years later, the Bharatiya Janata Party (BJP), the descendant of the party that had been systematically targeted during the Emergency, returned in strength under Narendra Modi, whose movement the author characterises as profoundly undemocratic.

Prakash's argument that the Emergency was above all a reflection of the Indian government's failure to live up to the promises of democracy makes this an uncomfortably timely book. India, the United States, Britain and a number of other European countries have elected leaders who want to overturn what significant numbers of voters see as a system that has let them down. In India – and potentially in those other countries as well – autocracy can slide quickly and easily into brutality and uncontrolled power. Where I think the author goes too far is in his implicit assumption that democracy has to be close to perfect in order to succeed. He is right on target, however, in the remarkable chapter on 'Freedom Behind Bars' that describes the strength of character adversity brought out in those who made it through imprisonment and other evils visited upon them.

Messengers of Hindu Nationalism: How the RSS Reshaped India
Walter Andersen and Shridhar D. Damle. London: C. Hurst & Co., 2019. £25.00. 405 pp.

Walter Andersen and Shridhar Damle wrote *The Brotherhood in Saffron*, the classic study of India's most prominent Hindu nationalist organisation, the Rashtriya Swayamsevak Sangh (RSS). Thirty years after its publication, the two authors have joined forces again. Their subject is still the RSS, but the story they tell is primarily about how that organisation has managed the transition of the Hindu nationalist movement to a dominant role in Indian politics.

This has been a surprisingly complicated transformation. Traditionally, the RSS was a movement devoted to the advancement of Hinduism and Hindu culture that was explicitly outside of the political-party framework. The BJP succeeded the Bharatiya Jana Sangh as the political party representing *Hindutva* (Hindu nationalism) in 1980. But the key event in forcing the RSS to deal with the BJP as a political party came in 2014, when Modi won a single-party majority for the BJP, the first such majority in decades, and then won an even bigger majority in 2019.

This was clearly a tremendous opportunity for the RSS, and for those who shared its view of India and of Hindu culture. The number of local RSS units, or *shakhas*, went up sharply whenever the BJP was in power. But having allies in power has also exposed the tensions within the RSS on a number of key points, and the tug of war between the RSS's view of economics and Modi's own view of how to shape the Indian economy.

Three examples illustrate the challenge. Traditionally, the RSS favoured economic self-sufficiency. The Modi government honours this tradition in its trade policy, which continues the basically cautious Indian approach to opening the country's market. But Modi has been interested in attracting foreign investment, which was more problematic to RSS economic purists. Government policy has won this competition. The second example shows a different balance. The RSS has had to accept that India has citizens of many different religions, but this has not come easily. One strand in the organisation wants to encourage those of other religions to 'come back home' to their presumed Hindu roots. The RSS has gone through its classic consultations on this issue, but it is noteworthy that Modi, while not associating himself with the 'reconversion' idea, has not publicly chastised those who lead it.

The Indian government's decision to revoke the limited autonomy enjoyed by Jammu and Kashmir provides a third example, in which Modi kept a campaign promise to erase the legal differences between India's only Muslim-majority state and the rest of the country. In the process, he opted decisively for the traditional RSS position that India was fundamentally a Hindu state. He also complicated his task of governing. The tension between those two goals is likely to endure.

This is an important and quite detailed account of how the intellectual superstructure of Modi's government works, and where one can expect tensions in the future. Andersen and Damle have organised the book by issues. This, and their practice of using the Hindi terms for many of the RSS's terms of art, mean that the book will probably appeal more to specialists than to the general public. But it will be hard to find a better telling of this story.

Many Rivers, One Sea: Bangladesh and the Challenge of Islamist Militancy
Joseph Allchin. London: C. Hurst & Co., 2019. £17.99. 237 pp.

When Bangladesh became independent and for several decades thereafter, the country was seen as being largely free of the Islamist militancy that had become a major feature of the political landscape in so many other Muslim-majority countries. Secularism was one of the founding principles articulated by the father of the country, Sheikh Mujibur Rahman, and by his Awami League.

Joseph Allchin, a journalist with extensive experience in Bangladesh, traces the transformation of the Bangladeshi scene, starting earlier than many people might have expected. His take-off point is the 1977 decision of General Ziaur Rahman, who became president after Sheikh Mujibur's assassination, to remove the word 'secular' from the country's formal title. The mobilisation of the Islamist movements took place over several decades, but the seed had been planted at the heart of the country's political competition. General Ziaur's Bangladesh Nationalist Party (BNP), inherited by his widow Khaleda Zia when he too was killed, allied itself with Jamaat-e-Islami.

The issue of militancy burst into public consciousness with two developments in 2013. The first was the establishment, at the insistence of Awami League prime minister Sheikh Hasina, Mujibur's daughter, of an International Crimes Tribunal to try those who were charged with atrocities during the country's 1971 independence war. There was a strong Islamist character to many of those accused and eventually executed. The second was the public assassination of a number of bloggers accused of being atheists. Three years later came the attack on the Holey Artisan Bakery, an upscale eatery in a Dhaka suburb where many expatriates lived. The fact that the perpetrators were upper-middle-class young men made clear beyond any doubt that violent extremism had come to Bangladesh.

Allchin argues correctly that asking whether the violence in Bangladesh came from an entrenched Islamic State (ISIS) presence or from local actors presents a false choice. Both were involved. He also notes, again correctly, that the government had ceded ground to the extremists. Sheikh Hasina, who now commands the Awami League and has alternated in power with the BNP's Khaleda Zia, continues to proclaim her adherence to secularism. But the Awami League too has sought to neutralise the religious issue by a tactical association with other Islamist organisations.

Bangladesh has known astonishing economic success, especially considering the economic collapse that attended its birth. Allchin's grippingly written account of the rise and modus operandi of its militant movements is sobering, and will add to the political challenges the country faces.

Middle East
Ray Takeyh

The English Job: Understanding Iran and Why It Distrusts Britain
Jack Straw. London: Biteback Publishing, 2019. £20.00. 400 pp.

The only people who think Britain is still a superpower are the Persians – so goes an old joke. Jack Straw, the former British foreign secretary, seeks to correct the record. His oddly titled *The English Job* is a mixture of history, biography and the usual lessons to be learned from a wise man of diplomacy. To his credit, Straw has leaned on academic literature and seems to know his way around a university library. This sort of intellectual curiosity is rarely displayed by former officials who are confident that the reports churned out by their bureaucracies contain all one needs to know.

Straw is at his strongest when he assesses the Pahlavi monarchs. He offers an informed account of Britain's intervention in Iran's politics and does so without the usual apologies for past imperial misdeeds. Iran was never a formal colony, but once the British navy switched from coal to oil, Persia suddenly became a scene of much British intrigue. (Straw leaves out the many reports filed by British envoys about the deficiencies of the Persian character.) The British Legation became the most important seat of power in Iran, as Her Majesty's representatives bribed, cajoled and manipulated the fractious Iranian aristocracy to their advantage. The Anglo-Iranian Oil Company (today BP) shared the spoils with Whitehall as Iran's oil served to fuel Britain's navy and economy while leaving little for the Iranians.

Straw's account weakens as he surveys the Islamic Republic and its many confrontations with the West. This is paradoxical given that, as foreign secretary, he had a front-row seat as the Iranians assaulted the regional order and routinely ransacked the British Embassy. For every instance of Iranian mischief there is an explanation that somehow blames the West, particularly the United States. All the usual tropes are here: Straw writes that the Western powers sided with Iraq during its war with Iran, but fails to mention that it was Tehran that abjured all offers of a ceasefire after the first two years of the war. In Straw's telling, Iran began subsidising anti-Israeli terrorist groups such as Hamas because the United States refused to grant it a role in its schemes to resolve the conflict between Israel and its Arab neighbours. This discounts the deep strain of anti-Semitism that permeates the Iranian clerical class. And, in the foreign secretary's reading of the Nuclear Non-Proliferation Treaty, Iran has a right to enrich uranium, despite the fact that no such right is explicitly acknowledged

Survival | vol. 61 no. 5 | October–November 2019 | pp. 178–184   DOI 10.1080/00396338.2019.1662155

in the accord. For Straw, Iran is a collection of moderates battling the hardliners who have always benefited from American truculence.

Straw's one refreshing departure from the standard narrative is his dismissal of the so-called grand bargain that Iran is said to have offered the Bush administration in 2003. Much ink has been spilt about how the Islamist leaders reached out to Washington to resolve all issues of contention between them. An American government enchanted by its shock-and-awe success on the battlefields of Afghanistan and Iraq is said to have dismissed this peace offering. Even someone as sympathetic to the Islamic Republic's talking points as Jack Straw seems to have trouble swallowing this tale.

Energy Kingdoms: Oil and Political Survival in the Persian Gulf
Jim Krane. New York: Columbia University Press, 2019.
£25.00/$32.00. 206 pp.

The Gulf monarchies have a simple survival strategy: offering their citizenry cradle-to-grave subsidies as a means of purchasing political passivity. This national compact is neither new nor original, as most states with externally generated income try some variation of this formula. But the model has gotten out of hand in the Middle East. Growing populations, volatile oil markets and the emergence of alternative fuels have raised questions about the compact's durability. Moreover, the complexion of the energy market is changing with the United States emerging as an oil producer in its own right, something that has not happened since the early twentieth century.

Jim Krane's important book suggests that the current pace of subsidies could actually endanger the monarchies. The Gulf kingdoms, particularly Saudi Arabia, are among the largest consumers of their own oil. Unlike the oil that they export, the vast quantities of oil supplied to the domestic market are given away almost free of charge. High rates of domestic consumption can be explained by the need to operate desalination plants in a region where rainfall is scarce, and by the need to cool houses year-round, as much of the region's electricity is powered by oil. Still, consumption has become unsustainable. These national compacts were negotiated at the turn of the century, when populations were small and wealth was great. That is no longer the case.

Much of the academic literature has suggested that any attempt to tamper with subsidy regimes is likely to provoke a revolt. Part of the bargain struck between the ruling elite and the citizenry was that the generous welfare state would compensate for a lack of participatory politics. Krane judiciously notes that the continuation of such practices is bound to deprive these regimes of needed funds, thus setting up the explosive political problem that the subsidies were designed to avoid in the first place. He suggests that the proponents of rentier-state theories need to readjust their assumptions given the changing landscape of the Gulf and of global energy markets. This sensible view seems to have penetrated the thinking of at least some in the region.

Paradoxically, two of the reformers that aggressively confronted the subsidy problem are among the most toxic political figures in the Middle East. President Mahmoud Ahmadinejad's tenure in Iran was beset with many crises of his own making, but he did address the issue of subsidies in a seemingly intelligent way by trying to gradually raise gas prices while providing direct cash outlays to those most in need. His reforms were not sustained by his successors, who feared the political price.

Muhammad bin Salman of Saudi Arabia introduced himself to the world as a reformer who would take on the Kingdom's entrenched problems that the elderly princes had long avoided. He surrounded himself with Western-educated advisers who were at ease with contemporary development models and paradigms, and was feted from Silicon Valley to the White House. He was seen as a man capable of saving Saudi Arabia from its own excesses, and he did in fact succeed in tempering Saudi profligacy. But his dark side was revealed by the murder of a journalist in 2018. It is unclear where his reforms stand today. The lesson here is that it is very difficult for leaders with authoritarian temperaments to be harbingers of positive change.

Krane's fine book illustrates the problems that no one interested in the stability of the Middle East should ignore.

The Quest for Authority in Iran: A History of the Presidency from Revolution to Rouhani
Siavush Randjbar-Daemi. London: I.B. Tauris, 2017. £85.00. 368 pp.

It seems that becoming president of Iran is not a good career move. Nearly every president of the Islamic Republic has become a non-person shortly after the expiration of his term. The one exception is Sayyid Ali Khamenei, who traded in the presidency for the more august office of supreme leader. Hashemi Rafsanjani was probably the most enterprising of all Iranian presidents, as he sought to transform the office into a consequential post. His failure should serve as a warning that the guardians of the revolution are not interested in sharing their power.

The Quest for Authority in Iran promises more than it delivers. Author Siavush Randjbar-Daemi does a credible job of chronicling the evolution of the office of the presidency. In the aftermath of the revolution, there were many debates about the structure of the new order and the nature of its institutions. The presidency was initially a largely ceremonial post that had to share executive power with the prime minister. This changed when the constitutional reforms of 1989 abolished the office of prime minister. The first man to hold the newly invigorated presidency was Rafsanjani, whose monopoly of power was cut short when Khamenei asserted his prerogatives and proved that in the Islamic Republic, the unelected branches can always subvert those who claim a popular mandate.

The most sustained effort to reform the regime came during the tenure of Mohammad Khatami. Iranian intellectuals and dissident clerics long believed that the theocracy could indeed be liberalised by relying on its own constitutional provisions. By contesting elections, expanding civil society and establishing a critical press, the reformers thought they could harmonise faith and freedom. Randjbar-Daemi's accounts of these exhilarating debates and the crushing disappointments that followed the collapse of the reform movement are the strongest sections of his book.

Ahmadinejad's presidency receives only a passing glance, even though it may turn out to be one of the Islamic Republic's most important turning points. Despite his crass anti-Semitism and nuclear brinksmanship, Ahmadinejad championed social justice and was the only president in Iran to tackle the thorny issue of subsidies in a serious way. He failed in all his adventures, both at home and abroad. In his own way, he demonstrated that the Islamic Republic's conservatives distrust populism as much as democracy.

Randjbar-Daemi ignores Hassan Rouhani's presidency altogether. This is not much of a loss, as Rouhani's tenure stands as one of the Islamic Republic's least consequential presidencies. His singular achievement was a contentious nuclear accord that had powerful detractors in both Washington and Tehran. Rouhani seemed to have hoped that the nuclear agreement would generate sufficient investments from abroad to obviate the need for structural reforms. This was always a risky bet, and proved even more so once America walked away from the accord and crushed Iran's economy.

The central lesson of all this is that the struggle for power between the elected and unelected branches of the Iranian government is now essentially over. In the aftermath of the 2009 Green Revolution, the Islamic Republic will no longer allow reformers and pragmatists to assume power. Randjbar-Daemi's unwillingness to grapple with this reality deprives his account of a logical conclusion.

Leap of Faith: Hubris, Negligence, and America's Greatest Foreign Policy Tragedy
Michael J. Mazarr. New York: PublicAffairs, 2019. $30.00.
528 pp.

It may come as a shock to many that in the 1990s there was a bipartisan consensus in Washington on the issue of Iraq. Both Republicans and Democrats wanted to change the regime in Baghdad. Bill Clinton called for such a change in 1998, and before long the Iraq Liberation Act was unanimously passed by the United States Senate. Bernie Sanders and John Kerry both supported a resolution that committed America to displacing Saddam Hussein. In 2000, the Democratic Party platform was even more vociferous than the Republican one in its condemnation of Saddam. Al Gore was an enthusiastic regime-changer, while George W. Bush spoke of a humble foreign policy that eschewed nation building. All this may have been cheap rhetoric, but the foundation for a muscular approach toward Iraq was constructed in the decade after the First Gulf War, whose outcome seemed to have left everyone unsatisfied.

Michael Mazarr's comprehensive and dispassionate account is a welcome addition to a field that too often yields to hysteria, if not libel. Despite all the chest-thumping, it was the 9/11 tragedies that made the invasion of Iraq possible. America wanted its revenge, and merely bombing Afghanistan seemed insufficient. Osama bin Laden proved elusive, while Saddam was all too available. The Bush administration was right to be concerned about the proliferation of weapons of mass destruction, and Saddam did himself no favours by impeding the work of international inspectors. Mazarr makes clear that the invasion was not a plot hatched by a secret cabal. He meticulously chronicles the litany of mistakes and misjudgements that doomed the entire enterprise. Still, the war was a mistake, not a crime.

The war came at a time when America's power was unrivalled. The United States had won the Cold War, and the roaring 1990s convinced everyone that Washington could condition outcomes in the Middle East and even transform its stubborn political culture. The invasion of Iraq was to set off the dominoes, bringing about the collapse of autocracies and the rise of pro-Western democracies. But the Iraqis were more eager to pursue their ancient religious feuds than to construct an inclusive republic. The sectarian civil war in Iraq polarised an already inflamed Middle East along religious lines. As America's fortunes changed, the erstwhile supporters of the war became its most severe critics. With the possible exception of George Bush himself, very few continue to believe in the correctness of the invasion and its grandiose mission of changing the Middle East. Those lofty ambitions are buried deep in the sands of Iraq.

Today, Washington is a capital struggling under Iraq's shadow. Democrats are traumatised by the war, while the Republicans seem intellectually chastised. No one wants to intervene in the Middle East, and regime change is a dirty word. The US recovered quickly from the once-debilitating Vietnam Syndrome because it could not take a vacation from the Cold War. It is hard to see what will cure the country's Iraq Syndrome. Such are the wages of losing a war of choice.

The Rise and Fall of Peace on Earth
Michael Mandelbaum. Oxford: Oxford University Press, 2019.
£18.99. 232 pp.

For decades, Michael Mandelbaum has proven to be one of the most astute and thoughtful observers of the international scene. In his latest book, he returns to the quarter-century after the Cold War, when it was casually assumed that trade and democratic expansion would create a stable world. America had prevailed over the Soviet Union, and American values were expected to be universally embraced. The question that Mandelbaum grapples with in this compact and important book is, what went wrong?

Three powers, China, Russia and Iran, stood aside from all the talk about the end of history and nursed their grievances. Russia was eager to reclaim its superpower status and quickly replaced messianic communism with crude nationalism as its guiding light. Whether the expansion of NATO triggered Russian suspicions is a question that will generate its share of debates and disagreements; what is certain is that Russia became the spoiler in Europe. Vladimir Putin offered his humbled citizens a vision of a future in which Russia mattered once more. The benefits of democratic rule and trade deals seemed less impressive to many Russians than regaining their lost empire.

In the Middle East, the Islamic Republic harboured its own suspicions. Unlike Russia, Iran did not abandon the revolutionary creed of its founder, Ayatollah Ruhollah Khomeini. In the 1990s, the country bided its time as the Clinton administration obsessed over the crafting of an agreement between the Israelis and the Palestinians. The rise of the reformers with the election of president Khatami in 1997 generated much excitement at the possibility that Iran might finally join the world community and embrace its values. Alas, this delusion was swept away as the hardliners reasserted their power both at home and in the region. The Bush administration's invasions of Iraq and Afghanistan served Iran's interests even as Russia was puncturing the lofty hopes of a peaceful post-Cold War order. Driven by religious extremism and Persian nationalism, Iran has embarked on an imperial journey that has left footprints from the Persian Gulf to the shores of the Mediterranean.

By far the most aggressive challenge came from China. With its double-digit economic growth rate and Belt and Road Initiative, China made clear that it had no intention of becoming another regional power under the American shadow. Chinese leaders saw America as a rival to displace, not a model to emulate. Although well integrated into the world trading system, Beijing is prepared to pursue its ambitions irrespective of American sensibilities.

Economy
Erik Jones

**Globalization Under and After Socialism: The Evolution of
Transnational Capital in Central and Eastern Europe**
Besnik Pula. Stanford, CA: Stanford University Press, 2018.
$65.00. 258 pp.

Communism has many legacies that have influenced the trajectories of post-communist development. One of the most powerful of these stems from the pattern of firm-level cooperation with transnational corporations based in the West. The more intensively firms under communism partnered with Western multinationals, the more widely economic actors in communist countries acquired the ability to communicate with foreign businesses, to produce at the level of quality expected in foreign markets, and to meet the contractual obligations required by foreign partners to deliver in full, on time and to specifications. All other things being equal, these capabilities are a boon to foreign investors. Thus, a record of successfully partnering with foreign multinationals in the past should make a national economy more attractive for foreign direct investment so long as any learned organisational competences can be expected to endure.

This claim lies at the foundation of Besnik Pula's fascinating reinterpretation of the patterns of post-communist development seen in the countries of Central and Eastern Europe over the past three decades. Pula shows how the ways in which communist governments attracted foreign partnerships and deployed foreign capital in one era shaped the way they were regarded by foreign investors in another. Of course, other factors also mattered, such as the size of the national market or the quality of its human capital. The pattern of privatisation played a role as well, particularly in the Czech case, where the government sold off large-scale enterprises in single transactions. Moreover, the 'organizational capital' that national economies inherited from their experience with Western firms under communism was ultimately a wasting asset, whose value diminished with the change of economic and technological circumstances both at home and abroad. Pula is not offering an enduring law to cover the structure of post-communist development. Instead, he shows only how some countries got a leg up on the competition depending on the implications of decisions taken two or three decades earlier.

The most interesting part of Pula's analysis is how he shows one sequence of events driving a series of further developments, like a multistage rocket. If the organisational legacies of communist interaction with Western multinationals can help explain the initial pattern of foreign direct investment under post-communism, then that pattern of investment can feed into the strategies chosen for development (import-led or export-oriented), which in turn help to explain the particular role the country would play in the wider European economy (as an assembly platform, a producer of intermediate goods, or some combination of both). Each sequence in this chain has its own initial conditions that it inherits from preceding events, and its own legacy to bequeath to the sequence that follows. Some countries end up doing surprisingly well as these chains roll into the present; others wind up in something like a developmental dead end. Crucially, however, Central and Eastern Europeans are the agents who set events in motion and who guide their countries' development. Foreign investors and Western multinationals create opportunities, but it is up to the Central and Eastern Europeans to exploit them.

Not everyone will be convinced by Pula's argument. There are too many variables, both included and omitted, and there are simply not enough cases to account for them all. There is also no reason why the causal sequences in every country need to be the same. If Central and Eastern Europeans truly have agency, they should be able to waste the advantages they gained through their experience under communism as well as exploit them. Such criticism aside, however, Pula offers an original interpretation of economic development both under and after socialism that deserves to be widely read.

Financial Citizenship: Experts, Publics, and the Politics of Central Banking
Annelise Riles. Ithaca, NY: Cornell University Press, 2018.
£11.99/$14.95. 108 pp.

Central-bank independence has lost its legitimacy – and central bankers know it. Central bankers may still believe that monetary policy is a technical enterprise and that by isolating themselves from politics they can make policy decisions that focus on the longer term, but the evidence is clear that people are starting to question why monetary policy should be held apart from political debate; why central bankers should be allowed to make decisions that hurt one part of society while benefiting another; and whether some new formula cannot be found to make monetary policy more accessible to stakeholders who are more aligned with Main Street than with Wall Street. The solution is not to hand monetary policy over to elected politicians – it is to reframe the narrative underpinning the legitimacy of central-bank independence. That narrative should have at its core a certain notion of 'financial citizenship', within which the people take responsibility for trying to understand monetary policymaking while central bankers take responsibility for engaging more systematically and more responsively with the public.

Annelise Riles makes a powerful case for this re-engineering of the argument for central-bank independence – and she is right both in her insistence that the current situation is unsustainable, and in her observation that central bankers are well aware that they can no longer count on a deferential public. Importantly, Riles also has a solution for bringing central bankers together with stakeholders from outside the financial sector and with the general public. She has developed a platform for engagement called 'Meridian 180' that she created originally to facilitate crisis response in the aftermath of Japan's Fukushima disaster and that she has now broadened to foster legitimating dialogue in other crisis situations. With a major financial catastrophe just behind us and the prospect of another looming, Riles has good reason to use her forum to seek more sustainable financial governance.

Riles points to her Meridian 180 platform only at the end of her argument, in her recommendations for how a new narrative to legitimate central-bank independence could be developed. That placement is unfortunate. Time and again in the build-up to her conclusion, Riles highlights statements from key actors that she collected at Meridian 180 events. Without specific knowledge of the organisation, it is easy to come away wondering whether there is some new Jackson Hole (Federal Reserve) or Sintra (European Central Bank) symposium that has popped onto the central-banking conference calendar. It is also difficult to appreciate the context within which those statements were made and hence the possibility that the precise choice of words might reflect this unique social environment.

None of this is to criticise Riles's underlying analysis. She makes a good point about the cultural distinctiveness of the central-banking community – not unlike the point made by Juliet Johnson in her book *Priests of Prosperity* on the expansion of central banking into Central and Eastern Europe. Riles also makes a good point about the too-close ties between central bankers and the finance community, much like Lawrence Jacobs and Desmond King do in *Fed Power*, their study of the Federal Reserve. Finally, Riles draws heavily on Paul Tucker's self-reflection after he left the Bank of England. Her focus is on Tucker's attitudes toward central-bank independence, but Tucker recast his thoughts in terms of independent agencies more broadly. An introduction to the Meridian 180 platform can – and should – be forgiven for not engaging more clearly and comprehensively with the many new voices challenging the isolation of policy-makers from democratic politics. A reorganisation of the material in this book would help readers better understand its contribution.

Currencies, Capital, and Central Bank Balances
John H. Cochrane, Kyle Palermo and John B. Taylor, eds.
Stanford, CA: Hoover Institution Press, 2019. $14.95. 350 pp.

Central bankers confront a wide range of problems related to the lack of coordination in monetary policymaking across countries, the impact of capital flows from one country to the next, the prolonged use of 'unconventional' monetary policies that have swelled the size of central banks' balance sheets, and a very imperfect understanding of how market participants shape their expectations about future inflation. Worse, these problems are all central to the tangled practice of monetary policymaking and financial-market supervision. Central bankers may dream of a world where they can set their policies using a rule for every occasion; more often than not, however, they have to exercise judgement in a way that most non-central bankers would find hard to distinguish from making a guess.

This situation is precisely what one would expect having read Annelise Riles's call for greater financial citizenship (see previous review). Nevertheless, it is worth reading this conference volume from the Hoover Institution to appreciate the difficulties that central bankers face. The volume is much better than the average edited volume, in which the papers rarely speak to one another. Here most of the text is transcript, which means the engagement is continuous. There are a few set pieces to start the conversation, but there are many more long comments and back-and-forth exchanges that are so artfully rendered as to give the reader a sense of being a fly on the wall. Even the papers read like they are being presented. What few formulas there are appear in a very slim annex; even the graphical presentation of data requires almost no explanation.

This format is important for a more general reader because it opens a door on the culture of central bankers that Riles (rightfully) finds so important to understand in her critique of central-bank independence. It also offers revealing insights on just how easily top members of the central-banking community are willing to concede the uniqueness of their position. An early exchange between former Bank of England deputy governor Paul Tucker and former Reserve Bank of India governor Raghuram Rajan is illustrative: in his paper, Rajan provides a proposal for rules that might govern how central banks think about and respond to the impact of their own policies on other countries; Tucker points out that Rajan's rules make more sense if central banks are seen as engaging in monetary politics rather than monetary economics; and Rajan concedes that economics is less important than perception – 'we need to be seen to be doing something … [M]onetary politics has been a central feature here' (p. 51).

Such asides show the political vulnerability of the central-banking community. They also show the limitations of central banking. Some of those limitations are mechanical. Central bankers cannot force banks in the private sector to loan money into the real economy, and they may have less leverage than they imagine in transmitting changes in interest rates through the banking sector to end users. Some of the limitations are also a matter of role play. Central bankers make monetary policy. In that sense, as one-time Federal Reserve governor Kevin Warsh observed, central bankers 'ought not to be fiscal policy makers with tenure'. Spending money may be necessary in a crisis, but in more normal times central banks should step back and allow elected politicians to make those sorts of decisions.

This collection also reveals the extent to which central bankers exist as a community, with overlapping personal relationships, a high awareness of one another's interests and achievements, and a deep respect for each other's contributions. Meanwhile, scholars from other disciplines who work on central banking and monetary policymaking are absent. As Riles argues, another challenge will be to widen the conversation. This is a readable collection that could have supported a more diverse set of participants.

Fighting Financial Crises: Learning from the Past
Gary B. Gorton and Ellis W. Tallman. Chicago, IL: University of
Chicago Press, 2018. £34.00/$45.00. 234 pp.

Another way to think about the political independence of central bankers is to imagine a world in which they do not exist. Such a world would still have banks and money; it just would not have monetary policy. This was the situation in the United States for much of the eighteenth and early nineteenth centuries. From the 1860s onward, the US government chartered national banks authorised to issue national currency, but it did not provide for centralised banking supervision, nor did it create facilities to bail out banks in trouble. Instead, the banks formed clubs to regulate and, when necessary, bail each other out. The US Federal Reserve System emerged from and in many ways improved upon those private arrangements. But anyone wishing to understand why central bankers are so close to large financial institutions should keep that historical development in mind. It is also important to recall the lessons learned by private bankers in the larger, more systemically important institutions about how to underwrite one another in hard times.

This is the opening premise of Gary Gorton and Ellis Tallman's fascinating exploration of the lessons of history for fighting the financial crises we face, and will face, in the present and future. Gorton and Tallman show how large, systemically important banks clubbed together in clearing houses – which are institutions in which banks net out their payments with one another to make the whole financial system work more efficiently. Banks that wanted to access these clearing houses, and the efficiencies they had to offer, had to subject themselves to close supervision by the other members of the club. When the financial system as a whole faced crisis, the clearing house would suddenly (and temporarily) transform itself into a large joint-stock financial institution – a giant bank, owned by the large banks that formed the core of the financial community – in order to ensure that each of the members had the money necessary to do business, and that any member that failed would do so in an orderly manner and without bringing down the entire system.

This private-sector arrangement did not eliminate the threat of financial instability. On the contrary, Gorton and Tallman find the 'national banking' period interesting because it was beset by frequent systemic crises. Nevertheless, the large banks and clearing houses did learn techniques to mitigate the impact of a sudden loss of confidence in the banking system. They learned to suspend the laws of contract, so that banks could stop redeeming short-term loans they had taken out (often in the form of 'deposits') in order to safeguard their liquidity; they learned to create new forms of liquidity underwritten by the system's major banks in order to act as a lender of last resort; and, more importantly, they learned how to manage information so that other participants in the marketplace would not know which banks – by name – were in trouble. In this way, the major bankers were able to shift popular attention away from specific institutions and onto the 'system as an entity' (p. 175).

Gorton and Tallman insist that the lessons of the past still apply. If policymakers want to prevent a crisis from taking down the financial system, they have to let systemically important banks break the laws of contract (temporarily); they have to ensure those banks have sufficient liquidity; and they have to manage access to information in order to force the public to look away from institutional accountability and to focus on the requirements for shoring up the system as a whole. These recommendations will be challenging for anyone looking for transparency in central banking. Gorton and Tallman agree that transparency is useful in the periods between crises, but argue that it is counterproductive when the financial system is in jeopardy. Their book is essential reading that should spark a wider conversation.

Why Not Default? The Political Economy of Sovereign Debt
Jerome Roos. Princeton, NJ: Princeton University Press, 2019.
£30.00/$39.95. 398 pp.

If there is a mystery in international finance, it is that governments do not default on their debts. This is the provocative assertion Jerome Roos offers at the start of his exploration of the development of sovereign-debt markets and the structural power of financial elites within them. Roos argues that there was a time when sovereign default was a regular event. With the progressive financialisation of international commerce running alongside the rapid expansion of the public sector, however, sovereign borrowers have found themselves increasingly at the mercy of their creditors. Governments cannot default because of the risk of being unable to borrow again in the near future; they cannot finance essential (or popular) public goods and services without borrowing; and they cannot face down either their big international creditors or the powerful states and international financial institutions that are their allies. As a result, debt becomes inviolable and democracy is subordinated to debt servicing.

Roos makes a powerful and provocative argument, one that updates the 'business power' literature from the 1970s by authors such as Robert Dahl and Charles Lindblom to include recent transformations in the relationship between banks and firms. Roos uses the notion of 'structural power', looking not only at why states rely on particular forms of finance, but also how this finance is underwritten by banks and financial markets. The case studies of Mexico, Argentina and Greece illustrate different underlying dynamics. Roos concludes with a plea for reconsideration of the balance between finance and democracy against the threat of popular rebellion. Given the current political climate, his argument warrants close consideration.

There is, however, a missing element that Roos could fold into future research as highlighted by Gary Gorton and Ellis Tallman's book (see previous review). This can be framed in terms of three questions: are there technologies that governments can use to ensure they have access to credit? If commercial banks can suspend their obligations in times of crisis, does the same privilege apply to states? What role do states play in the provision of 'indisputable' or 'risk free' short-term credit instruments at the heart of most financial transactions?

These are all questions that point toward the origins and functioning of central banks. Often, these banks – like the Bank of England – were created to ensure the sovereign could access credit. In exchange, the British Crown gave the Bank of England unique powers to stabilise the major banks at the heart of the financial system. Chief among these powers was the Bank of England's ability to issue indisputable or risk-free assets for use as liquidity in times of distress. This relationship started at arm's length, and the Bank of England formed as a limited-liability joint-stock company. Over time, however, the sovereign nationalised the Bank of England and then added its own assets – meaning government securities – to the list of indisputable credit instruments. In this telling of the story, the structural-power relationship flows from states to finance and not the other way.

Central banks continue to hold a pivotal position. Where governments control central banks, they can repudiate international obligations while maintaining domestic liquidity. This was the experience in Iceland. Where governments do not control central banks, the provision of liquidity is all that matters. Cyprus was forced to 'bail in' its foreign creditors by the European Central Bank (ECB). The Greek situation was also complicated by its relationship with the ECB. When Greece got into trouble in 2010, the ECB waived the requirements for the use of Greek debt as collateral. When Syriza was elected in 2015, the ECB took the waiver away. The 'defeat of the Athens Spring' owed much to that decision.

Letter to the Editor

The Two-state Quandary

Sir,

Benjamin L. Shaver and Guy Ziv's article 'A Near-consensus: Israel's Security Establishment and the Two-state Solution' in the June–July 2019 issue correctly describes the dominant instinct in the Israeli security establishment to separate from the Palestinians. But note that this does not necessarily translate into support for a two-state solution. The key issue is not whether such a solution is favoured in principle, but rather what the minimum Israeli security conditions are for allowing the establishment of a Palestinian state.

Two or three additional questions might have better clarified the political dispositions of the members of the Israeli defence establishment. For example: is military control from the Mediterranean Sea to the Jordan River an Israeli security imperative, or can Israel forgo control over the Jordan Valley? Should Israel withdraw unilaterally from parts of the West Bank given Palestinian unwillingness to enter peace negotiations? And, most importantly, can the Palestinians deliver peace?

Answers to these questions could have provided a richer and more nuanced report regarding the views of Israel's generals. Quoting the positions of far-left generals such as Ami Ayalon (who have an extremely limited following in Israeli politics) leaves the reader with an incomplete account of Israeli political discourse. While a large majority of Israelis and Israeli politicians theoretically are ready for territorial concessions, a huge majority of the public (over 70%) doubts the ability and willingness of Palestinians to live peacefully next to Israel. Hamas-ruled Gaza in the aftermath of a unilateral withdrawal best demonstrates Israel's concerns.

The authors of the article also fail to note that in recent decades Israel's defence establishment has had limited influence on government

Survival | vol. 61 no. 5 | October–November 2019 | pp. 193–196   DOI 10.1080/00396338.2019.1662157

policymaking and on public opinion. This counters the charges occasionally levelled that Israel is a militaristic state.

Professor Efraim Inbar
President
Jerusalem Institute for Strategy and Security

Reply from the authors

Professor Inbar correctly notes that the desire to separate from the Palestinians does not necessarily translate into support for the two-state solution. It is precisely for this reason that we tested explicitly for support for the two-state solution, as we explain in the study-design section (pp. 117–19).

Indeed, we found that 85% of senior veterans of Israel's security establishment unequivocally support the two-state solution, a conservative finding that would have been much higher had we tested for support for the more vaguely worded 'separation from the Palestinians'. For example, despite knowing that Ram Ben-Barak, a former deputy chief of the Mossad, supports the establishment of a Palestinian state, we adhered to our strict coding rule by coding his position on the two-state solution as 'inconclusive' given that his comments on this topic were not explicit in our dataset.

Moreover, as several of the interviewees pointed out, ex-security-establishment figures seeking to enter political life are often afraid that they might pay a political price for publicly supporting the two-state solution, and therefore refrain from doing so. As Professor Inbar mentions in his letter, a majority of the Israeli public is distrustful of Palestinian intentions vis-à-vis Israel. That the views of the security establishment are not in sync with those of the broader public is also why the actual percentage of former generals and spymasters who support the two-state solution is higher than what many of them have expressed publicly would indicate.

The other questions Professor Inbar suggests asking of former security officials, such as their position on the importance of retaining the Jordan Valley, were covered in our interviews. But we believe that the most significant factor – and the one that best lends itself to content analysis – is the breakdown of security-establishment veterans who support a two-state solution versus those who oppose it.

He also criticises us for failing to note that the security establishment has had limited influence on government policy, yet we point out that 'the near-consensus among Israel's top security officials is significant because it challenges claims by the ruling right-wing coalition that the two-state solution is neither desirable nor feasible' (p. 116). It is this paradox that we find most intriguing.

Finally, Professor Inbar's claim that we are quoting 'far-left generals such as Ami Ayalon' is tendentious and reflects his own biases. Ayalon is a former commander of the Israeli Navy – and a recipient of the Medal of Valor – and a former head of the Shin Bet who has identified in the past with the centre-left Labor Party, for which he once served as a member of the Knesset. We interviewed figures from across the political spectrum, including Netanyahu appointees and security veterans whose political views and affiliations remain unknown to us.

Benjamin L. Shaver and Guy Ziv

Closing Argument

Moral Compass of Central Europe

Jan Zdrálek

I

I arrived at Marble Arch precisely on time. Half a century ago, in 1968, a small group of emigrants had protested here against the Soviet-led invasion of Czechoslovakia. Now, another small group was rallying around national flags and home-made banners, calling for the resignation of Czech Prime Minister Andrej Babiš. Excitement was in the air; all the Czech expats in London knew that the biggest demonstration since the fall of communism was to take place in Prague that same day. I joined 80 compatriots in singing the national anthem. When we finished, someone shouted: 'There is a quarter of a million in Prague!'[1]

The record protest in Letná, a large park adjacent to the football stadium of Sparta Prague, was organised by the 'Million Moments for Democracy' movement led by a 26-year-old student, Mikuláš Minář. Letná was also the protest venue in 1989 when an estimated 500,000–800,000 people gathered there to resist the communist regime.[2] Just as in 1989, the 2019 event was publicly supported by actors and musicians, who performed on stage during the three-hour demonstration.[3]

Large-scale protests against the Czech prime minister intensified after the bewildering replacement of the government's justice minister. Marie Benešová took over from Jan Kněžínek, who resigned a day after Czech police recommended that the state prosecutor, which is independent yet

Jan Zdrálek is reporter–researcher for *Survival* and a master's student at the Johns Hopkins School of Advanced International Studies (SAIS).

Survival | vol. 61 no. 5 | October–November 2019 | pp. 197–204   DOI 10.1080/00396338.2019.1662159

technically administered by the Ministry of Justice, file charges against the prime minister. This added to a long list of troubles for Babiš, the second-richest man in the country, who is already facing a conflict-of-interest investigation and a criminal investigation for alleged abuse of European Union subsidies.[4] The prime minister denies the allegations and refuses to step down.[5]

Babiš's behaviour fits a pattern of political developments in Central Europe. Thirty years after the fall of communism, young democracies are threatened.

II

Developments in Poland and Hungary are especially worrying. In Poland, the governing Law and Justice party has since 2015 launched a string of radical and, at times, unconstitutional reforms to take over the country's judicial system.[6] In Hungary, Prime Minister Viktor Orbán fundamentally reformed the country's election law enabling him to gain a 'supermajority' in the parliament (that is, a majority sufficient for changing the constitution) and push through controversial, punitive laws targeting non-governmental organisations and educational institutions, notably the Central European University, which was driven out of the country.[7] Both governments came under scrutiny, in 2017 and 2018 respectively, when the EU invoked the so-called Article 7 procedure to sanction them for corroding democracy and failing to uphold fundamental EU values.[8] While the other two countries of the Visegrad Group, the Czech Republic and Slovakia, have thus far maintained a better democratic track record, things are starting to change.

In February 2018, Slovakia was shaken by the murder of Ján Kuciak, a young investigative journalist, and his fiancée. Kuciak wrote about corrupt Slovak businessmen and frauds related to the misuse of EU funds, allegedly implicating officials at the highest levels of Slovak politics. Following the government's unconvincing criminal investigation, Slovak citizens, supported by President Andrej Kiska, took to the streets and demanded the resignation of long-time prime minister Robert Fico,[9] who eventually stepped down and designated another member of his party, Peter Pellegrini, as his successor. This did not satisfy the protesters, who channelled their anger into support for the presidential campaign of Zuzana Čaputová, an anti-corruption lawyer who ultimately prevailed in the Slovak presidential election earlier this year. The political momentum activated by Kuciak's murder last year thus culminated in the election of Slovakia's first female president on a platform of 'humanism, solidarity, and truth'.[10] Many Czechs found reason to hope in her campaign, having observed the actions of their own president with increasing dismay.

One of the first warning signs for the Czechs was President Miloš Zeman's trip to China in October 2014. In an interview with Chinese state TV, Zeman claimed that he had not come to lecture the Chinese about human rights, but rather to learn how to stabilise society.[11] The president has flirted with other authoritarians too. For example, amid tensions in Ukraine in 2015, Zeman accepted Russian President Vladimir Putin's invitation to attend a military parade in Moscow commemorating the 70th anniversary of the end of the Second World War. He was the only EU head of state to attend.[12] On another occasion, he joked in front of Putin about 'liquidating' journalists because there were 'too many' of them. Putin himself had to temper Zeman's enthusiasm by adding that he would simply limit their numbers.[13] Meanwhile, Zeman has remained silent on important moral questions – refusing, for example, to publicly commemorate the 50th anniversary of the Soviet-led invasion of Czechoslovakia in 1968.[14] Despite this, he was re-elected for his second and final five-year term in 2018.

The second warning sign for Czechs took the form of the political movement ANO[15] under the leadership of Babiš. A billionaire of Slovak origin, Babiš was appointed prime minister in 2018 despite owning nearly half of Czech media outlets and being under investigation for the misuse of EU funds since 2017.[16] His impatience with democratic institutions has frequently been on display, as when he has described the Czech parliament as a 'talking shop' and advocated for the abolishment of its upper chamber, the senate.[17] Although the ANO movement remains constrained within a coalition government[18] and opposed by a number of viable political parties in parliament, it has become relatively powerful within the Czech political system.

A third and final warning lies in the tacit political symbiosis that has emerged between President Zeman and Prime Minister Babiš. The Czech political system is designed as a parliamentary democratic republic in which the prime minister wields executive power while the president plays a largely ceremonial role, merely confirming the prime minister's appointments. This relationship has given rise to controversy because Zeman seems always to meet Babiš halfway. In the recent controversial case, the president suggested that his long-time ally and adviser Benešová replace Kněžínek as justice minister. Benešová duly 'inherited' Kněžínek's task of overseeing the state prosecutor in filing charges against the prime minister.[19] Benešová's appointment sparked outrage, prompting thousands of citizens led by Million Moments for Democracy to gather in the largest Czech squares and demand the resignation of both the newly appointed justice minister and the prime minister.[20] The demonstrations will continue until Babiš resigns, according to Minář, who is already preparing for another big date: 17 November 2019, the 30th anniversary of the Velvet Revolution.[21]

III

In early 2019, Czechs and Slovaks commemorated the suicide by self-immolation of Jan Palach, a 20-year-old student of philosophy at Charles University who gave his life on Wenceslas Square in Prague in 1969. He wanted to awaken society from its lethargy following the Soviet-led invasion in August 1968, and his death has served as a powerful moral symbol ever since. In early 1989, students who took to the streets of Prague to honour his memory were beaten by the state militia. This brutal use of force, which has come to be called 'Palach's Week', precipitated the fall of Czechoslovakia's communist regime later that year.[22]

Palach himself was an engaged citizen. He was an enthusiastic supporter of the 'Prague Spring', a period in early 1968 of liberal reforms including the abolition of censorship and the loosening of the centrally planned economy. Spearheaded by the communist leader Alexander

Dubček, these reforms mobilised the entire country in an attempt to create 'socialism with a human face'. An invasion by the armies of the Warsaw Pact during the night of 20–21 August brought an abrupt end to the reformists' hopes. A shocked and submissive Dubček yielded to the Soviets and signed the Moscow Protocol, agreeing with the invasion and subsequent occupation of Czechoslovakia. Palach, who had only recently returned, disillusioned, from a summer trip to the Soviet Union, witnessed the invasion on the streets of Prague.[23] Deeply disappointed with the reaction of Czechoslovakia's leadership, as well as that of the general public, Palach sacrificed himself a few months later.

In his last letter, dated 16 January 1969, Palach called for an end to censorship and the dissemination of official propaganda.[24] Palach's friends from high school and university testified that he was a pensive student who enjoyed political debates and was generally well liked.[25] Zdenka Kmuníčková, a psychiatrist who recorded a brief interview with Palach shortly before his death, noted that he had a discernibly accentuated sense of justice.[26] On his deathbed, in great pain, Palach urged others not to follow him. Asked why he did it, he answered that 'people must fight against the evil they feel equal to at that moment'.[27]

Notes

1   Bohumil Vostal, Czech TV broadcast, 23 June 2019, available at https://twitter.com/BohumilVostal/status/1142816156664979456.

2   'Demonstrace 1989 vs. 2019. Srovnejte na fotografiích, jak to na Letné vypadalo tehdy a nyní', iRozhlas, 24 June 2019, https://www.irozhlas.cz/zpravy-domov/srovnani-demonstrace-letna-sametova-revoluce-1989-milion-chvilek-2019_1906240625_miz.

3   'Demonstrace za nezávislost justice a lepší vládu', iDNES.cz, 23 June 2019, https://www.idnes.cz/zpravy/domaci/online-on-line-reportaz-z-demonstrace-na-prazske-letenske-plani.B1007261.

4   Robert Tait, 'Communist Past Returns to Haunt Embattled Czech PM', Guardian, 19 February 2018, https://www.theguardian.com/world/2018/feb/19/communist-past-returns-to-haunt-embattled-czech-pm-andrej-babis.

5   'Czech Republic Protests: Andrej Babis Urged to Quit as PM', BBC, 23 June 2019, https://www.bbc.co.uk/news/world-europe-48737467.

6   Christian Davies, 'Hostile Takeover: How Law and Justice Captured Poland's Courts', Freedom House, May 2018, https://freedomhouse.

org/report/special-reports/
hostile-takeover-how-law-and-justice-
captured-poland-s-courts.

7   Patrick Kingsley, 'How Viktor Orban
    Bends Hungarian Society to His
    Will', *New York Times*, 27 March 2018,
    https://www.nytimes.com/2018/03/27/
    world/europe/viktor-orban-hungary.
    html.

8   David R. Cameron, 'EU Deploys
    Article 7 Against Poland & Hungary
    for Democratic Backsliding', Yale
    MacMillan Center, 17 September 2018,
    https://macmillan.yale.edu/news/
    eu-deploys-article-7-against-poland-
    hungary-democratic-backsliding.

9   Rob Cameron, 'Jan Kuciak:
    Murdered Slovakia Journalist
    Remembered', BBC, 21 February
    2019, https://www.bbc.co.uk/news/
    world-europe-47294178.

10 Shaun Walker, 'Slovakia's First
    Female President Hails Victory
    for Progressive Values', *Guardian*,
    31 March 2019, https://www.
    theguardian.com/world/2019/mar/31/
    slovakia-elects-zuzana-caputova-first-
    female-president.

11 Rob Cameron, 'Czech President
    Pelted with Eggs on Revolution
    Anniversary', BBC, 17 November
    2014, https://www.bbc.co.uk/news/
    world-europe-30086495.

12 Tony Wesolowsky, 'Czech President
    Breaks Ranks With Moscow Visit',
    Radio Free Europe/Radio Liberty, 11
    May 2015, https://www.rferl.org/a/
    czech-president-zeman-breaks-ranks-
    moscow-visit/27010077.html.

13 Damien Sharkov, 'Czech
    President and Putin Share
    a Joke About "Liquidating"
    Journalists', *Newsweek*, 15 May

2017, https://www.newsweek.com/
czech-president-and-putin-share-joke-
about-liquidating-journaalists-609216.

14 Krystof Chamonikolas, 'Czech Leader
    Stirs Ire with Silence on 1968 Soviet
    Invasion', Bloomberg, 21 August
    2018, https://www.bloomberg.
    com/news/articles/2018-08-21/
    czech-president-stirs-ire-with-silence-
    over-1968-soviet-invasion.

15 'Ano' means 'yes' in the Czech
    language.

16 Lili Bayer, 'Czech Police Recommend
    Charges Against Prime Minister
    in Fraud Case', Politico, 17 April
    2019, https://www.politico.eu/
    article/andrej-babis-czech-police-
    recommend-charges-against-prime-
    minister-fraud-case/.

17 Martin Ťopek and Veronika
    Neprašová, 'Vysněné Česko Andreje
    Babiše: zrušení Senátu, léčba na dálku
    a telefonující dálnice', Aktualne.cz, 19
    June 2017, https://zpravy.aktualne.cz/
    domaci/vysnene-cesko-andreje-Babiše-
    idealni-spolecnost-skvele-techn/r~a9d
    coada528b11e783fe002590604f2e/.

18 The coalition government is composed
    of ANO and ČSSD (Social Democrats).
    The government also signed an
    agreement with the Communist
    Party to ensure their tacit support
    in passing legislation. See Robert
    Tait, 'Czech Communists Return
    to Government as Power Brokers',
    Guardian, 12 July 2018, https://
    www.theguardian.com/world/2018/
    jul/12/czech-communists-return-to-
    government-as-power-brokers.

19 James Shotter, 'EU Finds Czech PM in
    Breach of Conflict-of-interest Rules',
    Financial Times, 31 May 2019, https://
    www.ft.com/content/52c97288-83c5-

11e9-b592-5fe435b57a3b.

20 'Protestující proti Benešové vyzvali na Václavském náměstí Babiše k demisi', IDNES.cz, 21 May 2019, https://www.idnes.cz/zpravy/domaci/demonstrace-milion-chvilek-demokracie-Benešová-Babiš-protest-praha.A190521_140615_domaci_fort.

21 Jane Dalton, 'Czechs Call on Prime Minister to Quit in Biggest Anti-government Demonstration Since Velvet Revolution', *Independent*, 23 June 2019, https://www.independent.co.uk/news/world/europe/czech-republic-protest-rally-andrej-babis-resign-fraud-a8971501.html.

22 Petr Blažek, 'Jan Palach's Week', Jan Palach – Charles University Multimedia Project, 2016, http://janpalach.cz/en/default/jan-palach/palachuvtyden.

23 Petr Blažek, 'The Prague Spring', Jan Palach – Charles University Multimedia Project, 2016, http://janpalach.cz/en/default/jan-palach/dk2.

24 'Poslední Dopis Jana Palacha', Modernidejiny.cz, 25 June 2013, http://www.moderni-dejiny.cz/clanek/posledni-dopis-jana-palacha/.

25 Jan Gazdík, 'Svatouškovský Pohled Na Palacha Mě Už Štval, Říká Jeho Kamarád Hamr. Proto Promluvil', Aktualne.cz, 14 January 2019, https://zpravy.aktualne.cz/domaci/svatouskovsky-pohled-na-palacha-me-uz-stval-rika-jeho-kamara/r~edf7f2eof7eb11e8a470ac1f6b220ee8/.

26 'Palach Učinil Velké Gesto, Poté Trpěl a Měl Velké Obavy, Aby Ho Lidé Pochopili, Říká Kmuníčková', DVTV, 16 January 2017, https://video.aktualne.cz/dvtv/otazky-na-rozhovor-s-popalenym-palachem-tezko-snasim-neslo-0/r~22116864db5a11e694810025900fea04/?redirected=1551612227.

27 Petr Blažek, 'Jan Palach: Death', Jan Palach – Charles University Multimedia Project, 2016, http://janpalach.cz/en/default/jan-palach/smrt.